French *Compagnies d'Ordonnance*, 1374–1480

The Birth of French Standing Military Units

Stéphane Thion

Helion & Company Limited
Unit 8 Amherst Business Centre
Budbrooke Road
Warwick
CV34 5WE
England
Tel. 01926 499 619
Email: info@helion.co.uk
Website: www.helion.co.uk
X (formerly Twitter): @helionbooks
Facebook: @HelionBooks
Visit our blog at helionbooks.wordpress.com

Published by Helion & Company 2026
Designed and typeset by Mary Woolley, Battlefield Design (www.battlefield-design.co.uk)
Cover designed by Paul Hewitt, Battlefield Design (www.battlefield-design.co.uk)

ISBN 978-1-804519-98-1

British Library Cataloguing-in-Publication Data.
A catalogue record for this book is available from the British Library.

For details of other military history titles published by Helion & Company Limited contact the above address or visit our website: http://www.helion.co.uk.

We always welcome receiving book proposals from prospective authors.

Contents

Introduction v

1 Sources 9
2 Historical Context 13
3 The First Milestones 21
4 The Fourteenth Century and The First Founding Ordinances 25
5 The Beginning of the Fifteenth Century: Unrest and Reconstruction 45
6 Charles VII and the *Ordonnance* of 1439 52
7 The Ordinances of 1445 And The Creation of Permanent Mounted Troops 62
8 The *Francs-Archers* and Artillery in The Standing Army 93
9 *Compagnies d'Ordonnance, Francs-Archers* and Artillery Under Louis XI 99
10 Appearance and Equipment of the Men-At-Arms of the *Compagnies d'Ordonnance* 112
11 In The King's Service 129
Conclusion 151

Appendices:
I *Ordonnance* of 13 January 1374 155
II *Ordonnance* of 22 April 1411 on the Matter of Artillery 159
III Excerpts from the 13th account of Hémon Raguier, Treasurer of Wars, Relating to the Siege Of Gallerande in July 1426 161
IV Copy of the 1445 Order 163
V Poitou, to House Men-of-War, *Ordonnance* of 26 May 1445 167
VI *Ordonnance* of 28 April 1448, 28 November 1451 and 1459 Establishing the *Francs-Archers* 170
VII The King's Entry into Rouen on 10 November 1449, According to Gilles (Jacques) le Bouvier 177
VIII Order from Charles VII to The Generals and Financial Advisers to Pay, For Three Months and Without Watches, Through Macé De Launay, 600 Lances and 450 Small Wages, Intended for The Expedition to Guyenne. La Guerche, 21 April 1451 180
IX Regulations for the Maintenance and Discipline of Men-at-Arms, dated 6 June 1464 182

X Schedule of the State of the Troops in the King's Pay for the Year Beginning 1 January last and Ending on 31 December 1464 186
XI *Ordonnance* of 1466 Establishing Four Captain Generals of The Francs-Archers 191
XII Instruction by Aymar Cadorat (*c.* 1466) 196
XIII Letters Concerning the Clothing of the *Francs-Archers* and the Sums Levied by Their Captains, Paris, 12 January 1474 198
XIV Letters Concerning the Raising, Pay, Armament and Obligations of the *Francs-Archers*, 30 March 1475 201

Colour Plate Commentaries 206
Bibliography 209

Introduction

At the end of the Middle Ages, the French monarchy underwent a period of political and institutional restructuring, with the Hundred Years' War providing both the context and the catalyst. From 1337 to 1453, the conflict was not limited to dynastic rivalry: a process of destruction and reconstruction, it tested the crown's ability to mobilise men on a long-term basis, finance the war, maintain internal order and, more broadly, exercise effective sovereignty over a kingdom long troubled by feudalism, regional particularisms and princely rivalries.

The defeats of the French knights, the irregularity of feudal service, the slowness of recruitment, and the rise of new warfare practices (raids, prolonged sieges, the increased role of artillery) revealed the limitations of a military organisation based on individual prowess and vassalage. Added to these weaknesses was a decisive phenomenon: the proliferation of demobilised troops – *routiers*, *grandes compagnies* and *écorcheurs* – who ravaged the countryside and undermined the King's authority, transforming military disorder into a lasting social and political crisis. It was in this context that Charles VII began the process of creating a standing army, generally associated with the establishment of the *compagnies d'ordonnance* (1445), the creation of the *francs-archers* (1448) and the affirmation of a structured royal artillery. Such a transformation could not be built from scratch. In order to establish this type of institution and overcome the strong opposition that existed at the time, it must be considered within a broader framework, that of a long process of evolution, in which milestones were gradually laid down.

The question posed by this book is that of the origins and explanatory factors behind this change: how and why did the French monarchy come to replace the feudal model of the host and *arrière-ban* with a more stable, paid, controlled military system that was permanently attached to the state? The answer cannot be attributed to a single cause. It requires us to consider, on the one hand, the accumulated experience of the crises of the fourteenth century – which led to an increase in regulations, controls and ordinances aimed at regulating the military – and, on the other hand, the specific situation of the fifteenth century, marked by the gradual restoration of royal power after the darkest years (civil war, English occupation, territorial fragmentation). Charles VII's reforms thus appear to be the culmination of a long process of professionalisation and centralisation: warfare became less of an intermittent seigneurial duty and more of a function supervised by the crown, requiring permanence, financial regularity, administrative procedures and a more stable hierarchy.

The challenges of this transformation go far beyond military history alone. Establishing a standing army was first and foremost a matter of public order: reducing the role of private warfare and curbing the forms of predation associated with demobilisation by channelling armed violence into regular frameworks. It was also a fiscal and administrative issue: paying troops on an ongoing basis required sustainable resources, payment logistics, control agents – in short, a strengthened state infrastructure. Finally, it is a major political issue: by establishing forces directly dependent on the King – ordnance companies for the professional core, *francs-archers* as a source of infantry, artillery as a technical and strategic instrument – the monarchy increased its ability to impose its decisions on both the English and the great princes, and gradually consolidated its monopoly on legitimate force. These measures marked a fundamental shift: war, which had long been a defining feature of the nobility's identity and feudal power struggles, was becoming a matter of state, subject to standards, inspections, accounting and governmental rationality.

The outcome of this process, as it will be examined here, is twofold. On the military front, it led to improved cohesion, availability and discipline among the royal forces, which contributed to the momentum of reconquest and the affirmation of French power in the final phase of the Hundred Years' War, thanks to the increased effectiveness of siege operations and the decisive role played by artillery. Institutionally, it marked a turning point in the history of the monarchy: the organisation of permanent units and the supervision of recruitment contributed to the construction of a more centralised state, capable of coordinating taxation, administration and the armed forces within a single project of sovereignty.

To answer the question posed, the book will follow a four-step progression. First, it will present the sources used and the methodological precautions they require. It will then place the reforms in the historical context of the Hundred Years' War, emphasising the military and political crises that made the emergence of a stable army conceivable – and then necessary. Next, it will analyse the 'first institutional milestones': professionalisation, earlier ordinances, pay and control mechanisms, which paved the way for the upheaval of the mid-fifteenth century. Finally, it will study the concrete implementation of Charles VII's reforms – ordnance companies, *francs-archers*, and artillery – as well as their effects on the government of the kingdom and the evolution of warfare at the end of the Middle Ages. Numerous appendices supplement this work as supporting documents.

A note on terminology

Throughout this book, I have chosen to retain the expression *Compagnies d'Ordonnance* rather than adopt the more idiomatic English form of 'Companies of Ordinance', and I consistently use the French word *ordonnance* in place of ordinance. This choice is deliberate, as it preserves the historical and linguistic specificity of the original French terminology.

Medieval and early Renaissance French sources also frequently use the expressions *hommes d'armes, gens d'armes*, and *gens de guerre*. In the usage of the period, *gens d'armes* and *gens de guerre* referred broadly to those engaged in warfare and were, in that sense, largely interchangeable. While these terms might be translated into modern English as "soldiers," such a rendering would be historically misleading, since the word would be anachronistic in this context. Likewise, although *gendarme* would later evolve into a term replacing *homme d'armes*, it had not yet assumed that meaning during the period examined here. For this reason, I translate *hommes d'armes* as men-at-arms, and *gens d'armes* and *gens de guerre* as men-of-war.

1

Sources

Apart from recognised secondary sources, such as Jean Favier and Philippe Contamine, primary sources have mainly been used. Here is presented a description of the main primary sources.

Thomas Basin, *Histoire de Charles VII et de Louis XI* (Paris: J. Quicherat, 4 vols, Société de l'Histoire de France, 1855–1862): this is a major source for the reign of Charles VII, written in the 1460s and 1470s. Thomas Basin was born in 1412 in Caudebec, Normandy. At the age of 12, his father sent him to study at the University of Paris, where he obtained a Master of Arts degree at the age of 17. He then went on to study in Louvain and Pavia before returning to Caudebec. He entered the priesthood and returned to Louvain to study canon law. During those troubled years, Thomas Basin was a direct witness to the restoration of the monarchy.

Gilles (or Jacques) le Bouvier, *Recouvrement de Normandie*, contained in *Les chroniques de Normandie* (Rouen: Hellot, 1881). These are chronicles printed in Rouen in 1487 by Guillaume le Tailleur. This book contains a third part entitled 'Recouvrement de la Normandie', the short work written by Gilles le Bouvier, known as the Herald of Berry as he was Charles VII's herald from 1420 onwards.

Jean de Bueil, *Le Jouvencel* (Paris: Renouard, 1887): this is a somewhat fictionalised work based on real events, the experiences of Jean de Bueil, who became captain of one of Charles VII's companies of infantry. The historical and personal events recounted by de Bueil in fictionalised form and in random order are contextualised and reorganised at the end of the book by Guillaume Tringant, one of the author's servants. Jean de Bueil lost many members of his family at Agincourt and earned his spurs at the Battle of Verneuil in 1424. He was trained in the art of war by Guillaume II, Viscount of Narbonne, who was killed in the latter battle, and then by Étienne de Vignolles, known as La Hire. One could not have dreamed of a better mentor to introduce de Bueil to the art of war. The two men, master and pupil, earned the nickname 'Scourge of the English'. De Bueil was knighted in 1434. From 1427 onwards, he took part in a series of sieges and battles, including Orléans and Patay in 1429, the capture of Château-du-Loir in 1431, the Siege of Saint-Célerin and the Battles of Beaumont and Vivoin in 1432, the raid on Chinon in 1433, another Siege of Saint-Célerin and the Battle of Grand-Hormeau in 1434, the Siege of Saint-Denis in 1435, and the Cotentin campaign in 1436. He was captain general of the *écorcheurs* between 1436 and 1438, took Sainte-Suzanne in 1439, took part in the Siege of Pontoise in 1441 and the unfortunate affair of Craon in 1443, then was appointed captain general of the expedition against the Swiss under the Dauphin, the future Louis XI, and was victorious over the forces of Basel at the Battle of Saint-Jacques in 1444. It was, among other things, the excesses of this campaign that prompted Charles VII to carry out a radical reform of the army. From 1451 to 1476, de Bueil was captain of a company of one hundred lances. In *Le Jouvencel*, Jean de Bueil expresses 'in moving and eloquent terms, that sincere love of arms which is the characteristic trait of his individuality,' writes his biographer. 'Through his faults as well as his qualities, our character was a man of his time,' he continues.[1] *Le Jouvencel* is considered a 'veritable treatise on military and moral education, supported by historical examples and allusions.'[2] The aim of the author, who died in 1478, was to share his experience. As such, this source, even if fictionalised, remains invaluable.

Alain Chartier, *Le Quadrilogue de maistre Alain Chartier* (BNF): This is a treatise written in 1422, which the introduction describes as: 'Here begins a notable and excellent treatise on the subject of war, correcting and revising each point of faith. This treatise is called a quadrilogue because it was compiled by four people, including the late venerable, discreet and wise Master Alain Chartier, who during his lifetime was a Doctor of Decree and secretary to King Charles VII.' Alain Chartier, brother of Jean (see below), and of Guillaume, Bishop of Paris, was a renowned poet of the fifteenth century who was employed by Charles VII as his secretary in around 1419.

Jean Chartier, *Chronique de Charles VII, Roi de France* (Paris: P. Jannet, 1858): Jean Chartier was the brother of Guillaume Chartier, Bishop of Paris, and of Alain Chartier. He was probably born in Bayeux at the very beginning of the fifteenth century. In 1435, he was commander and hostelier of the Abbey of Saint-Denis, a position he probably owed to the favour of Charles VII. The King resided in part at the Royal Abbey of Saint-Denis in 1437. It was on this occasion that Jean was appointed, on 18 November 1437, official historiographer of the kingdom by letters patent. He was paid 200 *livres parisis* in wages for the position. However, unlike Froissart, Jean Chartier, sheltered in his monastery, was not a direct witness to the events he describes. The date of his death is unknown, but he is still mentioned in a document dated October 1470. *The Chronicle of Charles VII* is the only known work he authored.

Mathieu de Coussy (or d'Escouchy), 'Chroniques,' in *Choix de Chroniques et Mémoires relatifs à l'Histoire de France* (Paris: Delagrave, 1835): Mathieu

1 Léon Lecestre, 'en introduction de Jean de Bueil,' *Le Jouvencel* (Paris: Renouard, 1887), Tome premier, p.ccixxxvij.

2 Lecestre, *Le Jouvencel* Tome premier, p.ccixxxviiij.

de Coucy was born in Le Quesnoy in Hainaut in the first half of the fifteenth century. This chronicler recounts the scenes he witnessed with sincerity, as a witness of his time. His chronicle is one of the few sources we have on the deliberations that led to the *ordonnance* of 1445 and its content. This source is even more valuable for this reason.

Philippe de Commynes, 'Mémoires sur les règnes de Louis XI et Charles VIII' in J. A. C. Buchon, *Choix de Chroniques et mémoires sur l'histoire de France* (Paris: Desrez, 1836), edition presented and translated by Joël Blanchard. This is an essential source covering the period from 1464 to 1498, i.e. the reigns of Louis XI and Charles VIII.

Jean Froissart, *Chronicles*, (Brussels: Kervyn de Lettenhove, 25 vols., 1867–1877): This essential chronicle covers the first half of the Hundred Years' War. Another edition of Jean Froissart's Chronicles was also used for this work, published by J. A. Buchon in the *Collection des chroniques nationales françaises* (Paris: Delagrave, 1825). Jean Froissart's Chronicles form a lively and literary account, reflecting the chivalric mentality of the period that preceded it and helping to understand the process of forming the *compagnies d'ordonnance*.

Guillaume Gruel, author of *Chronique de Richemont, connétable de France, duc de Bretagne* (Paris: Société de l'histoire de France, 1890): Guillaume Gruel, born in the first decade of the fifteenth century, was raised in the household of the Lord of Montauban, *Maréchal* of Brittany. He entered the service of Richemont when the latter was already Constable of France. He attended the marriage of the Constable and Jeanne d'Albret on 29 August 1442. Guillaume Gruel took an active part in the Normandy campaign and fought alongside the Constable at Formigny, making his chronicle a valuable source.

Jean de Haynin, author of his memoirs entitled *Les mémoires de messire Jean, seigneur de Haynin et de Louvegnies* (Mons: E.M. Hoyois, 1892), was a Burgundian knight and chronicler. Born in 1423, he was an officer in the armies of Philip the Good and Charles the Bold. He left us a detailed description of the Burgundian Army and the Battle of Montlhéry (1465). He died in 1495.

The *Memoirs* of Olivier de la Marche (in *Nouvelle collection des mémoires pour servir à l'histoire de France*, volume three, Paris: publisher not stated, 1837): Olivier de la Marche, born in 1425 or 1426, was a Burgundian captain and chronicler at the court of Burgundy. His *Memoirs* cover the period from 1435 to 1488. They provide an interesting perspective on the impression left by the *ordonnance* of 1445 and its implementation, notably mentioning an interesting consequence.

Jean Molinet, author of *Chroniques* (Paris: J.A. Buchon, 1828): Born in 1435, Jean Molinet was a poet and musician, but also a chronicler attached to Charles the Bold, Duke of Burgundy. His *Chroniques* cover a period from 1474 to 1504 and provide a detailed description of the Battle of Guinegatte and the Burgundian Army.

Enguerrand de Monstrelet, author of the *Chronique d'Enguerrand de Monstrelet*, in J. A. Buchon, *Collection des chroniques nationales françaises*,

11 volumes (Paris: Delagrave, 1824–1826): Enguerrand de Monstrelet was a Picard nobleman and squire, whose year of birth is unknown, but is thought to have been at the end of the fourteenth century, and who died in 1453. His chronicles begin in 1400, the year for which he obtained information from 'trustworthy' sources. He was the historian of Philip of Burgundy. He was appointed bailiff of the Chapter of Cambrai in 1436, then provost of the same city in 1444 and provost of the city of Wallaincourt in the same year. His chronicle covers the years 1400 to 1444.

Jean de Roye dit Troyes, author of the 'Chroniques du règne de Louis XI' in M. Petitot, *Collection complète des mémoires relatifs à l'histoire de France*, volume XIII, (Paris: Foucault, 1820): born around 1425, he was a Parisian bourgeois, lawyer, and author of a 'scandalous chronicle' of the reign of Louis XI.

The Ordinances of the Kings of France of the Third Race, vol. XIII–XV, (Paris, Imprimerie Royale, 1723–1849): This is a collection of royal ordinances. The regulations for soldiers of 30 April 1351 and 13 January 1374, as well as those of 2 November 1439, are included.

Valérie Bessey's work, *Textes fondateurs des institutions militaires* (Turnhout: Brepols Publishers n.v., 2006) also presents several ordinances and regulations of interest for the period in question, notably the ordinances of 2 November 1439, 26 May 1445, 5 January 1446 and 28 April 1448.

The Cabochian Ordinance (1413) – Documents sur le règne de Charles VI (Clermont-Ferrand: Paleo, 2008) is also an interesting source for understanding the evolution of the process of building a standing army.

Auguste Vallet de Viriville, 'Notices et extraits de chartes et de manuscrits appartenant au British Museum de Londres', Bibliothèque de l'École des Chartes (1847) 8, pp.110–147. This document reveals some passages from the *ordonnance* of 26 May 1445 issued in Louppy-le-Château and that of 4 December 1455, *Letters from King Charles VII, by which he appointed five commissioners in the seneschalsy of la Marche to collect, according to a new method, a levy for the pay of men-at-arms.*

Finally, to mention a fundamental academic article published in 2015 in Stéphane Péquignot's *Revue Historique*: 'De la France à Barcelone. Une version catalane de "l'ordonnance perdue"' de Charles VII sur les gens d'armes (1445)' (Presses Universitaires de France, 2015). This scientific article reveals a copy of the 1445 ordinance, in Catalan, discovered in the Historical Archives of the City of Barcelona, 'by chance during research on a completely different subject.'[3] This is a copy of the 1445 *ordonnance*, which had been lost, and Stéphane Péquignot published it in full in the appendix to his paper. It is reproduced here as Appendix IV.

3 Stéphane Péquignot, 'De la France à Barcelone. Une version catalane de "l'ordonnance perdue" de Charles VII sur les gens d'armes (1445)', *Revue Historique*, 4:276 (2015), p.794.

2

Historical Context

The Hundred Years' War

The Hundred Years' War, which spanned the period from 1337 to 1453, was a fundamental period in French and European medieval history. Torn apart by a long series of conflicts, the French monarchy, weakened and sometimes contested, underwent profound military, political and institutional changes over the decades, against a backdrop of dynastic conflict with England.

When what chroniclers would later call the Hundred Years' War began in 1337, the French monarchy was at the height of its feudal power and on the threshold of a structural crisis from which it would not emerge until the mid-fifteenth century. The long confrontation between the Kings of France and England cannot be reduced to a dynastic conflict: it was the expression of a change in sovereignty, a transformation of the relationship between war and the state. Through a century of defeats, alliances and reconquests, the late Capetian monarchy, followed by the Valois dynasty, experienced unprecedented weakness before laying the foundations for the modern administrative monarchy in the second half of the fifteenth century.

From the French perspective, the Hundred Years' War was first and foremost an existential crisis: a challenge to the very principle of Capetian legitimacy, the fragmentation of the kingdom, the disruption of the feudal order and a radical transformation of military structures. It highlighted the fragility of the feudal system and the slow emergence of a centralised state capable of monopolising legitimate violence.

To understand the subsequent creation of the *ordonnance* companies under Charles VII, we must first trace the origins of this crisis: how the feudal rivalry between the Capetian and Plantagenet kings led to a total war that shook the kingdom; how the military collapse of the fourteenth century led to a profound disorganisation of the armed forces and the tax system; and how, through a century of struggle, a new conception of royal power and warfare gradually took shape.

The roots of the conflict can be traced back to the feudal ambiguities inherited from the Norman conquest of England and the complex relations between the French crown and its vassals across the Channel. Since the twelfth century, the Kings of England, heirs of William the Conqueror, had been both independent sovereigns on their island and vassals of the King of France for their Continental possessions, notably Guyenne. At the beginning of the fourteenth century, the Capetian monarchy seemed triumphant: Philippe le Bel had imposed his authority on the papacy the great fiefdoms and the nobility. But the successive deaths of his three sons, all without male heirs – Louis X in 1316, Philippe V in 1322, Charles IV in 1328 – triggered a major dynastic crisis.

Applying Salic Law, the peers of the realm rejected Edward III of England – grandson of Philippe le Bel through his mother Isabella – in favour of a Capetian cousin, Philippe of Valois, who was crowned King as Philippe VI. This choice, legally sound but politically explosive, placed the Plantagenets in the position of rejected pretenders. Added to this rivalry over rights was economic and political tension: the English wool trade, vital to Flemish clothiers, made the cities of Flanders dependent on London. However, Flanders was under the authority of the King of France: this intertwining of interests created a breeding ground for confrontation. When Philippe VI supported the anti-Flemish policy of Count Louis de Nevers, the Flemish cities revolted and turned to Edward III.

In 1337, after a series of incidents in Guyenne – confiscation of the duchy by the King of France and Edward III's refusal to submit – war broke out. To legitimise his enterprise, Edward publicly claimed the French crown and proclaimed this in his acts from 1340 onwards. From then on, the conflict took on the dimensions of a struggle for total sovereignty.

The first cycle of the war (1337–1360) was dominated by English military superiority and French political disorganisation. Despite appearances of a classic feudal war, it was a conflict that revealed the structural weakness of the kingdom: slow mobilisation, the weight of princely rivalries, the absence of a standing army and a chronic financial crisis. From the very first campaigns, Edward III imposed a different model of warfare. The English, with their more consistent military discipline and systematic use of the longbow, practised a form of warfare known as chevauchée: devastating, rapid raids aimed at ruining the country and undermining the legitimacy of the French King.

The naval Battle of Sluis (1340) marked the first major English victory. English naval superiority paved the way for landings on the Continent. But it was the campaign of 1346 that symbolised the collapse of the French system: at Crécy-en-Ponthieu, on 26 August, Philippe VI suffered a crushing defeat. Froissart gives a gripping account of the battle, describing the confusion among the French troops, the hasty cavalry charges and the hail of English arrows.[1] This battle marked the end of a certain feudal chivalry, attached to

---

1 Jean Froissart, 'Chroniques', in Jean Yanoski (ed.), *Collection de chroniques,*

individual prowess, in the face of the disciplined tactics of archers. The fall of Calais in 1347 sealed France's defeat. Now an English possession, the city became a lasting bridgehead on the Continent.

The situation worsened with the Black Death (1348–1350), which decimated the population and ruined tax revenues. When Jean le Bon succeeded Philippe VI in 1350, he inherited a weakened, exhausted kingdom threatened with disintegration. The disaster at Poitiers in 1356 had proved the impotence of the feudal system: King Jean was taken prisoner by the Black Prince, and the French army, composed of poorly coordinated contingents, was swept away by English discipline.

The King's captivity triggered a major political crisis: the Dauphin Charles, the future Charles V, had to govern a devastated kingdom, while the Estates General demanded reforms and the limitation of royal power. The Grand *Ordonnance* of 1357, spearheaded by Étienne Marcel, attempted to place taxation and the army under the control of the Estates. It was a premature attempt at representative government, which failed amid the chaos of revolts and the restoration of princely rule. The failure of royal power was also evident in the military sphere. Gangs of demobilised soldiers, known as the *grandes compagnies*, ravaged the country, living off plunder and ransom. These companies already foreshadowed the fundamental problem that would lead, a century later, to the creation of a permanent standing army.

The Treaty of Brétigny in 1360 sealed France's defeat. Jean II, released in exchange for a ransom, ceded vast territories: Guyenne, Poitou, Limousin, and part of Saintonge and Périgord came under English rule. Edward III renounced the French crown, for a time, in exchange for this full sovereignty. For the French monarchy, it was an unprecedented humiliation, revealing the collapse of the feudal system and the failure of the traditional *levée en masse*.

The period following the Treaty of Brétigny was one of reconstruction. The kingdom, stripped of its south-western provinces, had to rebuild itself under a weakened royal authority. Paradoxically, the relative peace exacerbated military disorganisation: demobilised troops turned into independent armed gangs, pillaging the territory. These companies embodied the decline of the feudal system, which was incapable of controlling the violence. They were not only a social scourge: they were also a political symptom. The King had no standing army; each campaign required costly mandates and slow feudal appeals, which were often ineffective. The kingdom lived under the constant threat of its own soldiers.

When Jean II died in 1364, his son Charles V inherited a desperate situation. This learned and prudent prince, who would later be called 'the Wise', understood that the restoration of royal power required a profound reform of military and financial structures. Under the impetus of his constable, Bertrand du Guesclin, the King undertook a methodical

---

mémoires et autres documents (Paris: Firmin Didot Frères, 1865), pp.72–85.

reconquest. Far from the disastrous battles of his predecessors, he favoured a war of attrition, administrative reconquest and the use of paid troops. Charles V's reforms – a permanent tax on salt and the *taille*, the creation of an embryonic royal treasury, and the centralisation of military command – initiated a transformation. War became a matter of state and no longer a feudal enterprise. But these advances remained fragile.

Charles V's work was based on two pillars: the restoration of financial control and the professionalisation of warfare. In 1363, he re-established the *taille royale*, a permanent direct tax, to pay the troops and maintain the fortifications. He also put an end to the disorder of the companies by employing them abroad – notably in the wars in Spain, where du Guesclin put their energy at the service of the royal cause. This policy of expelling uncontrolled forces allowed the kingdom to breathe and the monarchy to rebuild a core of regular armies. Charles V's success can be measured by the reconquest of territory. Between 1369 and 1380, the English lost almost all of the gains of the Treaty of Brétigny, apart from Calais, Bordeaux and Bayonne. The King of France avoided large pitched battles and favoured sieges, positional warfare and diplomacy. This strategy, in contrast to that of Crécy and Poitiers, proved to be extremely effective.

At the same time, the monarchy strengthened its symbolic authority. Charles V saw himself as the embodiment of Capetian continuity, commissioning the writing of new sections of the *Grandes Chroniques de France*, which presented his reign as a restoration of the providential order. The King also ordered the construction of the Louvre and the Château de Vincennes, symbols of rational power and centralised government. When Charles V died in 1380, the kingdom was at peace, the economy was recovering, and the crown was surrounded by prestige. But this stability was still based on a fragile balance: the reforms were not institutionalised, and political cohesion depended on an exceptional King.

The minority and subsequent madness of Charles VI plunged France into political and military chaos from which it would take decades to recover. This tragic reign, oscillating between periods of lucidity and mental crises, saw the dislocation of the kingdom under the effect of princely rivalries. The early years (1380–1388) were marked by the regency of the King's uncles – the Dukes of Anjou, of Berry, and of Burgundy – who seized power and finances. Popular discontent exploded in Paris in 1382 with the Maillotins revolt. This social unrest, brutally suppressed, revealed the exhaustion of the kingdom and the growing divide between the monarchy and the people.

When Charles VI personally took power in 1388, he attempted to continue his father's work, surrounding himself with the former advisers of Charles V, the Marmousets. But in 1392, on his way to Brittany, the King suffered his first bout of madness. From then on, the monarchy sank into a latent civil war between the princes of the blood. Two factions formed: the Armagnacs, supporters of the House of Orléans, and the Burgundians, led by the Dukes of Burgundy, John the Fearless and then Philip the Good. This division ruined any attempt at resistance against England. The two parties clashed in Paris and in the provinces in a bitter struggle, while

Men-at-arms in battle *c.* 1380–1390. Illumination from the *Chroniques de Saint-Denis*, British Library Ms Roy 20C-VII f. 001. (Public Domain)

royal power was paralysed by the King's illness. On 23 November 1407, the assassination of Duke Louis of Orléans by the men of John the Fearless plunged the kingdom into a spiral of revenge. The Armagnacs, led by Bernard VII of Armagnac, seized the capital in 1413, imposed an authoritarian government, and were then driven out. Meanwhile, England, unified under Henry V, prepared its offensive.

Taking advantage of French discord, the King of England resumed his plans for conquest. In 1415, he landed in Normandy. The French army, weakened and divided, suffered a disaster at Agincourt on 25 October 1415, comparable to Crécy and Poitiers. This tragic episode for French chivalry saw it once again decimated on the battlefield by English archery tactics, this time combined with muddy terrain. Agincourt marked the beginning of the darkest phase of the war for France. The losses among the high nobility were immense: the cream of French chivalry lay in the mud, mowed down by English archers. After this massacre, the kingdom collapsed. The Burgundians, triumphant, recaptured Paris in 1418 and handed the capital over to the English.

In 1420, the mad King and Queen Isabeau signed the Treaty of Troyes with Henry V, which disinherited the Dauphin Charles in favour of the King of England, who was proclaimed heir and regent of France.

This treaty marked the complete downfall of the French monarchy: the King was mad and France was divided between the English and the Burgundians. The territorial collapse was spectacular: Normandy, Champagne and Picardy came under English control, while Burgundy dominated the north and east of the kingdom. The Dauphin Charles, who had taken refuge in Bourges, retained a small domain south of the Loire – hence the ironic expression 'King of Bourges'. It was during this period of humiliation that the generation of Charles VII's servants was formed – the men who would later lay the foundations of the army of *ordonnance*: La Trémoille, Dunois, Alençon, Bureau and Richemont. However, resistance seemed futile until 1429.

The English laid siege to Orléans, the last stronghold on the Loire. It was then that Joan of Arc emerged. Her intervention changed the course of the war. The episode of Joan of Arc was the symbolic turning point in the recovery of the nation's destiny. Coming from Domrémy, convinced of a divine mission, she presented herself to Charles VII in Chinon in 1429, galvanised the royal army and effected the lifting of the Siege of Orléans on 8 May 1429, a major event in the psychological reversal of the conflict. The Dauphin was then taken to Reims and crowned King under the name Charles VII on 17 July 1429. The monarchy, symbolically restored, regained its spiritual and national legitimacy: the coronation in Reims marked the rebirth of French sovereignty.

Joan of Arc's intervention did not immediately end the war, but it did reverse the political dynamic. After her death in 1431, burnt at the stake in Rouen, the royalist movement continued to organise itself. Charles VII, now recognised by most of the kingdom, undertook a methodical reconstruction. The King, long indecisive and distrustful of those around him, gradually asserted himself. He surrounded himself with new men from the middle nobility and the administrative bourgeoisie: Dunois, Richemont, and the treasurer Jouvenel des Ursins. These advisers understood the need for a stable army and regular taxation. The years 1430–1440 saw the slow establishment of the instruments of modern monarchy: the creation of a permanent tax (the taille), the reorganisation of the Treasury, the restoration of the Parliaments, and the reform of the currency. Charles VII's 1439 *ordonnance* on military service thus foreshadowed that of 1445, which permanently established the *ordonnance* companies. On the military front, the reconquest accelerated. Thanks to recruitment reforms and improved troop discipline, France recaptured Paris in 1436, Normandy in 1449 and Guyenne in 1453. The artillery, led by the Bureau brothers, played a decisive role. The victory at Castillon (17 July 1453) completed the reconquest: it was the effective end of the Hundred Years' War.

The period following the Treaty of Arras in 1435, which sealed the alliance with the Dukes of Burgundy, marked a decisive turning point for the French monarchy. Charles VII, freed from internal strife and strengthened by the Burgundian alliance, was now in a position to extend and consolidate his authority over the entire territory, which had previously been fragmented by civil war and occupied by English troops. The gradual

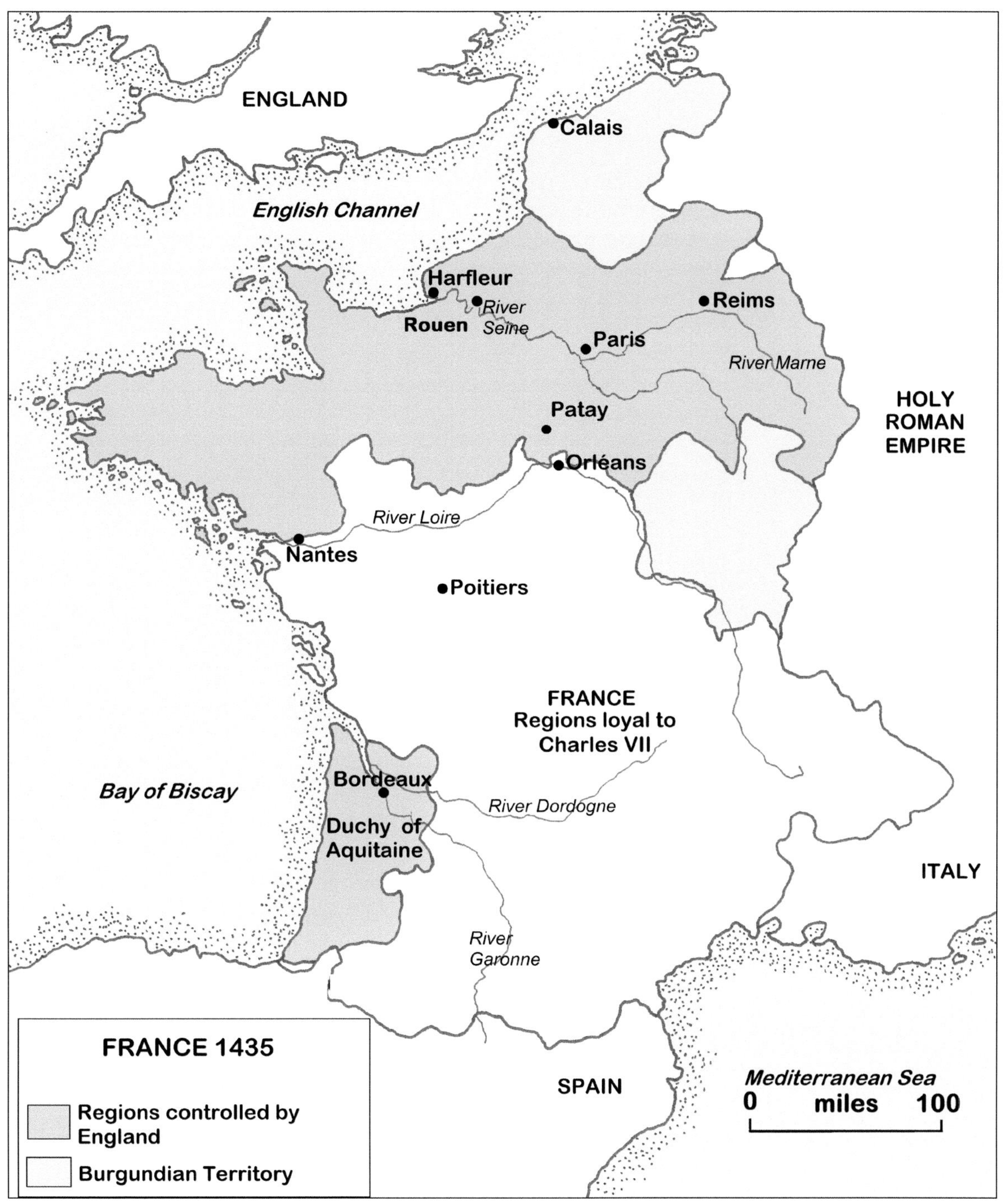

France in 1435. (Reproduced from, Peter Hoskins, *The Battle of Castillon 1453*, Warwick: Helion & Co., 2023 ©)

return of Paris to royal obedience in 1436, followed by that of the north of the kingdom, symbolised the process of monarchical restoration, which was now based on a more coherent administrative structure and royal officials devoted to the crown. The monarchy reactivated the system of royal officers: bailiffs, seneschals and receivers-general, to restore public order and the kingdom's finances. Taxation by the *taille*, now perceived as a permanent royal tax, gradually replaced the exceptional levies of the Estates General. This increased centralisation of the kingdom was accompanied by close surveillance of the great feudal lords, whose participation in the royal armies was no longer voluntary but enforced by royal policy.

The century of the Hundred Years' War radically transformed the political and military structures of the kingdom. In 1337, the Capetian monarchy was still a feudal aggregate; by 1453, it had become a centralised administrative power capable of maintaining a standing army and a stable tax system. The experience of disorder – companies, civil wars, looting – convinced the monarchy that only institutional control of war could guarantee peace. This military centralisation was accompanied by a change in the relationship between the King and his subjects. Military service ceased to be a feudal duty and became a public function. War, once the foundation of the nobility, became an instrument of government. The end of the Hundred Years' War was therefore not only the end of a conflict, but the birth of a new political system: the French monarchy became a sovereign, autonomous power, capable of maintaining order by regular means.

3

The First Milestones

The End of Chivalry

Fourteenth century France was characterised by a complex network of seigneurial and princely powers. The fragmentation of the kingdom, illustrated by the pre-eminence of the great vassals, gave the Hundred Years' War the character of a civil war as much as a foreign war. The Dukes of Burgundy, allies or adversaries depending on the phase of the conflict, took advantage of the institutional weaknesses of the monarchy. The King had to deal with princes, bishops and towns, whose loyalty fluctuated according to circumstances. The feudal system, based on vassalage and reciprocal services, gradually crumbled under the pressure of collective disasters: wars, famines, demographic crises and, above all, the Great Plague of 1347–1351. Military mobilisation, based on the call of vassals, showed its limitations in the face of the necessities of a prolonged large-scale confrontation.

Crécy and Poitiers saw the defeat of the proud French knights, who had once been victorious. And it took a long time for the lesson to be learned. At the end of the Battle of Crécy, which pitted King Philippe VI of Valois against Edward III Plantagenet on 26 August 1346, 1,500 knights were dead, including Duke Raoul of Lorraine, Louis de Dampierre, Count of Nevers and Flanders, Charles II of Valois, Count of Alençon and Perche and brother of the King of France, Henri IV of Vaudémont, Louis de Châtillon, Count of Blois, Enguerrand VI de Coucy, Louis II de Sancerre, Jean IV d'Harcourt, Jean Ier de Luxembourg, known as 'the Blind', Count of Luxembourg and King of Bohemia, Hugues d'Amboise, Jean II d'Auxy and Robert de Rambures, to name but a few.

Ten years later, at Poitiers on 19 September 1356, between 500 and 700 men-at-arms were killed, while the King of France and 17 counts were taken prisoner.[1] Among the dead were the Constable of France, Gauthier

1 Froissart, 'Chroniques' in *Collection des Chroniques*, p.132.

VI de Brienne, Jean de Clermont, *Maréchal de France*, Geoffroy de Charny, bearer of the Oriflamme, the Bishop of Châlons, Pierre Duke of Bourbon, Guichard de Beaujeu, Jean de Landas, Guillaume de Nesle, Eustache de Ribemont, Guillaume de Montagu, and Guichard d'Angle. 'And there died, as was recorded, all the flower of French chivalry, which greatly weakened the noble kingdom of France,' lamented Froissart.[2]

Nearly 60 years later, on 25 October 1415, Agincourt would once again be the graveyard of thousands of knights. Among the casualties were Charles I d'Albret, Count of Dreux and Constable of France, Hugues VII d'Amboise, Chamberlain to the King, and his son, Hugues VIII d'Amboise, Edward III, Duke of Bar, Jean Ier, Duke of Alençon and Count of Perche, Baudoin d'Ailly, Vidame of Amiens, Philip, Count of Burgundy, Antoine of Burgundy, Duke of Brabant and Limburg, Jean de Montaigu, Archbishop of Sens, and Ferry I, Count of Vaudémont, to name but a few. A little less than 10 years later, at Verneuil on 17 August 1424, hundreds more knights were killed, including the Count of Aumale, the Count of Ventadour and the Viscount of Narbonne.

It might appear from this grim tally that none of these lessons were learned. That is not the case. In fact, the early years of the fourteenth century saw the beginning of the professionalisation of armies. Philippe le Bel, following the disaster of Courtrai on 11 July 1302, accelerated this professionalisation towards paid armies, a process that culminated in the *Ordonnance* of Nancy of 1445 under Charles VII. In drafting his ordinances of 1445, the *Bien Servi* drew inspiration from what his predecessors had put in place. The *compagnies d'ordonnance*, created by Charles VII in 1445, did not therefore arise out of nowhere: they were the logical response to a century of crises. Their creation marked the victory of royal sovereignty over feudalism and private warfare. They embodied the rationalisation of violence in the service of the state.

The Thirteenth Century and the Concept of the King's *Hôtel*

From the thirteenth century onwards, certain knights and sergeants received a salary without being considered mercenaries. Thus, between 1250 and 1253, the expenses of Saint Louis show sums of money paid for the wages of the 'people of the Hôtel' and for the 'crossbowmen and sergeants of arms of the *Hôtel*' of the King.[3] A few years later, the 'summary of expenses incurred on the Aragon road in 1285' lists the sums paid for the wages of the knights of the '*hôtel*' and for the King's '*varlez*'.[4] In fact, in the thirteenth century,

2 Froissart, 'Chroniques' in *Collection des Chroniques*, p.132.

3 *Recueil des historiens des Gaules et de la France*, Tome 21 (Paris, 1855), pp.512–513.

4 *Recueil des historiens des Gaules et de la France*, Tome 21, pp.515–517.

the core of a royal army was primarily made up of the King's men, whose headquarters was the '*Hôtel*'.

'The *Hôtel* was first and foremost the structure that enabled the daily life of the King, his family and his entourage. .... From the chancellor to the lowest servant, several hundred people were employed at the *Hôtel*' Xavier Hélary explains.[5] Within this *hôtel*, there were around 30 'sergeants-at-arms of the King', two or three 'usher-in-arms of the King' and 25 crossbowmen. The 'knights of the *Hôtel*', generally close advisers, acted as bodyguards. Philippe Contamine considers bodyguards to be part of the typology of permanent forces.[6] There were few men at the *Hôtel* in peacetime, around ten. This number could rise to several dozen knights in wartime.[7] Thus, a list of knights who fought alongside Saint Louis in 1269 includes 128 names, including the constable, three marshals, the master of the crossbowmen, a seneschal, the cupbearer and the chamberlain. This same list distinguishes between knights in the King's service who will eat 'at his *Hôtel*', 'at the King's *Hôtel*' or 'at court' and other knights who 'will not eat at court.'[8] Another list of 'knights of the *Hôtel le roi croisiés*', probably dating from 1270, has 29 names, including the constable, the cupbearer, the Duke of Burgundy, the Count of Eu, the Count of Auxerre and the Count of Dammartin.[9]

These knights, sergeants or crossbowmen, paid and fed by the King, cannot be considered vassals, nor can they be considered mercenaries.

> *Cette notion d'entourage du roi semble évoluer au début du XIVe siècle, alors qu'il est demandé aux chevaliers de l'hôtel convoqués d'amener avec eux un certain nombre d'hommes d'armes* (This concept of the King's entourage seems to have evolved in the early fourteenth century, when knights summoned to the royal court were required to bring a certain number of men-at-arms with them).[10]

This is shown by this list of summonses during the reign of Philippe Le Long, for 29 May and 15 July 1317:

> From the King's *Hôtel*: Mignot de Vielh Pont, X [i.e. 10 men-at-arms]. Monseigneur Jehan de Gaillon, X. Le comte de Bouloigne, XL. Monseigneur Robert de Boloigne, XX. Le comte de Blais, LX. Le seigneur de Bauçay, XV. Gauvion de Bauçay, XV. Monseigneur P.

5 Xavier Hélary, *L'armée du Roi de France – La guerre de Saint Louis à Philippe le Bel* (Paris: Perrin, 2012), p.90.

6 Philippe Contamine, *La guerre au Moyen Âge* (Paris: Presses Universitaires de France, 2me édition, 1992), p.297.

7 Hélary, *L'armée du Roi de France – La guerre de Saint Louis à Philippe le Bel*, pp.90–91.

8 *Recueil des historiens des Gaules et de la France*, Tome 20 (Paris, 1840), pp.306–308.

9 *Recueil des historiens des Gaules et de la France*, Tome 23 (Paris, 1876), p.733.

10 Contamine, *La guerre au Moyen Âge*, p.205.

> de Garancières, XV. Sancey de Baucey, XV. Le sire de Baufremont, X. Le sire de Lor, X. Le sire de Saint Palaiz, X. Monseigneur Hugue d'Augeron, V. Le seigneur de la Tour.[11]

Although these close associates of the King were paid and fed, they could not constitute a standing army. Their numbers and probably the length of their service were too limited.

11 *Recueil des historiens des Gaules et de la France*, Tome 23, p.808.

4

The Fourteenth Century and the First Founding Ordinances

The *Ordonnance* of 1351

Soldiery, or the 'monetisation of military service' to use Xavier Hélary's term,[1] continued to develop during the fourteenth century. Thus, at the dawn of the Hundred Years' War, armies were already engaged in a process of professionalisation. In England, Edward I, drawing on experience gained during the Scottish Wars, particularly at the Battle of Bannockburn in 1314, enlisted his troops under contracts written on parchment, known as indentures.[2] In France, Philippe le Bel, marked by the defeat at Courtrai in 1302, began this transformation towards paid troops, hired by contract and financed by taxation. Thus, after the Treaty of Athis was signed on 23 June 1305, ending the war between Philippe le Bel and Guy of Dampierre, Count of Flanders, the King of France was required to maintain a permanent troop presence on the Flemish border. On 6 June 1312, Pierre de Galard, Master of the Crossbowmen, was appointed captain in Flanders. Five years later, the *ordonnance* of 12 March 1317 established captains in all the towns of the kingdom:

> And they have requested that we, upon this, make and issue a suitable order and, in each of the good towns, appoint at our expense a good and capable captain who, to the said towns and their people, shall take an oath that they, their towns, their country and the people thereof loyally, well and sufficiently in his power, and the people of the towns and countries shall also swear an oath to the said captain to obey him well and loyally and to assist him in the said guard. And

---

1 Xavier Hélary, 'Pourquoi combattre?', in G. Traina (ed.), *Mondes en Guerre, Tome I: De la préhistoire au Moyen Âge* (Paris: Perrin, 2025), p.534.

2 Jean Favier, *La guerre de Cent Ans* (Paris: Marabout, 1980), pp.79–80.

> nevertheless, in each bailiwick or region, appoint a captain general at our expense, who shall do so, and they shall swear an oath to him in the manner described above, and they shall obey and assist the other captain and all the people of the said towns of the said bailiff or region. And we, for the good of our kingdom, have granted and agreed to this, and especially to appoint the captains, however, as the time is now ripe and the need is great, we command you to immediately, without delay, elect and establish in the cities and towns of Rouen, Pont-de-l'Arche, Pont-Audemer, Pont-l'Evêque, Orbec and all other castles and towns in your bailiwick where we have *châtellenies* or viscounties, by the council of the burghers, elders and sufficient persons of these towns, cities and castles, as many as you deem appropriate, certain persons in this regard who know all the people of the said cities, towns and castles, and of the other towns that belong to and depend on their castellanies and viscounties; who, by virtue of their power and status, will be able to maintain horses and men-at-arms, each according to their status and means, and likewise the lesser men, who will be able to have armour for foot soldiers, each according to their status and means, and according to what they report to you in order to maintain, guard and accomplish.[3]

This *ordonnance* concerns the Bailiwick of Rouen, but others were sent to the Bailiffs of Orléans, Senlis, Vermandois, Caen, Sens, Caux, Gisors, Troyes, Cotentin, Meaux and Amiens.[4] As can be seen, it organised the supervision of urban militias by a captain appointed and paid by the King, in this case Philippe V the Long. Previously, towns and cities were responsible for military authority, appointing their own captains.

As early as 1297, during the first War of Flanders, the garrison of Calais was commanded by a captain of the place, Henri Le Marquis, and consisted of one mounted constabulary and eight foot *connétablies*, the *connétablie* being a unit with a theoretical strength of 45 men at the time. These *soudoyers* (paid soldiers, usually mercenaries) seem to have served for varying periods, ranging from 26 to 90 days.[5] The period of service therefore remained very short and differed little from the 40 days of feudal service required of the King's vassals in the thirteenth century. However, the length of service would evolve and could reach four months, as in the 1303 *ordonnance* issued by Philippe le Bel to the Bailli d'Auvergne.[6]

---

3 Valérie Bessey, *Construire l'armée française*, (Turnhout: Brepols Publishers n.v., 2006), Tome I, p.54.

4 Bessey, *Construire l'armée française*, Tome I, p.53.

5 Hélary, *L'armée du Roi de France – La guerre de Saint Louis à Philippe le Bel*, pp.188–189.

6 Gilles André de la Roque, *Traité du Ban et Arrière-ban* (Paris: Michel le Petit, 1676), p.97.

It should be noted here that, within the framework of the *ban* and *arrière-ban*, men-at-arms were placed under the authority of captains and paid by the day by the lord or by a royal officer – such as the marshal or the master of crossbowmen – responsible for their recruitment. Before pay was issued, troop musters, known as *montres*, were organised to control the presence and equipment of the soldiers. The main objective was to verify that the troops serving the King had the agreed number of men. Military service was the subject of formal contracts, known as letters of retention, which specified the nature and duration of the commitment, as well as the amount of remuneration. An amount on pay, known as a loan, was generally paid in advance. In addition, these contracts also set out the compensation payable in the event of loss or hurt of horses during operations, known as *restor*.

It was not until the defeat at Crécy that the organisation and control of the army began to evolve. Jean le Bon attempted to structure his army through the *ordonnance* of 30 April 1351. The objective was twofold: to organise the army into coherent companies under the authority of captains selected for their skill, and to regularly check the strength and equipment of these units. This *ordonnance* therefore introduced *revues* (reviews); periodic and unannounced inspections aimed at reviewing the strength and readiness of the troops. The purpose of these regular checks was to prevent fraud, particularly the practice of listing the same man-at-arms in several places at once, when logically he could only serve in one company. Similarly, they prevented several units from sharing the same military equipment. To ensure the effectiveness of these checks, inspections were carried out without warning. Each soldier was identified by name and nickname, each horse by its markings and coat colour, and even by the type of bit or harness. Pay could then be issued on the spot, at the end of the inspection.

Given that these *Regulations for soldiers of April 1351* constitute a fundamental text for understanding the evolution of the professionalisation of the royal army in the fourteenth and fifteenth centuries, a summary of the main articles is presented below:[7]

1. A banneret shall receive forty *sols tournois* per day; a knight twenty sols tournois, an armed squire ten *sols tournois*, and a valet armed with a hauberk, a bascinet with a camail, a gorget, and gauntlets five *sols tournois*.
2. The men-at-arms shall be organised into large bands comprising at least twenty-five, thirty, forty, fifty, sixty, seventy or eighty men-at-arms, depending on the resources of the *chevetaines* [chieftains] and lords who command them. The constables, marshals, masters of crossbowmen and stewards shall receive

7 Mr Secousse, *Ordonnances des Roys de France de la troisième race, quatrième volume* (Paris: 1734), pp.67–70.

the muster rolls or may appoint suitable, knowledgeable and sworn persons to receive these muster rolls loyally. At each muster, the *chevetaine* and his men, knights, squires and armed valets shall be present on their warhorses. Each man will be called, his name and nickname written down, as well as the colour of the coat, the markings, the sign and the price of the horse he is riding. Each horse on the same route shall be branded with the same iron and registered only if its price exceeds thirty *livres tournois*, or twenty *livres tournois* for the horse of an armed valet. These inspections shall be carried out frequently, armed and unarmed, at least twice a month, without warning, in order to prevent the borrowing of horses or harnesses.

3. Men-at-arms shall swear not to leave their captain's company for another without the permission of the constable, marshal or master of crossbowmen. Battle commanders shall swear that they will maintain the number of men-at-arms and haubergeons as well as their armour and mounts in accordance with the muster, without fraud. They shall take this oath before the constable, the marshal or their delegate. The bannerets belonging to each battle, as well as all knights, squires and haubergeons dependent on these bannerets, shall also take this oath. Each banneret shall know the names and surnames of the men-at-arms and haubergeons belonging to their company.
4. All men-at-arms and haubergeons must participate in the parade and all must have a master or *chevetaine*. The constables, marshals, masters of crossbowmen or other delegates shall appoint a knight as chevetaine to command a route of twenty-five or thirty men-at-arms. This knight and his company shall make a *montre* as specified in the preceding articles. This knight shall take care of his power and ensure that his company has no faults. The company of this knight shall have a pennant with a tail, bearing his arms, and shall receive wages equivalent to those of a banneret.
5. A horse registered for inspection may not be purchased, exchanged, given away or disposed of without the authorisation of the constable, a marshal or other delegate during the period of pledges. No horse may be registered unless it has been presented for inspection.
6. No man-at-arms or haubergeon may take leave from the battle commander without the authorisation of the constable, marshal, master of crossbowmen or other delegate, or unless the banneret, knight or squire received in review has previously informed and notified the battle commander.
7. Anyone who has or sees a horse received for display that is lost, frightened or dead must immediately notify the constable, marshal, master of the crossbowmen or their delegates so that

the restor can be applied as soon as possible, enabling the horse to serve and receive its wages.

8. Concerning the foot soldiers of the kingdom, crossbowmen equipped with a good crossbow, a good baldric, and armed with plate armour, a *cervellière*, a gorget, a sword, a knife, armour, iron and leather arm guards shall receive three *sols tournois* per day in wages; a pavise bearer armed with plate armour or a hauberk, a bascinet with a camail, a gorget, armour, arm guards, gauntlets, a sword, a knife, a lance, a pavise or other armour shall receive two and a half *sols tournois* per day in wages. The foot soldiers shall be organised into companies of twenty-five or thirty men. Each *connétable* (commander of a *connétablie*) shall receive double pay and shall parade before those who are appointed or delegated to this task. Each constable shall have a pennant with a tail, bearing the arms or insignia of his choice. All crossbowmen and pavise bearers, armed with the armour they are required to wear, shall parade where their names and surnames shall be recorded, as well as that of the constable who commands them. The person receiving the parade shall verify that each foot soldier, crossbowman or pavise bearer has all his weapons, as recorded. He shall punish and fine any offender, and the offence and fine shall be notified to the crossbowmen's clerk. Inspections shall be carried out twice a month.
9. The marshals, masters of crossbowmen and other delegates shall inspect and receive the montres, especially at the beginning, so that the men-at-arms pay more attention to performing loyal and well-timed *montres*.
10. All lords and *chevetaines* who have armed forces shall swear before the King, his lieutenants, constables, marshals or their captains, or those whom the King delegates, to serve loyally and to continually maintain in their service the number of armed men for whom they have taken pledges. This oath shall be taken before the King or those to whom he has delegated authority.

This regulation is of interest to us in two ways in respect of the context of the evolution of the royal army towards a standing army.

On the one hand, it is a regulation that attempts to regulate the organisation as well as the composition (staff, equipment, mounts) and control of combat formations. Article 2, in particular, pays special attention to how *montres* and *revues* are carried out: who is authorised to carry out these *montres* and *revues*, what must be shown and recorded, and how often they must be carried out. Moreover, Jean II le Bon, did not stop at this *ordonnance*. To ensure its application, on 28 January 1356 he appointed 12 commissioners to regulate the inspections that the States of Languedoc undertook to provide him with. And the Great Charter of 1356 specified for the payment of wages that:

> The superintendents of the States shall attend the *montres*; that no one shall be believed on his written word or his word of honour, except the signatories and princes of the blood; that nothing shall be paid except to those who actually present themselves in arms, that the horses shall be marked and that the commissioners shall make proper note of everything in their revues.[8]

This regulation thus foreshadows the numerous regulations that would follow and would continue through into the eighteenth century.

Men-at-arms in battle, dated to the end of the fourteenth century. Illustration taken from the *Chroniques de Saint-Denis*, British Library Ms Roy 20C-VII f. 030. (Public Domain)

On the other hand, he established a real organisation within the royal army that foreshadowed the regulations of the fifteenth century: the army, commanded by the King or his lieutenant (the constable or marshal), was divided as in the past into *batailles*, themselves commanded by *batailles* commanders (usually bannerets). But these batailles were now broken down into smaller units called *routes*, commanded by a *chevetaine*. These *routes*

8 Jean Milot, 'Évolution du Corps des Intendants Militaires (des origines à 1882),' *Revue du Nord*, 198 (1968), p.383.

generally consisted of 25 or 30 men but could number up to 90 men in the cavalry. In the infantry, these units of 25 or 30 men were called *connétablies* or companies and were commanded by a *connétable*. These regulations also authorised *chevetaines* and *connétables* to carry a pennant with a tail on their lances. We already know that the post of *connétablie* that existed under Philippe le Bel: remember here that in 1297, the garrison of Calais had nine *connétablies*, including one cavalry unit. Additionally, Guillaume Guiart, a French chronicler and poet who fought at the Battle of Mons-en-Pévèle and died around 1316, describes *connétablies* of soldiers (verses 7393 and 10,563)[9], *connétables* (verse 10 649)[10] and *chevetaingnes* (verse 7650).[11] Regarding the *route*, verse 6774 of Guillaume Guiart's chronicle refers to it ('Whose entire company is already among the Flamenz, *mut cil de Fieules* and his *route*, like battle-hardened men')[12] as well as verse 7007 ('Let them guard against Renaut de Pinquegni coming, and about sixty others! Their *route* between Flamens stands...'),[13] verse 7717 ('God! May we return in good route, and beautiful stream of people, Monsieur Renaut de l'Aiglentier!')[14] or verses 8500, 8528 and 11,381.[15] The term actually dates to the mid-thirteenth century, as it is found in Philippe Mousket's rhyming chronicle to refer to soldiers organised into bands.[16] This unit is mentioned even earlier, in *Yvain*, or *The Knight of the Lion*, a novel written in 1176 by Chrétien de Troyes:

> Welcome, they say, 'to this *route*,
> Which is full of valiant people!
> May he who drives them be blessed,
> And who gives us such good hosts![17]

---

9 J.A. Buchon, *Branche des royaux lignages, chronique métrique de Guillaume Guiart*, Tome VIII (Paris, 1828), pp.285 & 407.

10 Buchon, *Branche des royaux lignages, chronique métrique de Guillaume Guiart*, Tome VIII, p.410.

11 Buchon, *Branche des royaux lignages, chronique métrique de Guillaume Guiart*, Tome VIII, p.295.

12 Buchon, *Branche des royaux lignages, chronique métrique de Guillaume Guiart*, Tome VIII, p.261.

13 Buchon, *Branche des royaux lignages, chronique métrique de Guillaume Guiart*, Tome VIII, p.270.

14 Buchon, *Branche des royaux lignages, chronique métrique de Guillaume Guiart*, Tome VIII, p.297.

15 Buchon, *Branche des royaux lignages, chronique métrique de Guillaume Guiart*, Tome VIII, pp.327, 328 et 438.

16 Centre national de Resources Textuelles et Lexicales: https://www.cnrtl.fr/etymologie/routier//1

17 Chrétien de Troyes, '*Yvain* ou *le chevalier au lion*', in A. Pauphilet (ed.), *Poètes et Romanciers du Moyen Âge* (Paris: Gallimard, Bibliothèque de la Pléiade, 1952), p.222.

The term *rotte* or *rote* refers, in Old French, to a small path traced by the passage of animals, whether herds or wild animals. This would be an evolution of the Latin *rupta*, which means broken or scattered. However, in our context, the word *route* most likely comes from the Old German *rotte* or *rote*, which means a military group of varying size, a clan, or a band of thieves or vagabonds.[18] The German etymological dictionary writer Wolfgang Pfeifer defines the term *rotte* as a group, a crowd and, more specifically, in High German, a gang, horde or criminal gang. In Middle High German (*c.* 1050–1350), the meaning evolved to refer to a group of warriors or a cooperative. In Middle Low German, this term also refers to a group or division.[19] Finally, it should be noted that the German term also comes from the Latin *rupta*. The term *route* to designate a unit comprising several dozen men, or even a few hundred, was used until the end of the century. Thus, in 1385, Froissart reports that the Duke of Bourbon 'left Moulins in Bourbonnais and rode with a fine *route* of knights and squires.'[20] He also reports that, for the expedition to Castile in 1386, two knights, Guillaume de Lignac and Gauthier de Passac, were appointed captains of Louis de Bourbon's vanguard, and that they 'put themselves in good order, themselves and their *route*, and in very good *ordonnance*.'[21] Thus, the term *routiers* evolved to refer to members of irregular companies who ravaged France until the mid-fifteenth century.

While this organisation is not entirely new, Article 3 of the April 1351 regulation becomes particularly interesting when it specifies that men-at-arms 'shall swear that they will not leave their captain's company', and then, further on, that the *chefs de batailles* must swear that none of the men-at-arms and haubergeons of their company will do the opposite (of what they have sworn). Furthermore, Article 8, which deals with the infantry, specifies that 'all foot soldiers shall be organised into companies of twenty-five or thirty men.' This regulation therefore paves the way, albeit clumsily at times due to the confusion of the terms used, for companies commanded by captains. We find the term *chevetaine*, this time written as '*chiefvetaine*', in the '*Ordonnance* made as a result of the Assembly of the Three States of the Languedoc' dated 28 December 1355.[22] Finally, the *ordonnance* of 30 March 1356 refers to captains in Article 35, placing them before the

---

18 Nicolas Savy, *Bertrucat d'Albret ou le destin d'un capitaine gascon du Roi d'Angleterre pendant la guerre de cent ans* (Pradines: Archeodrom, 2015), p.15.

19 *Digitales Wörterbuch der deutschen Sprache*, https://www.dwds.de/wb/zusammenrotten; *Etymologische Wörterbuch des Deutschen* (Strasbourg: Karl J. Trübner, 1883 pour la première édition, 1915 pour la 8e édition).

20 Jean Froissart, 'Les chroniques de Jean Froissart' in *Collection des Chroniques Nationales Françaises*, livre second, Tome IX (Paris: Delagrave, 1824), Chapter 215, p.72.

21 Jean Froissart, *Les chroniques de Jean Froissart*, (Paris: A. Desrez, 1835), Livre III, Chapter 53, p.549.

22 Mr Secousse, *Ordonnances des Roys de France de la troisième race, Troisième volume* (Paris, 1732), p.35.

constable: 'none of the lieutenants, captains, constables, marshals, admirals, masters of crossbowmen...'[23] However, the term captain is probably used here to refer to the commander of a place or stronghold, as we have seen was the case under Philippe le Bel, and not as the commander of a *route*.

To what extent was the ordinance of 1351 applied, and did it take effect on the eve of the Battle of Poitiers (1356)? We do not really know. Froissart, who echoes the chronicle of Jean le Bel, recounts in his chronicles that the nobles of the kingdom present in the army gathered:

> There they deliberated at length on how they would defend themselves. It was therefore ordered that all men should arm themselves immediately, and that each lord should raise his banner and advance, in the name of God and Saint-Denis, and that they should prepare for battle, as if to fight at once.... Three large *batailles* were ordered on the advice of the Constable of France and the marshals: each had sixteen thousand men, all of whom were experienced and proven men-at-arms. The first was led by the Duke of Orléans, with thirty-six banners and twice as many pennants; the second by the Duke of Normandy and his two brothers, Sir Louis and Sir John; the third was to be commanded by the King of France.[24]

Based on the first battle, each banner would have had 400 to 500 men and each pennant more than 222 men. With the pennant representing the *route*, the figures here seem far removed from those prescribed by the 1351 *ordonnance*. However, Froissart clearly states that the men were indeed 'shown to be men-at-arms'. It therefore seems that the *ordonnance* was applied. However, this did not produce any results in terms of effectiveness. Further on, Froissart himself asserts that the arrangements made for the Battle of Poitiers were better than those for Crécy:

> But in my opinion, the Battle of Poitiers was fought much better than that of Crécy; and all kinds of men-at-arms had more time to observe and consider their enemies than they had at Crécy; for the said battle of Crécy began late in the evening, without preparation or order, and that of Poitiers began early in the morning, and was quite well organised, if fortune had been on the side of the French.[25]

According to the chronicler, despite being outnumbered seven to one, the English were able to use the terrain to their advantage to overcome this

23 Mr Secousse, *Ordonnances des Roys de France de la troisième race, Troisième volume* (Paris, 1732), p.139.

24 Froissart, 'Chroniques' in *Collection de chroniques*, p.102.

25 Froissart, 'Chroniques' in *Collection de chroniques*, pp.119–120.

disadvantage. It was therefore thanks to their superior command that they won this victory.

The Time of Companies

After the defeat at Poitiers, the Treaty of Brétigny of 8 May 1360 left many soldiers unemployed. These *routiers*, who had previously been trained in the *routes*, formed companies of up to 200 men, led by a captain who became a war entrepreneur:[26] Bertrucat d'Albret, Seguin de Badefol, Mouton de Blainville, Arnaud de Cervole known as the Archpriest, Bertrand du Guesclin, Jean de Grailly known as the Captal de Buch and Bernard de la Salle are the main examples. Some, such as Mouton de Blainville, Bertrand du Guesclin and Jean de Grailly, were loyal to the King who paid them, while others sold their services to the highest bidder. According to Philippe Contamine:

> ...when the companies were formed after the truce concluded in May 1360 in Brétigny between the English and the French – it was indeed initially a voluntary and, in some respects, artificial creation, rather than the simple survival of formations that already existed as such before – it was they themselves who gave themselves this name, deliberately reviving a term that had already been used, albeit rarely, in previous years to refer to similar formations. In order to impress the people and the authorities and to emphasise their numerical importance, they even called themselves 'The Great Company'. Its members referred to each other as 'companions'.[27]

The names of these companies could vary: '*Grans Compaignes*' in 1360, '*Compaignes*', '*gens des compaignes*', '*Bretons et gens de compaignes*', '*gens de Compaignes*', '*gens de la Grant Compaigne*' and '*Gascoings de compaignes*' to give just a few examples.[28] The *Grandes Chroniques de France* recounts that in 1365,

> Monseigneur Bertrand du Guesclin negotiated with several companies of men, English, Gascon, Breton, Norman and other nations who were in the Kingdom of France and held several fortresses there, some since the time of the war with the King of England, and others that had been occupied by the said companies

26 Favier, *La guerre de Cent Ans*, p.301.

27 Philippe Contamine, 'Les compagnies d'aventure en France pendant la Guerre de Cent Ans' in *Mélanges de l'École française de Rome*, 87:2 (1975), p.369.

28 Contamine, 'Les compagnies d'aventure en France pendant la Guerre de Cent Ans', pp.370–371.

> since the peace made between the Kings of France and England; and many had damaged and were damaging the said kingdom of France every day.[29]

The strength of these companies of *routiers* – a pleonasm, as Nicolas Savy rightly points out, since the terms *compagnie* and *route* refer to the same type of unit[30] – varies, but are frequently in the range of 100 to 200 men. They could then join forces to attack better-defended locations: between two and six companies, or even more, could assemble for a limited period. Thus, Bertrucat de Labret (or d'Albret) brought together six Anglo-Gascon companies, numbering around 1,000 men, in September 1379 to pillage and ransom Beaucaire and Béziers areas.[31] It was in his order dated 19 July 1367 that Charles V used this term to refer to these bands: 'We have been assured by several trustworthy sources that many members of the company had and still have the intention, desire and intention to return to our Kingdom.'[32]

The term companies already existed in the twelfth century,[33] as in the anonymous epic poem *Le charroi de Nîmes*,[34] or the novel *Yvain* by Chrétien de Troyes,[35] but it is true that at that time, the term was used more in the sense of 'in the company of'. It was not until the fourteenth century, and particularly the Jean le Bon *ordonnance* of 1351, that the term came to refer to a military unit, even if it did not then designate a unit with a specific number of personnel.

When Charles V ascended the throne on 8 April 1364, he had to act quickly against these companies. According to Philippe Contamine,

> to undertake his reconquest, Charles V did not seek to use new types of combatants: his forces consisted mainly of men-at-arms (recruited primarily from different regions of the kingdom) and crossbowmen,

29 Paulin Paris (ed.), *Les grandes Chroniques de France*, Tome sixième (Paris: Techener, 1838), p.237.

30 Nicolas Savy, *La guérilla anglaise en Languedoc, Auvergne et Limousin – Les cavaliers de l'Apocalypse (1369–1393)* (Pradines: Chez L'auteur, 2022), p.19. It should be noted that Froissart refers to "companions keeping route": Froissart, *Les chroniques de Jean Froissart, livre troisième*, Chapter 17, p.348. Froissart also uses both terms without distinguishing between their meanings: "for on all sides companies and routes riden": Froissart, *Les chroniques de Jean Froissart, livre troisième*, Chapter 17, p.355.

31 Savy, *Bertrucat d'Albret*, pp.325–326.

32 Secousse, *Ordonnances des Roys de France de la troisième race*, cinquième volume, p.15.

33 Contamine, 'Les compagnies d'aventure en France pendant la Guerre de Cent Ans', p.369.

34 Anonymous, 'Le charroi de Nîmes', in A. Pauphilet (ed.) *Poètes et Romanciers du Moyen Âge* (Paris: Gallimard, La Pléiade, 1952), p.127.

35 Chrétien de Troyes, *Romans de la Table Ronde*, p.286; Chrétien de Troyes, 'Yvain', p.222.

> either on foot or on horseback, of French or foreign origin (Italy, Spain). These were the basic types, to which were added only a small number of archers, on horseback or on foot, as well as sergeants and pavisiers occasionally provided by urban communities.[36]

And to organise these men, Article 4 of the *Ordonnance* of 19 July 1367 stipulates that:

> Each of these captains, or countries where he is commissioned, shall inquire and ascertain without delay what men-at-arms he may have, and how many could help him to lead out, both those residing in the country of his captaincy and those outside the neighbouring places; the places and fortresses that remain garrisoned; and as soon as he can, he shall certify this to Us, so that, if necessary, We may know and be able to know how many and what kind of men We could be provided with: those men who are chosen, the captains shall ensure that they remain garrisoned and ready, to be available whenever they are summoned: and when summoned, they shall be paid their wages from the funds in the dioceses to which they belong.[37]

Article 7 adds specific provisions concerning the infantry to be mobilised:

> We hereby order and command all archers and crossbowmen residing in our good towns to prepare themselves, and that the governors of each of these towns let it be known how many archers and crossbowmen there are, and how many could be had, if need be, and let them make a register in each town, and certify this to us as soon as they can; and with this, let them enjoin and induce all young men to practise, continue and learn the art and manner of shooting.[38]

An *ordonnance* of 23 May and 3 April 1369 prohibiting games of chance also enjoined Parisians to practise archery and crossbow shooting.[39]

Charles V's primary objective was to recapture the territories ceded to the English. Thus, the royal troops began to gain ground from 1369 onwards. But above all, he needed men to hold all the strongholds in

36 Philippe Contamine, 'La Guerre de Cent Ans: le XIVe siècle. La France au rythme de la guerre', in A. Corvisier (ed.), *Histoire militaire de la France: 1, Des origines à 1715* (Paris: Presses Universitaires de France, 1992), pp.125-152.

37 Secousse, *Ordonnances des Roys de France de la troisième race,* cinquième volume, p.16.

38 Secousse, *Ordonnances des Roys de France de la troisième race,* cinquième volume, p.16.

39 Secousse, *Ordonnances des Roys de France de la troisième race,* cinquième volume, p.172.

the kingdom. These permanent forces were then supplemented by new retinues during the months of military activity dedicated to the reconquest. Philippe Contamine estimates the number of troops at 3,400 for two-thirds of the year between 1369 and 1380, rising to 5,400 for the third of the year corresponding to the months favourable for campaigning.[40] Thus, although the King sometimes resorted to general summonses, these special convocations corresponded to specific expeditions, such as those to counter the expeditions of the Duke of Lancaster in 1369 and 1373 or those of Buckingham in 1380. Apart from these specific occasions, Charles V's army was mainly composed of volunteers whose captains were retained in his service by letters of retinue. Here we see a trend towards centralisation, as it appears that these letters were only issued by two people: Charles V, of course, for most of the kingdom, and Louis d'Anjou for Languedoc.[41] The King of France therefore had limited forces at his disposal, a few thousand men at most, but they were regular troops, paid.[42] Various ordinances, including that of 7 December 1369, were thus intended to finance the war.[43] Then, to stack the odds in his favour, on 2 October 1370, the King appointed Bertrand du Guesclin as Constable of France.[44]

At that time (1369–1380), wages were 60 francs per month for a knight banneret, 30 francs for a knight bachelor, 15 francs for a squire or 'well-equipped' archer, 12 francs for a mounted crossbowman, 8 francs for a foot crossbowman, 30 francs for a captain of mounted or foot crossbowmen, 24 francs for a constable of mounted crossbowmen and 16 francs for a constable of foot crossbowmen.[45] However, Philippe Contamine notes exceptions with examples of 40, 35 and even 15 francs per month for a knight, and exceptions of 25, 20, 18 and even 12 francs per month for a man-at-arms.[46]

The decade from 1369 to 1380 was therefore a period of reconquest. It was a slow reconquest, achieved by avoiding battles and cavalry charges. Bertrand du Guesclin, Olivier de Clisson, Jean de Vienne, Mouton de Blainville, Louis d'Anjou and the Duke of Bourbon were the architects of this reconquest. The army led by these men was, according to Jean Favier,

---

40 Philippe Contamine, 'La Guerre de Cent Ans: le XIVe siècle. La France au rythme de la guerre', in A. Corvisier (ed.), *Histoire militaire de la France: 1, Des origines à 1715* (Paris: Presses Universitaires de France, 1992), pp.125-152

41 Philippe Contamine, 'La Guerre de Cent Ans: le XIVe siècle. La France au rythme de la guerre', in A. Corvisier (ed.), *Histoire militaire de la France: 1, Des origines à 1715* (Paris: Presses Universitaires de France, 1992), pp.125-152.

42 Xavier Hélary, 'Combats et opérations militaires', in G. Traina (ed.) *Mondes en Guerre – Tome I: De la préhistoire au Moyen Âge* (Paris: Perrin, 2025), pp.577–78.

43 Paulin Paris, *Les grandes Chroniques de France*, Tome sixième, pp.321–322.

44 Paulin Paris, *Les grandes Chroniques de France*, Tome sixième, p.325.

45 Philippe Contamine, *Guerre, État et Société à la fin du Moyen Âge. Tome 2. Études sur les armées des rois de France 1337–1494* (Paris: EHESS, 2024), Annexe VI.

46 Contamine, *Guerre, État et Société à la fin du Moyen Âge. Tome 2. Études sur les armées des rois de France 1337–1494*, Annexe VI.

an 'army of professionals born out of the break-up of the old companies and the knightly army resurrected after the tragedies of Crécy and Poitiers.'[47] But, he continues, 'the feudal army was practically a thing of the past.... The King retains professional soldiers, pays them and keeps them.'[48] Charles V knew how to choose his captains, regardless of their origin, such as Du Guesclin or Clisson, and he knew how to keep them in his service. 'As for the troops, they are battle-hardened and accustomed to manoeuvring together. By constantly renewing the retainers, the King of France maintained what was almost a permanent army from 1369 onwards,' Favier concluded.[49]

French footmen in battle, end of fourteenth century. Illustration from the *Chroniques de Saint-Denis*, British Library Ms Roy 20C-VII f. 133. (Public Domain)

The *Ordonnance* of 1374

To organise this army of reconquest, ensure the presence of soldiers, and prevent fraud and misdeeds, the legislative framework had to be updated. Never mind that Charles V issued a first mandate on 17 October 1373 in which he ordered each captain to present only the men-at-arms from their *hotel* at each *montre* or review. The combatants in his retinue were then to be divided into *chambres*, each of which was to have no more than 10 men-at-arms. The captain then received wages for each *chambre* and

47 Favier, *La guerre de Cent Ans*, p.341.
48 Favier, *La guerre de Cent Ans*, p.341.
49 Favier, *La guerre de Cent Ans*, p.342.

each *montre*.[50] These initial provisions were then incorporated into the *ordonnance* of 13 January 1374, for the Regulation of Troops. The King justified this *ordonnance* on the grounds that, in times of war, some captains of men-at-arms,

> ...did not maintain the number (of men) they claimed to have and took payment. And that often the money they received was not paid to their men according to what they had received; and also that when these men left before the time they were supposed to serve, they made no mention of it to the war treasurers, their lieutenants and clerks of montres.[51]

The main articles of these regulations are given in Appendix I.

With this regulation, which reiterates and updates that of 1351, Charles V ordered that the men-at-arms in his employ be divided into *routes* of 100 men each; each *route* being under the command of a captain, who himself reported to a lieutenant of the King. This regulation differs from that of Jean II only in the size of these *routes*, which must now necessarily be 100 men, and in the name of their leader, the term captain replacing that of *chevetaine*. The title 'captain' thus clearly extends from the military command of a stronghold, as was previously the case, to the command of a *route*. This *ordonnance* also notes the appearance of a small unit, the *chambre*. This division of the *route* or company appears in documents from 1368 onwards.[52] This order also confirms the payment of wages per *chambre* (Article 11).

Charles V then endeavoured to monitor the implementation of this *ordonnance* and the number of troops. Several examples illustrate the application of this *ordonnance* in the years that followed. For example, on 24 August 1375, Charles V retained Alain de Beaumont in his service with 100 men-at-arms in Brittany. Beaumont was then retained with 50 men in 1376, 1377 and 1378 to serve in Angoumois, Limousin, Périgord and Saintonge. Jean, Duke of Berry, was ordered to provide 300 men-at-arms on 28 April 1373, then 100 men-at-arms on 19 December 1374. Jean de Mauquenchy, known as Mouton de Blainville, was retained for a company of 300 men-at-arms on 12 September 1369, then for 100 men-at-arms in

50 Philippe Contamine, 'La Guerre de Cent Ans: le XIVe siècle. La France au rythme de la guerre', in A. Corvisier (ed.), *Histoire militaire de la France: 1, Des origines à 1715* (Paris: Presses Universitaires de France, 1992), pp.147–148.

51 Secousse, *Ordonnances des Roys de France de la troisième race*, cinquième volume, p.658.

52 Contamine, 'La Guerre de Cent Ans,' p.147.

1371, 1375 and 1379.[53] Finally, Olivier de Clisson's company was inspected from January to August 1376 in Vannes for 200 men-at-arms.[54]

Some *montres* from this period also highlight the control of sub-units known as *chambres*. For example, a *montre* received in Amiens from the company of Gauvinet de Bailleul, knight, on 13 March 1379, lists only himself and 8 squires.[55] The *montre* of Hugues d'Arquenay, a knight bachelor, included another knight bachelor and 10 squires on 1 January 1380 in Brittany. However, there are *montres* that are more difficult to place within this organisation. For example, that of Jehan Darien, squire, also compiled in Brittany on 29 April 1380, had 15 squires with him.[56] As another example, the *montre* of 'Messire Maurice Mauvinet, knight bachelor,' received in Amiens on 1 September 1386, lists only 2 knights, including Mauvinet, and 26 squires.[57] These muster rolls therefore probably reflect garrisons in border areas (Brittany, Picardy) rather than *routes*.

A man-at-arms around 1380. His head is protected by a bascinet. Drawing from Viollet-le-Duc, *Encyclopédie médiévale*. (Public Domain)

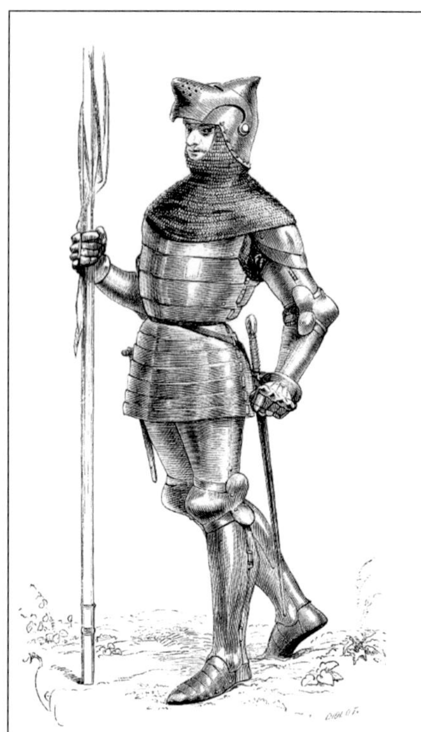

Not only did Charles V want to maintain control, but he also tried to pay wages regularly: between 800,000 and 1,000,000 francs were allocated each year to pay the soldiers. Thus, Étienne Braque, treasurer of wars, paid Bertrand du Guesclin 127,000 *livres tournois* (i.e. francs) in 16 instalments between 20 May 1373 and 31 March 1374 for 400 men-at-arms present between March and November 1373, 600 men-at-arms in December, and 700 men-at-arms in January and February 1374.[58] In this way, the King of France managed to retain the loyalty of his captains over several years, as well as the men in their companies. The latter took up winter quarters in strongholds and garrisons between different campaigns. Among Charles V's captains, we regularly find Bertrand du Guesclin, Olivier de Clisson, Louis de Sancerre, Alain de Beaumont, Owen of Wales, or the 20 men-at-arms of Hue du Boulay and the 24 mounted crossbowmen of Étienne Présent forming the King's bodyguard.[59]

53 Contamine, *Guerre, État et Société à la fin du Moyen Âge. Tome 2. Études sur les armées des rois de France 1337–1494*, pp.532–593.

54 Philippe Contamine, 'La Guerre de Cent Ans,' p.148.

55 Victor de Beauvillé, *Recueil de documents inédits concernant la Picardie*, deuxième partie (Paris, 1867) Chapter I, p.95.

56 'Montres inédites de gens d'armes Bretons', Extrait de la *Revue Historique de l'Ouest*, années 1885 à 1887. https://tudchentil.org/spip.php?article531

57 Beauvillé, *Recueil de documents inédits concernant la Picardie*, deuxième partie, Chapter IX, pp.102–103.

58 Philippe Contamine, 'La Guerre de Cent Ans: le XIVe siècle. La France au rythme de la guerre', in A. Corvisier (ed.), *Histoire militaire de la France: 1, Des origines à 1715* (Paris: Presses Universitaires de France, 1992), pp.125-152.

59 Philippe Contamine, 'La Guerre de Cent Ans: le XIVe siècle. La France au rythme de la guerre', in A. Corvisier (ed.), *Histoire militaire de la France: 1, Des origines à 1715* (Paris: Presses Universitaires de France, 1992), pp.125-152.

Philippe Contamine identified 40 captains of men-at-arms who were retained by Charles V between 1369 and 1380 for a period of at least two years or during four different years, thus paving the way for a standing army: Pierre dit Hutin d'Aumont, who commanded up to 70 lances between 1368 and 1388; Robert le Baveux, who commanded between 40 and 60 men-at-arms between 1375 and 1379; Alain de Beaumont, who commanded up to 300 men-at-arms between 1368 and 1382; Jean de France, Duke of Berry, who commanded up to 800 men-at-arms between 1369 and 1374; Jean de Mauquenchy, known as Mouton de Blainville, who commanded up to 100 lances between 1364 and 1388; Guillaume de la Boissière, known as Parrigny, who commanded companies from 1377 to 1394, including 40 lances in 1377; Guillaume des Bordes, who commanded up to 200 men-at-arms from 1368 to 1379; Hue du Boulay, who commanded companies between 1364 and 1392 and commanded the 20 men-at-arms of the King's guard in 1369; Louis, Duke of Bourbon, who commanded between 200 and 400 men-at-arms between 1369 and 1379; Jean III de Bueil, who commanded up to 100 men-at-arms from 1368 to 1388; Hue de Châtillon, who commanded up to 400 men-at-arms between 1364 and 1388; Olivier de Clisson, who commanded up to 400 men-at-arms between 1370 and 1392; Hervé le Coich, who commanded up to 44 lances from 1375 to 1393; Enguerrand VII de Coucy, who commanded up to 200 men-at-arms from 1377 to 1392; Colart d'Estouteville, who commanded up to 40 men-at-arms from 1369 to 1388; Jean, Lord of La Ferté-Frênel, who served from 1369 to 1394; Owen of Wales (Owain Lawgoch), who commanded up to 200 men-at-arms and 100 crossbowmen from 1369 to 1378; Bertrand du Guesclin, who commanded up to 900 men-at-arms, including the 100 men-at-arms of his *hotel* from 1364 to 1380, in addition to his army commands; Alain de la Houssaye, who commanded up to 40 men-at-arms from 1368 to 1378; Guillaume de la Houssaye, who was retained for 20 men-at-arms from 1376 to 1379; Jean du Juch, who commanded up to 40 men-at-arms between 1371 and 1380; Guillaume de Laigue, who commanded 10 men-at-arms and 4 crossbowmen from 1376 to 1377 and was captain until 1392; Jean, Count of la Marche, who commanded up to 300 men-at-arms from 1370 to 1392; Guillaume de Mareuil, who commanded up to 80 men-at-arms, 10 mounted crossbowmen and 20 foot crossbowmen from 1372 to 1385; Raymond de Mareuil, who served from 1370 to 1394; Olivier Le Moine, who served from 1371 to 1385; Jacques de Montmor, who commanded up to 60 men-at-arms and 40 foot crossbowmen from 1377 to 1394; Gaucher de Passac, who commanded up to 250 men-at-arms and 50 crossbowmen from 1372 to 1391; Renaud VI de Pons, who commanded up to 300 men-at-arms between 1370 and 1416; Olivier du Pont, who commanded up to 50 men-at-arms between 1377 and 1384; Thibaud du Pont, who was retained for up to 100 men-at-arms from 1371 to 1377; Bureau de la Rivière, who commanded up to 200 men-at-arms from 1372 to 1392; Alain VIII, Viscount of Rohan, who was retained for up to 25 lances from 1377 to 1392; Jean, Viscount of Rohan, who commanded up to 200 men-at-arms from 1374 to 1386; Louis de Sancerre, who was retained for up to 500 men-at-arms from 1369 to 1380 before being appointed Constable of France in 1397; Jean de Sempy, who commanded up to 200 men-at-arms from 1372 to 1382; Maurice de Tréséguidy, who commanded up to 40 men-at-arms from 1374 to 1392; Pierre Trousseau, who commanded at least 24 men-at-arms from 1371 to 1373; Jean de Vienne, who commanded up to 200 men-at-arms from 1369 to 1388; Jean Wyn, of Welsh origin, who commanded up to 100 lances from 1369 to 1384.[60]

Men-at-arms in battle, end of fourteenth century. Illustration from the 'Chroniques de Saint-Denis', British Library Ms Roy 20C-VII f. 035. (Public Domain)

Most French 'armies' at that time were what we would today call expeditionary forces: they did not exceed a few companies in size and were mainly composed of men-at-arms and crossbowmen. In June 1381, for example, the Duke of Berry raised 400 men-at-arms and 400 crossbowmen in Gévaudan, Velay, Vivarais and Valentinois.[61] Although the young King Charles VI requested in 1386 that an army of 6,000 men-at-arms and 6,000 crossbowmen be raised to invade England, this project was quickly abandoned.[62] However, this ratio of one man-at-arms to one crossbowman was exceptional, as the latter were generally in the minority. In May 1381, *Maréchal* Louis de Sancerre raised 480 men-at-arms and 100 crossbowmen, again to defend Gévaudan, Velay and Rouergue against irregular companies.[63] Other examples are the 40 lances and 60 crossbowmen commanded by Jean Moulin sent in 1383 by the Count of Flanders to defend

60 Contamine, *Guerre, État et société à la fin du Moyen Âge: études sur les armées des rois de France, 1337–1494*, Tome 2, pp.562–593.

61 Savy, *La guérilla anglaise en Languedoc, Auvergne et Limousin*, p.226.

62 Froissart, *Les chroniques de Jean Froissart*, Livre III, Chapter 52, p.548.

63 Savy, *La guérilla anglaise en Languedoc, Auvergne et Limousin*, p.241.

Le Moûtier near Menin,[64] or in May 1385 when Admiral Jean de Vienne led 1,000 men-at-arms and 600 crossbowmen for a landing in Scotland.[65] We can also mention the 400 men-at-arms and 200 crossbowmen commanded by Enguerrand de Coucy, sent to Auvergne by the *Maréchal de* Sancerre in May 1389[66] or the 400 to 600 men-at-arms and 120 Genoese crossbowmen commanded by Robert de Béthune in Auvergne in 1390.[67]

However, these expeditionary forces may not have included crossbowmen, particularly when mobility was a priority. Valets and *gros* valets appear regularly in the *Chronicles of Jean Froissart*, but their numbers are not usually mentioned.[68] Indeed, the latter did not seem to fight regularly. Froissart recounts the following anecdote, which took place in 1388 in Gascony:

Men-at-arms in battle, end of fourteenth century. Illustration from the *Chroniques de Saint-Denis*, British Library Ms Roy 20C-VII f. 134. (Public Domain)

64 Froissart, *Les chroniques de Jean Froissart*, Livre II, Chapter 210, p.277.

65 Savy, *La guérilla anglaise en Languedoc, Auvergne et Limousin*, p.285. For its part, Froissart mentions 100 lances and 500 crossbowmen in *Les chroniques de Jean Froissart*, Livre II, Chapter 225, p.329.

66 Savy, *La guérilla anglaise en Languedoc, Auvergne et Limousin*, p.342.

67 Savy, *La guérilla anglaise en Languedoc, Auvergne et Limousin*, p.363.

68 For example, Froissart mentions, 'a thousand lances, knights and squires, not counting crossbowmen and gros varlets' for the 1385 expedition to Scotland (Froissart, *Les chroniques de Jean Froissart*, Livre II, Chapter 223, p.308).

> Ernauton de Sainte-Colombe had a valet who watched the battle, neither fighting nor being asked to do so; when he saw his master being treated so badly, he became very angry, and went to his master and took the axe in his hands.... and when he had the axe, he went to the squire and struck him on the bascinet.[69]

It therefore seems that *gros* valets refers to valets armed for combat. Froissart thus refers to 'the valets and foragers of the Gascon and French knights' in 1385.[70] Further on, referring to the troops sent to Toulouse to fight the irregular companies in 1388, he recounts that they 'found these men-at-arms to be well equipped when they were all assembled, about four hundred lances and a good thousand carrying shields and gros valets.'[71] According to Philippe Contamine, the *gros* valet, considered a combatant, actually appeared in the 1380s.[72]

Artillery, for its part, was reserved for sieges.

Within the army, there was a distinction between *d'ordinaire* (i.e. regular) and *de crue* (i.e. temporary) personnel, with the latter intended to serve for shorter periods. The former therefore had their wages maintained for a period of at least one year. According to Philippe Contamine, 'this new structure encouraged the training of professional soldiers, for whom serving the King was not a temporary occupation or a sideline, but a genuine profession.'[73]

69 Froissart, *Les chroniques de Jean Froissart*, Livre III, Chapter 9, pp.389–390.

70 Froissart, *Les chroniques de Jean Froissart*, Livre III, Chapter 19, p.422.

71 Froissart, *Les chroniques de Jean Froissart*, Livre III, Chapter 23, p.440.

72 Contamine, *La guerre au Moyen Âge*, p.243.

73 Philippe Contamine, 'La Guerre de Cent Ans: le XIVe siècle. La France au rythme de la guerre', in A. Corvisier (ed.), *Histoire militaire de la France: 1, Des origines à 1715* (Paris: Presses Universitaires de France, 1992), pp.125-152.

5

The Beginning of the Fifteenth Century: Unrest and Reconstruction

Charles VI and the Cabochian *Ordonnance* of 1413

A man-at-arms around 1395, drawing taken from Viollet-le-Duc, *Encyclopédie médiévale*. (Public Domain)

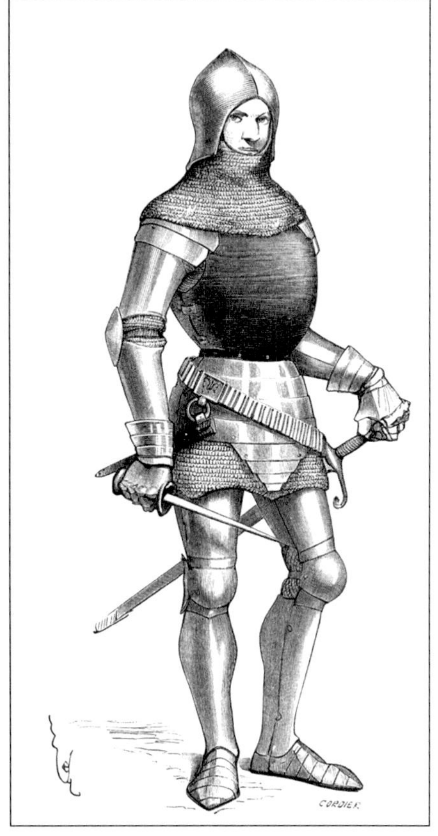

The death of Charles V in 1380 unfortunately changed the situation. His son Charles VI was still a minor, and his uncles divided the regency between them. Charles V had prepared his succession: Louis d'Anjou, the eldest of his brothers, was to be regent of the kingdom, while Philip of Burgundy and John of Berry were to be guardians of his son Charles VI. However, these princes agreed to keep Charles VI out of power well beyond his coming of age in 1381. They shared power and, above all, tax revenues. This struggle for income was the cause of the civil war between the Armagnacs and the Burgundians. It was not until October 1388 that Charles VI recalled his father's former advisers and gained power. On the military front, multiple ceasefires and truces were signed between 1389 and 1400, even after Henry of Lancaster dethroned his cousin Richard II in 1399.

The regency, resistance to taxation, the urban revolts of 1378 and 1379 in Languedoc and Flanders, and those of 1382 in Paris and Rouen, the King's madness, and the civil war between the Armagnacs and Burgundians had disastrous consequences for the kingdom's finances. Philip of Burgundy, known as the Bold, died on 26 April 1404. The duchy then passed to his son, John the Fearless, but the duchy's coffers were empty. In 1412, John the Fearless, who supported Charles VI, urged him to fight against the enemies of the kingdom. To finance the army, he persuaded the King to convene the Estates General of *Langue d'oïl*.[1] Through his manipulations, the Duke of Burgundy sought to attack the officers who had enriched themselves and make the princes pay, particularly those of the Armagnac party. He therefore increased the pressure in the streets of Paris. On 27 April 1413, a riot was organised by Simon le Coutelier, nicknamed Caboche, a butcher by profession. The *Cabochiens* were in fact a popular Parisian faction affiliated with the Burgundian party. However, these events did not prevent the Estates General from completing their work: the *ordonnance* was finally ready. It was read to King Charles VI in two sessions on 26 and 27 May 1413. The King approved all of its provisions on the evening of 27 May. The Estates General therefore published the *ordonnance* known as the 'Cabochian Ordonnance', comprising 259 articles.

This *ordonnance*, which was revoked a few months later, sought to reduce the royal treasury's expenditure, particularly the wages of captains of strongholds and castles. Its content is of interest to us for several reasons. Several articles of this *ordonnance* notify the reduction in the salaries of captains of strongholds, which confirms that the institution of captains paid by the central government still existed. Thus, Article 51 states that 'Barbasain and his companions will no longer receive the five hundred *livres tournois* that they had each year from the treasury.'[2] Article 53 similarly stipulates: 'How the captain of Chastel de Creil shall no longer receive Vc *livres tournois* for his captaincy'[3]. Articles 54 to 58, 60, 63 to 65, 67 to 82, and 84 to 86 address the captains of localities or castles who see their wages reduced[4] whereas Article 87 requires every captain to hold only one capitaincy.[5] Articles 250 to 258 of the *ordonnance* concern men-at-arms.[6] Article 250 forbids soldiers, men-at-arms, archers and crossbowmen from gathering in the kingdom without authorisation, under penalty of the crime of *lèse-majesté*. Article 251 adds the prohibition of pillaging. Articles 252 and 253 are addressed to captains of men-at-arms, archers and crossbowmen who have received higher wages than they should have and who have committed fraud during muster rolls. Article 254 forbids all captains from living off the land.

The *ordonnance* confirms that there were permanent troops, particularly in castles and strongholds, whose captains and their 'companions' were paid by the royal treasury. There are 32 captains who appear in this *ordonnance* for the year 1413 and who have had their wages reduced: Arnault Guilhem de Barbasain (Barbazan), Guillaume Bataille and Clignet de Brabant, knights, Archambault de Villiers and Yvon de Katins, squires (Article 51),

1 The countries where the *langue d'oïl* is spoken refers to Northern France, while the countries where the *langue d'oc* is spoken refer to southern France.

2 *L'ordonnance cabochienne (1413) – Documents sur le règne de Charles VI* (Clermont-Ferrand: Paleo, 2008), p.42.

3 *L'ordonnance cabochienne (1413)*, p.42.

4 *L'ordonnance cabochienne (1413)*, pp.43–49.

5 *L'ordonnance cabochienne (1413)*, p.50.

6 *L'ordonnance cabochienne (1413)*, pp.193–201.

the captain of the castles of Creil (Article 53), Beauquesne (54), Péronne (55), Crécy (56), Airanes (57), Hélicourt (58), Villeneuve le Roy (60), the castles of Tours (63), Chastillon (64), Crèvecœur en Brie, Bar sur Seine (67), Vitry (68), the bridge of Saintes (69), Rochefort en Saintonge (70), Rouen (71), Molyneaulx (72), Avranches (73), Regnierville (74), La Roche Tesson (75), the castle of Nogent le Roy (76), the market of Meaux (77), Le Vivier en Brie (78), the new castle of Lincourt (79), Neaufle (80), Gaillard (81) and Gisors (82), and Valoignes (84).[7] These captains were, of course, duly appointed and commanded by the King.[8]

This reduction in pay probably had a disastrous effect on the leading captains of the royal army. But the royal coffers were empty, and military discipline was at an all-time low. Thus, in 1422, Alain Chartier berated the captains in his quadrilogue:

> Many of the knights and nobles cry out for arms, but they run instead to money.

and then further on:

> What is the discipline of chivalry if there is no law ordained and upheld in the exercise of arms and battles under the command of the leader and for the public good? .... And if no one inquires to find out what no one could ignore, when we have seen them disobey orders, break defences, come when they please and leave when they please, abandon their guards to guard abandoned things, surrender without cause the fortresses that had been delivered by force, failing when needed and surrendering when not needed, sending away their companions, forming separate companies?

He laments that,

> everyone wants to form their own company and be their own leader, and there are so many chevetaines and masters that they can hardly find companions or servants.

Chartier then demands that no one be allowed to become a squire unless he has performed a feat of valour, that no man-at-arms receive wages unless he has taken prisoners, and that no one be captain unless he knows how to wear a sword and don a coat of mail. He concluded by demanding that:

7 *L'ordonnance cabochienne (1413)*, pp.43–49.
8 *L'ordonnance cabochienne (1413)*, p.196.

> the obedience and discipline of chivalry, which is currently being criticised, be seriously restored.[9]

The reign of Charles VI thus ruined Charles V's efforts to professionalise the army. The French nobility rediscovered the pleasures of military expeditions (Louis I of Anjou's expedition to Italy in 1382, the Barbary Crusade in 1390 and the Nicopolis Crusade in 1396, and the conquest of Liguria by Louis d'Orléans, the King's brother, in 1395) and jousting. Even the summoning of the *arrière-ban* was put back on the agenda. This was notably the case on 1 May 1418.[10] Thus, 'for reasons that were primarily financial, the outline of a permanent mobile army created by Charles V did not survive his death,' Philippe Contamine noted,[11] and the administrative organisation disintegrated after Agincourt.

Nevertheless, at that time, some of the troops were still retained and paid. This was the case for the garrisons in the border regions with English possessions, placed under royal authority through lieutenants and captain generals.[12] Thus, in 1412, the Lord of Richemont was given 'a very fine and large company' of 1,600 knights and squires.[13] Even if they did not receive their pay regularly, the troops assigned to defend the strongholds were therefore maintained. However, Charles VI did not yet have the manoeuvring force required to carry out offensive operations.

The numbers of troops in each unit, particularly *chambres*, were constantly monitored. On 25 December 1415, 'Jean des Marquez, squire, gave receipt for a sum of one hundred and fifty *livres tournois* which he had received for himself and nine squires in his company, charged with defending the town of Boulogne.'[14] And on 13 June 1419, 'Aubert de Raineval, knight bachelor, gives receipt for one hundred and forty-two *livres* ten *sous tournois* for his wages, those of another squire bachelor, and eight squires employed in the service of the King in Picardy.'[15] Figures of around 10 or even 15 knights or squires appear in numerous muster rolls

9 Alain Chartier, *Quadrilogue* (BNF).

10 Philippe Contamine, 'La Guerre de Cent Ans: le XVe siècle. Du "Roi de Bourges" au "Très Victorieux Roi de France"', in A. Corvisier (ed.), *Histoire militaire de la France: 1, Des origines à 1715* (Paris: Presses Universitaires de France, 1992), pp.171–208.

11 Philippe Contamine, 'La Guerre de Cent Ans: le XVe siècle. Du "Roi de Bourges" au "Très Victorieux Roi de France"', in A. Corvisier (ed.), *Histoire militaire de la France: 1, Des origines à 1715* (Paris: Presses Universitaires de France, 1992), pp.171–208.

12 Valérie Bessey, *Construire l'armée française*, t. I, p.26.

13 Guillaume Gruel, *Chronique d'Arthur de Richemont* (Paris: Société de l'histoire de France, 1890), p.9.

14 Beauvillé, *Recueil de documents inédits concernant la Picardie, deuxième partie*, CXX, pp.124–125.

15 Beauvillé, *Recueil de documents inédits concernant la Picardie, deuxième partie*, CXXI, p.125.

from Brittany compiled between 1412 and 1419.[16] Men-of-war[17] remained divided into two main categories: men-at-arms and men-of-trait (shooting men, a trait meaning a bolt), the latter generally being crossbowmen on foot or on horseback. Thus, before the Battle of Agincourt, the Duke of Alençon was retained for 800 men-at-arms and 400 men-of-trait, the Count of Vendôme for 300 men-at-arms and 150 men-of-trait, and the Duke of Berry for 1,000 men-at-arms and 500 men-of-trait.[18]

Men-at-arms in battle, c. 1400. Illustration from the *Chroniques de Froissart*, Bibliothèque nationale de France Ms 2663 f. 145v. (Public Domain)

Probably appearing in Italy in the 1360s as an administrative unit, the 'lance' or '*armure de fer*' (lit. iron armour) consisted only of the man-at-arms accompanied by two horses. The figures above indicate a ratio of two men-at-arms to one crossbowman or archer. This ratio of two men-at-arms to one man-of-trait appears in many other examples: in 1403,

16 'Montres inédites de gens d'armes Bretons', https://tudchentil.org/spip.php?article531

17 French documents use two different words: '*gens d'armes*' to refer to all soldiers and '*homme d'armes*' to refer specifically to the heavily equipped men-at -arm. From hereon, I have translated '*gens d'armes*' as men-of-war and '*hommes d'armes*' as men-at-arms.

18 Philippe Contamine, 'La Guerre de Cent Ans: le XVe siècle. Du "Roi de Bourges" au "Très Victorieux Roi de France"', in A. Corvisier (ed.), *Histoire militaire de la France: 1, Des origines à 1715* (Paris: Presses Universitaires de France, 1992), pp.171–208.

Maréchal Boucicaut, Governor of Genoa, after sacking the cities of Batroun and Beirut on 9 August, planned an expedition to Alexandria. To this end, he planned to recruit 1,000 men-at-arms, 1,000 armed valets, 1,000 crossbowmen and 200 archers.[19] At the time, there is no indication that these three categories, men-at-arms, armed valets and men-of-trait, together formed a basic unit. According to Froissart, this was clearly not the case. Thus, for the Siege of Taillebourg in 1385, he reports that when 'all these men-at-arms were brought together, there were seven hundred lances, not counting the Genoese [crossbowmen] and the gros valets; and there were in all two thousand combatants.'[20] These lines reveal that the 'lances' are clearly distinguished from the '*gros valets*' and that the total reveals a ratio of 1,400 crossbowmen and squires to 700 lances, or two to one. It is worth noting here the difference with the English, who had a ratio of two archers to one man-at-arms within their corps or companies. In regions further away from the seat of power, particularly in south-western France, these ratios between types of combatants could vary. Jean Froissart reports that in 1388, the Bastard of Cornillac, Guillonnet de Harnes, Perrot Boursier, Jean Calemin de Baselle, the squire Le Rouge, and 'forty lances, and all their squires, *pillards*, and others' headed for the town of Lourdes.[21] The term *pillards* (looters, marauders) is commonly used by Froissart to refer to members of irregular companies, or *routiers*, who are not considered men-at-arms.

Under Charles VI, the men-of-trait equipment gradually incorporated bows alongside crossbows, but the latter remained more highly valued. Thus, from 1382 until the beginning of the fifteenth century, the accounts of the treasurers-at-war systematically mention payments to 'men-at-arms, archers, mounted and foot crossbowmen,' 'men-at-arms, crossbowmen and others,' or 'men-at-arms, archers, and crossbowmen,' before grouping them together, at least from 1418 onwards, as payments to 'men-at-arms and men-of-trait with projectile weapons.'[22] Thus, an extract from the military treasurer's accounts of 16 November 1422, specifies that:

> for the payment of the men-at-arms and men-of-trait who served the King in his wars, to whom 60 francs were paid per banneret, 30 francs per knight bachelor and squire banneret, 15 francs per simple squire, 30 livres per captain of mounted and foot crossbowmen,

19 Philippe Contamine, 'La Guerre de Cent Ans: le XVe siècle. Du "Roi de Bourges" au "Très Victorieux Roi de France"', in A. Corvisier (ed.), *Histoire militaire de la France: 1, Des origines à 1715* (Paris: Presses Universitaires de France, 1992), pp.171–208.

20 Froissart, *Les chroniques de Jean Froissart*, Livre second, Tome IX, Chapter 215, p.73.

21 Froissart, *Les chroniques de Jean Froissart*, Livre troisième, Chapter 9, p.281.

22 See for example, Léon Mirot, 'Dom Bévy et les comptes des trésoriers des guerres; Essai de restitution d'un fonds disparu de la Chambre des Comptes', *Bibliothèque de l'École des Chartes* (1925) 82, pp.341–348.

> 24 livres per constable (i.e. head of the constabulary), 12 livres per mounted crossbowman, 8 livres per foot crossbowman, 10 livres per mounted archer and 7 livres per foot archer, all per month.[23]

The crossbowman, as we can see here, is better paid than the archer.

At the end of Charles VI's reign, the letter of retinue, with no time limit, remained the norm. However, whereas in the previous century ordinances distinguished between captains of men-at-arms and captains of men-of-trait, a company now combined both types of troops.

Men-at-arms in battle, c. 1400–1425. Illustration from the 'Grandes Chroniques de France,' Bibliothèque nationale de France Ms 783 f. 177v. (Public Domain)

23 See for example, Léon Mirot, 'Dom Bévy et les comptes des trésoriers des guerres, p.348.

6

Charles VII and the *Ordonnance* of 1439

The Early Years of Charles VII's Reign (1422–1444)

Following the defeats at Agincourt and Verneuil, by 1428 Charles VII had only a few small companies of soldiers at his disposal. His primary concern was to find financial resources, however he managed to obtain subsidies from the Estates of Auvergne and the city of Poitiers.[1] At the same time, there was a change in the military's organisation. As we have just seen, 'there were no longer any companies of men-of-trait, no more captains or connétablies of crossbowmen.'[2] Within the remnants of the armies inherited by the King, there was no longer any distinction between bannerets, knights, squires, crossbowmen and archers; but of course there were still companies commanded by captains. These captains could be knights or squires. Thus, in May 1436, the Constable of France, Richemont, laid siege to Creil with companies whose captains were both knights and squires. Among these were the Duke of Alençon; John II, Count of Aumale; Guillaume d'Albret, *Maréchal de France*; Jean de Torsay, Master of Crossbowmen; succeeded by Jean, Lord of Graville; Louis de Culant, Admiral of France; Amaury, Lord of Séverac and *Maréchal de France*; Jean de Brosse, Lord of Sévère and *Maréchal de France*; Jean, Bastard of Orléans[3] or La Hire. Alongside these French captains were many foreigners, such as the Lombards Théaude, Luquin Russe, Caqueran and Martin d'Arblay, Bernard Albert from Aragon, Rodrigue de Villandrando from Castile, and Archibald Douglas and John Stuart, Earl of Buchan, from Scotland.[4]

1 Philippe Contamine, *Charles VII* (Paris: Perrin collection Tempus, 2021), p.187.
2 Favier, *La guerre de Cent Ans*, p.482.
3 Contamine, *Charles VII*, p.124.
4 Contamine, *Charles VII, pp.*124–125.

It is now difficult to determine the number of troops behind the term company. In Jean Chartier's *Chronique de Charles VII*, all forces numbering a few hundred men, but which may number more than a thousand, are referred to as companies, while armies are still broken down into *batailles*.[5] Thus, in 1423, the Count of Aumale brought together several captains, including Louis de Loré and Louis Tromargon, who commanded 700 or 800 lances between them.[6] In 1429, during the siege of Orléans, Étienne de Vignolle, known as La Hire, and Ambrois de Loré skirmished together with 120 lances.[7] However, Philippe Contamine mentions Gilles de Rais and eight other captains in the same year, commanding a total of nine companies with 212 men-at-arms and 238 archers or crossbowmen, who were reinforced by eight other companies totalling 150 men-at-arms and 150 archers.[8] These were companies comprising 19 to 23 men-at-arms and as many archers. Another example is a letter dated 26 October 1430 written by Jean de Bueil, who was then lieutenant to Charles d'Anjou, Count of Maine, showing that he was 'captain of men-at-arms and archers stationed and organised in the castle, town and island of Sablé.' The same letter later mentions '120 *paient*' (120 men), suggesting that this company – even though the letter does not use the term 'company' – probably had 120 men at the time.[9] In 1431, according to Gilles (or Jacques) le Bouvier also known as Berry, Poton de Xaintrailles commanded 120 'lances and the archers' whereas, the same year, Guillaume de Barbazan ordered 200 lances 'with the *gens de trait*.'[10] In 1432, Ambrois de Loré and Jean de Bueil 'and their enseigns' had no more than 120 to 160 lances and 100 to 120 archers.[11] In 1438, Jean de Dunois, Bastard of Orléans, was paid 1,200 livres tournois for the pay of 100 men-at-arms and 100 archers whom the constable had asked him to bring to the Siege of Creil [12] whereas Gahache Janebé, 'captain of men-at-arms', had only 16 men-at-arms and 5 archers for the same siege.[13] After the capture of Orléans and the coronation of Charles VII in 1429, that is, from the moment he was able to gather new resources, whether moral or financial, it seems that the strength of a company was commonly 100, 120, or 200 lances with at least as many archers.

5 Jean Chartier, *Chronique de Charles VII, Roi de France* (Paris: Vallet de Viriville, 1858), Tome I, pp.103–104.

6 Chartier, *Chronique de Charles VII*, Tome I, p.35.

7 Chartier, *Chronique de Charles VII*, Tome I, p.79.

8 Contamine, *Charles VII*, p.206.

9 Jean de Bueil, *Le Jouvencel* (Paris: Renouard, 1889), Tome second, pp.310–312.

10 Denis Godefroy, *Histoire de Charles VII par Jean Chartier, Jacques le Bouvier dit Berry, Roy d'armes, Mathieu de Coucy et autres auteurs du temps* (Paris: Imprimerie Royale, 1661), pp.382 and 383.

11 Godefroy, *Histoire de Charles VII*, p.390.

12 Gruel, *Chronique d'Arthur de Richemont*, pp.249–250.

13 Gruel, *Chronique d'Arthur de Richemont*, pp.250–251.

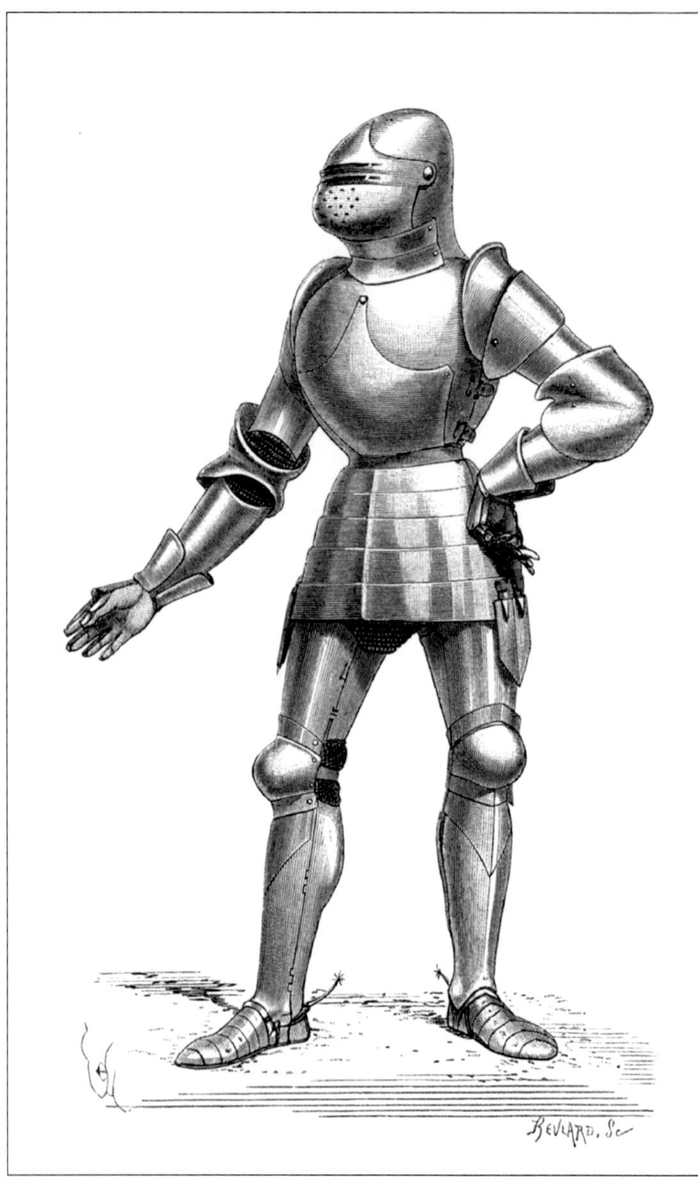

A man-at-arms *c.* 1400. Drawing from Viollet-le-Duc, *Encyclopédie médiévale*. (Public Domain)

During this troubled period, these companies could be made up of mercenaries recruited from outside France: Aragonese, Castilians, Scots, or Lombards. At Verneuil in 1424, 7,000 Scots commanded by John Stuart, Earl of Buchan, and Archibald Douglas, along with 2,000 Lombards, fought for the King of France. These mercenaries expected payment, even if Jean Chartier downplayed its importance. He wrote, when his protector Charles VII asked the Duke of Alençon in May 1429 to raise an army to accompany Joan of Arc and recapture Orléans:

> In the hope that she had come from God, for no more wages or other profit than they had from the King, a large company of men-at-arms and archers gathered with the Duke of Alençon and the said Joan the Maid, in whom all the men-at-arms had great hope: the Bastard of Orléans, the Lord of Boussac, *Maréchal de France*, the Lord of Graville, Master of the Crossbowmen, the Lord of Culent, Admiral of France, Sir Ambrois, Lord of Loré, Étienne de Vignolle known as La Hire, Gautier de Brussac, and several other captains.[14]

However, the same author informs us that Joan of Arc's men-at-arms received 2 to 3 francs each in June 1429 before Gien.[15] Consequently, this period saw a decline in the wages of men-at-arms. Thus, the monthly pay of a man-at-arms or squire fell from 50.8 to 33.5 grams of gold between 1411

14 Chartier, *Chronique de Charles VII*, Tome I, pp.81–82.
15 Chartier, *Chronique de Charles VII*, Tome I, p.90.

and 1400, while that of a foot soldier fell from 27.12 to 16.75 grams of gold over the same period.[16]

It is interesting to note that in *Le Jouvencel*, Jean de Bueil refers mainly to knights, captains, and paid soldiers: 'It is not only the good and valiant knights, captains, and *soudoyes* who must undertake and lead the difficult tasks of battle'.[17] A company could therefore be commanded by a knight or a squire, as Jean Chartier indicates in this example from 1430:

> And for this purpose [i.e., to confront the English in Champagne], Monseigneur Eustache de Conflans, knight captain of the said place of Châlons, a squire named Versailles, another squire, Pierre Martel, captain of Sept-Saulx, and several other captains of men-at-arms from the surrounding garrisons were assembled with the said Barbazan.... And while the said battle was taking place, a squire named Henri de Bourges, captain of the castle and town of Sarry-lès-Châlons, was sent for by the said Barbazan.[18]

Within the company, the two basic units remained the lance, composed of the man-at-arms and probably his page, and the man-of-trait. But the latter was now dominated by the archer, at least in the northern half of the country. The ratio of men-at-arms to archers seems to have evolved gradually, moving first toward a proportion of one man-at-arms to one man-of-trait, and subsequently to one man-at-arms for every two men-of-trait, most of whom were archers. Thus, the 'Excerpts from the 13th account of Hémon Raguier, treasurer of wars, relating to the Siege of Gallerande in July 1426,'[19] listing companies of captains led by Arthur de Richemont for this siege gives figures ranging from five men-at-arms for nine archers to 91 men-at-arms for 68 archers. In this list, men-at-arms are in most cases more numerous than archers. In total, there are 567 men-at-arms and 349 men-of-trait listed, giving a ratio of 1.62 men-at-arms per man-of-trait. The detailed list is reprinted in Appendix III. For its part, the muster of Bueil's company, carried out in 1428 by the Count of Vendôme in the presence of the authorities of Tours and recorded in the city's register of deliberations, lists 21 men-at-arms and squires, a similar number of archers and 1 foot crossbowman,[20] a man-at-arms for an archer. Subsequently, Jean Chartier frequently mentions two archers for every man-at-arms in his *Chronique de Charles VII*. Thus, in 1429, the Constable of Richemont assembled a 'very

16 Contamine, *Guerre, État et société à la fin du Moyen Âge*, Tome 1, pp.234–276.

17 De Bueil, *Le Jouvencel*, Tome premier, p.14.

18 Chartier, *Chronique de Charles VII*, Tome I, pp.128–129

19 René Planchenault, 'La Conquête du Maine par les Anglais: les campagnes de Richemont 1425–1427', *Revue historique et archéologique du Maine*, 2:13 (1933), pp.149–151.

20 Léon Lecestre in Jean de Bueil, *Le Jouvencel*, p.xxij.

fine company' of '400 lances and 800 archers.'[21] During an expedition in 1432, Chartier noted 60 to 80 lances and 100 to 160 archers: 'the lords of Loré and Bueil and their troops had no more than sixty to eighty lances and one hundred or one hundred and eighty archers.'[22] The same year, Ambrois de Loré commanded 50 lances and 100 archers.[23] In December 1435, the constable sent 400 men-at-arms and 600 archers against the *écorcheurs* which suggests that this ratio of two archers to one man-at-arms was not universally respected.[24] In the same vein, Jean de Bueil wrote, in episodes in *Le Jouvencel* set in the years 1428–1432, that he took with him 'one hundred men, that is to say, forty men-at-arms and sixty archers'[25] and later, probably for the Siege of Saint-Célerin in the Orne region in 1432, that his '200 men-at-arms with 300 archers took part in the siege...'[26] Further on, in Chapter 9 of the second part of *Le Jouvencel*, which deals with 'good practices' for fighting the enemy while 'in *bataille* on foot,' he suggests placing the men-at-arms in the middle and the archers and other ranged-armed soldiers on the flanks, which suggests two archers for every man-at-arms.[27]

Man-at-arms, c. 1415. Drawing from Viollet-le-Duc, *Encyclopédie médiévale*. (Public Domain)

It was in the period following Agincourt that the *coustillier* seems to have replaced or joined the valet within the companies. It should be emphasised once again that when Jean de Bueil refers to a lance, he is referring only to the man-at-arms who actually carries this weapon, and not to the additional personnel such as archers and any valets. Thus, he writes that 'the Count of Parvanchières (a false name perhaps referring to Jean d'Orléans, Count of Dunois, or Charles d'Anjou, Count of Maine) made his order and gave Jouvencel the garrison of Crathor (Orléans) and reinforced it with two hundred lances and archers'[28] or further on, 'came and charged among them and the number of people with him up to the number of forty or fifty, as many lances as archers and *coustilliers*.'[29] But it seems that the companies now included men-at-arms, valets or *coustilliers*, and archers. The ratio between these combatants seems to vary from one man-at-arms for one or two archers to one man-at-

21 Gruel, *Chronique d'Arthur de Richemont*, p.69.
22 Chartier, *Chronique de Charles VII*, Tome I, p.137.
23 Chartier, *Chronique de Charles VII*, Tome I, p.151.
24 Chartier, *Chronique de Charles VII*, Tome I, p.216.
25 De Bueil, *Le Jouvencel*, Tome premier, p.106.
26 De Bueil, *Le Jouvencel*, Tome premier, p.138.
27 De Bueil, *Le Jouvencel*, Tome premier, p.153.
28 De Bueil, *Le Jouvencel*, Tome premier, p.212.
29 De Bueil, *Le Jouvencel*, Tome premier, p.214.

arms for one *coustillier* or valet and one to two archers. We can thus see this ratio evolving in the first half of the fifteenth century without really stabilising.

This change in the composition of the company stemmed from the need to understand the enemy and the terrain to avoid any surprise for the captains. These provisions had indeed been overlooked for too long in the past. Thus, according to Jean de Bueil, King Charles VII sent him a long letter by one of his envoys, which included the following:

> Firstly, as it concerns a *bataille* on horseback, you know full well that you need *découvreurs* [scouts]. Then you need *coureurs* [runners], and you willingly put them at the front so that they repel the enemy coureurs, preventing them from seeing your dispositions and your strength. And if yours are the strongest, they will see those of your enemies, and your enemies will not see yours. After that, you set up a battle called the vanguard; you place two wings on either side; and each wing has *coureurs*, so that they are not taken by surprise. The main battle comes next with the banners and standards, and there the leader is located. After that, there is a small battle called the rearguard. And after this rearguard, there must be a small troop of men, so that no one comes from behind to cry alarm, nor does anyone run upon them, for a noise that comes from behind does more harm than one that comes from the front. One should have a small hidden *bataille*, either in a valley or in the shade of a small wood, which comes after all the battles are assembled, to help where they see the need; and this is often the cause of victory in battle, for your enemies have as many *batailles* as you do, and if God has given you the grace of this advantage, it is a great gain for you. But be careful that your enemies have not done the same as you; at least you will have yours to counter theirs; thus you cannot fail to have it. The Italians have even more than half of it, for they always fight on horseback, which other nations do not do. And if you have to deal with them, you will need to have more. But generally, other nations do not have more. However, if you see something new, take new counsel again.
>
> … The way to arrange your *bataille* on foot is to choose the most advantageous position possible, then place a large *tourbe* [unit] of armed men in the middle; and in front of and around your banners, there should be a good number of men-at-arms, so that they cannot be easily brought down; and on both sides, all the men-of-traits, so that they can attack the flanks of the enemy's *bataille*; and at both ends of your men-of-trait, a number of men-at-arms to guard them; behind your main *bataille*, a good *tourbe* of men-at-arms to ensure that no man retreats and also that no noise is made against you and that they can resist, if anyone wants to give you any trouble, and also, when the main *bataille* is in melee, to help where they see that it is needed, although you must place the rear of your battle in a very advantageous position, if you can. Your *tourbe* of traits and

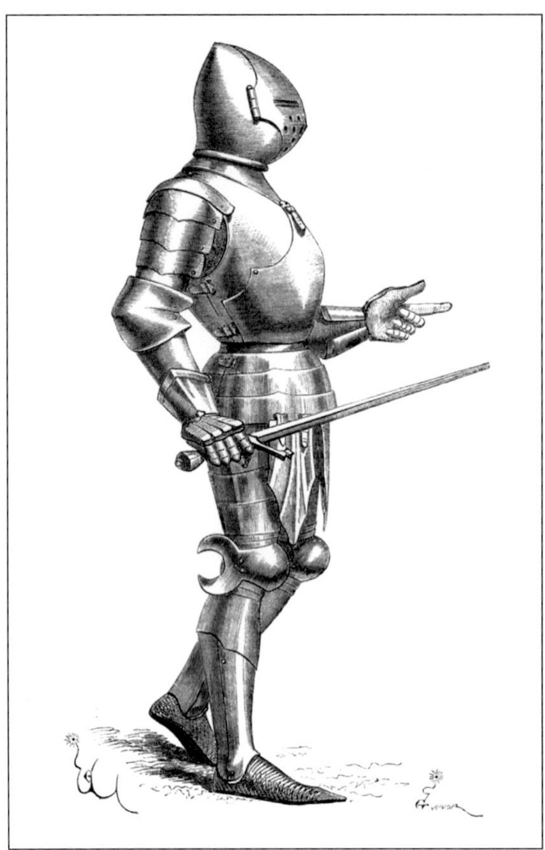

Man-at-arms in white armour, wearing a *bicoque* head protection, c. 1425. Drawing from Viollet-le-Duc, *Encyclopédie médiévale*. (Public Domain)

> your wings must charge on the sides when the great battle is assembled.... And for this reason, I am of the opinion that your *bataille* should be in *tourbe* formation.[30]

These excerpts are among many other pieces of tactical advice. It is difficult to date precisely the years to which these passages refer, as *Le Jouvencel* was written between 1470 and 1477, but these various anecdotes seem to take place between 1429 and 1432. These pieces of advice to the king are interesting for several reasons. They show that at that time, the French army was gradually adopting English tactics, notably by placing archers on the wings and men-at-arms in the centre. The Battles of Agincourt and Verneuil were therefore clearly a catalyst for the evolution of French practices. They also suggest the emergence of a temporary unit, the *tourbe*, probably a subdivision of the *bataille*. This unit does not appear in other sources. Finally, it should be noted that, in Jean de Bueil's narrative, these tactical opinions and dispositions, whether real or fictional, emanating from the King, would be based on the author's practices and experiences.

The accommodation of his troops was another concern for King Charles VII, and it was regularly mentioned in the introduction to his ordinances. But even before the future ordinances, we can already see how practices had evolved under his influence. In a passage from *Le Jouvencel* referring to the year 1429, Jean de Bueil describes the following events:

> Thus the lords marched, each to his own quarter, and lodged quietly, without any noise or shouting among the host. The Count of Parvanchières (this false name actually refers to either the Count of Dunois or Charles d'Anjou, Count of Maine) had a very good way of doing this, as he did in all matters of war, and was wise and valiant. His way of doing things with regard to lodgings was that in all his companies, each man had a *maître-logeur* [quartermaster]. And this *maître-logeur* carried a small banner, one and a half feet square, with his captain's livery. And as soon as they left the battlefields to go and find lodgings, no horseman dared to leave to go to the lodgings on pain of death, except those who had a banner in their hands. Thus, only the *logeurs* [lit. lodgers; billeting officer] went, and the

30 De Bueil, *Le Jouvencel*, Tome second, pp.35–38.

> captains had no trouble keeping their men in line. And when it came time to find lodging, each *logeur* went ahead and waited where each man was to lodge, whether in fields, houses, or bushes. The *logeurs* put up a small pole, and there each man found his lodging, without anyone having to call his page, and without making any noise. But all lodged where they had been ordered to. And when the *logeurs* had arrived at their lodgings, whether in the city, village, or fields, each one placed his banner, which was on a stick or a small pole, in the window of his lodgings or on a bush, if there were any bushes. And when the army arrived, everyone looked upstream and downstream, and where they saw the sign of their *logeur*, they went straight there, and their *logeur* showed them where they should camp. So there was no shouting or booing, nor did any man call his page or his valet. But everyone lodged where they were ordered, and by this means there was no noise or storm.[31]

This passage shows that, even in Joan of Arc's era, accommodation for soldiers was well organised within the royal army.

Man-at-arms, first half of fifteenth century. Drawing from Viollet-le-Duc, *Encyclopédie médiévale*. (Public Domain)

The *Ordonnance* of 1439

During those years, the country continued to suffer depredations. Reducing the excesses and pillaging committed by soldiers was a fervent desire of Charles VII, and his actions would mark his reign. He believed that soldiers and their captains had lived off the people for too long, as 'it has been said and shown to the King by the people of the three Estates of his Kingdom, now assembled in this city of Orléans.'[32] Even before the *ordonnance* regulating the *compagnies*, Charles VII had confirmed the organisation of the royal army into companies commanded by captains since, by the 'Pragmatic Sanction' of 2 November 1439, intended to 'prevent the pillaging and vexations of soldiers,' he ordered that:

> Firstly. Because a great number of captains have exceeded their authority and assembled large numbers of men of arms and of traits

31 De Bueil, *Le Jouvencel*, Tome premier, pp.178–179.

32 Vilevault, *Ordonnances des rois de France de la troisième race*, treizième volume (Paris: 1782), p.306.

without the King's permission or licence, which has caused great harm and inconvenience, the King, wishing to establish good order and discipline in warfare and to restrict such practices, has ordered that a certain number of captains of men-at-arms and of traits be appointed to conduct the war, which captains shall be appointed and elected by the King, prudent and wise men who shall be elected by him to the office of captain of men-at-arms and war; and each captain shall be given a certain number of men who shall be elected by him from among those who are in fact or by office captains of men-at-arms and war; and he forbids them to name themselves or bear the name of captains, on pain of the penalties declared below.

(1) *Item.* And shall be taken and chosen by their captains or other persons appointed by the King, from among the men-at-arms appointed, men-at-arms and of trait, and other persons of war who are most notable, sufficient, and best skilled, for whom and for their government their captain shall be held responsible.

(2) *Item.* Defend the King to all, on pain of incurring the crime of *lèse-majesté*; namely, on pain of being stripped, dismissed, and deprived forever, he and his descendants of all honours and public offices and the rights and prerogatives of nobility, and of confiscation of body and property, that no one of any rank whatsoever shall be so bold or daring as to raise, lead, conduct, or receive, and neither raised, led, conducted, nor received any company of men-at-arms, nor of trait, or other men-of-war, except with the leave, licence, consent, and order of the King and by his letters patent; and likewise that no one shall bear arms or join any captain or other person, except under one of the said captains who shall be elected by the King, and within the number that shall be ordered to him.

(3) *Item.* Defend the King, that none of the said captains shall receive in his company the people of another captain without his consent, & on the said penalties; and that no man-at-arms, gentleman or other, or men-of-trait or other men-of-war, depart from their captains, on pain of being deprived of honour, and confiscation of property, and of promptly losing their horses and armour, which shall be committed and won over to the captain whom they have abandoned.

(4) *Item.* The King forbids any captain from taking or accepting into his company any man-at-arms, of trait, or other man-of-war beyond the number assigned to him, on pain of being deprived of his office as captain and having his property confiscated.[33]

33 Vilevault, *Ordonnances des rois de France de la troisième race,* treizième volume, pp.306–307.

Other articles follow, prescribing everything that captains and soldiers are forbidden to do, to a total of 47 articles. Among them, Article 26 is of interest here: the King orders that 'captains and men-of-war shall be stationed and established in garrisons at border posts facing the enemies, as ordered by the King.'[34] The similar applied to Article 30, which stipulated:

> And as for the fact that certain lords, barons, and other captains place and maintain in their fortresses and castles, men-at-arms and of trait, and also in other fortresses, such as churches, forts, and others, or in lands subject to the King, who are daily causing great oppression to the King's subjects, the King orders and commands that all such garrisons vacate those places, and that the lords of those places provide sufficient men, at their own expense, without harm to the people, and that the other places and fortresses be returned to those to whom they belong.

According to Gilles le Bouvier, known as Berry, from that year onwards, following the lifting of the siege of Avranches by the Constable of Richemont,

> Charles VII "ordered, after careful deliberation by his council, that all his men-at-arms be quartered at the frontiers, each man-at-arms having three horses and two archers, likewise with three horses, and no more, and that they be inspected and paid every month; and that all the rest of the useless mouths be driven out. And in order to implement and begin to observe this useful *ordonnance*, the King had money, provisions, and artillery delivered to all the captains.'[35]

It is difficult to say whether Berry is confusing the *ordonnance* of 1439 with the forthcoming *ordonnance* of 1445. However, he is probably referring to an initial draft *ordonnance*, since he would later present the new *ordonnance* at the end of 1444.[36]

With this 'Pragmatic Sanction,' Charles VII sought to take matters into his own hands by banning irregular companies in the country and replacing them with captains appointed by him. The same applied to the positions held by these companies, which had to be vacated as quickly as possible and occupied by royal garrisons. However, it was not until the truce of 28 May 1444, that Charles VII was able to finalise and implement his reorganisation plans.

34 Vilevault, *Ordonnances des rois de France de la troisième race,* treizième volume, p.310.

35 Godefroy, *Histoire de Charles VII,* pp.406–407.

36 Godefroy, *Histoire de Charles VII,* p.427.

7

The Ordinances of 1445 and the Creation of Permanent Mounted Troops

Thus, between 1317 and 1444, the conditions gradually came together that would lead to the creation of a standing army: the appointment of captains paid by the royal authority in the towns; the creation of units called *routes* and then companies, commanded by a captain and numbering up to a hundred men or more; practices inspired by the *routiers*, who were paid by local communities over long periods of time through the use of *patis*, and virtually becoming permanent units,[1] but on behalf of the King of England when not on their own account; the increasingly common practice of paying wages to soldiers; the professionalisation of warfare through the replacement of the old noble knighthood by experienced warriors, whether knights, squires, or simple men-at-arms; and finally, Charles VII's desire to replace the irregular bands of *routiers* with captains and men-at-arms in his pay, which materialised in the Pragmatic Sanction of 1439. These were the milestones that led to the ordinances of 1445.

The *Ordonnances* of 1445

As we have seen, in the first half of the fifteenth century, irregular companies continuing their depredations across the country remained a major problem for the King of France. Thus, in January 1436, Jean Chartier recorded,

1 *Patis* were treaties signed between highway companies and communities, whereby the former provided protection for the latter in exchange for payment of a certain amount. Savy, *Bertrucat d'Albret*, pp.56–57.

Portrait of Charles VII by Jean Fouquet (1450–55). Oil on wood, Louvre Museum, Paris. (Public Domain)

> ...three to four thousand men-of-war came to the Champagne region, some of whom had come from the fortresses that the constable had surrendered, and they caused great damage to the country. There was no man, woman or child whom they did not strip, provided they could find them to their advantage, down to their shirts; and when they had pillaged everything, they ransomed the villages. A man named de Chabannes and two bastards of Bourbon were their captains, and the people commonly and vulgarly called them the écorcheurs.[2]

These excesses, those of the Swiss campaign of 1444, and the failure of the attempt to 'clientelise' the *écorcheurs*, led King Charles VII to undertake a radical reform of the army.[3] The *ordonnance* of 1439 only partially did so, mainly because it did not detail the provisions. Thus, in early 1445, Charles VII convened his Council. Mathieu de Coussy described this event:

> In the year one thousand four hundred and forty-five, the King of France, during his stay at the said place of Châlons, assembled the members of his council on several and various occasions to obtain advice, deliberation and conclusions on certain major and important matters.... particularly concerning the matter of war and his men-at-arms, he desired with all his heart that a good solution and method be found whereby his soldiers could be paid and bribed in sufficient numbers and placed and settled in the towns and fortresses of his kingdom, wherever he saw fit, and that all other pillagers, thieves and wicked people, of whom there were a great number of useless ones, who knew and did nothing else but destroy, steal and plunder his vassals and his own subjects, would be driven out and dismissed, and that it would be said and ordered to them that in a short time, each of them, on pain of death, withdraw and return to the places from whence they came, and that they resume ploughing and doing their work, each according to their condition. The aforementioned manner and opening was practised and put forward several times in

2 Chartier, *Chronique de Charles VII, Roi de France,* Tome I, p.216.

3 De Bueil, *Le Jouvencel,* Tome premier, p.cxxvii.

> the presence of the King, as is said, where several great lords of his blood and other noble men were with him, councillors and captains of great authority, who, each in turn, when asked and questioned, responded according to their opinion and understanding, and according to what they thought was and should be done for the best.[4]

There was, of course, much debate, and the Council raised two objections: the threat that these soldiers could pose, given their numbers and power, if they did not submit, and the state of the royal finances, as the country was in ruins. Although Charles VII listened attentively to these objections, the project was very dear to his heart. He was supported by his son the Dauphin, by René d'Anjou, King of Sicily, and his son the Duke of Calabria, by Charles d'Anjou, Count Arthur de Richemont, Constable of France, the Counts of Clermont, Foix, Saint-Paul, Tancarville and Dunois, as well as by ecclesiastical and secular advisers. It is also highly likely that the Constable of Richemont and Pierre de Brézé contributed to the development of this project.[5] Guillaume Gruel thus asserts that Arthur de Richemont ordered 'the captains who have always lasted since.'[6]

Olivier de la Marche suggests that Pierre de Brézé may have been the instigator: 'The *ordonnance* begun by King Charles, his father (i.e. father of the Dauphin Louis), was put into effect and very well organised: and it was said that Sir Jean de Brézé, Lord of Varenne, had been the cause of the said *ordonnance*, which was a very fine and profitable thing for the kingdom.'[7] Less convincing, Philippe de Commynes writes that the 'lords of Italy', namely René and Charles of Anjou, were behind this *ordonnance*: King Charles VII 'inflicted a cruel wound on his kingdom that will bleed for a long time, & a terrible band of paid men-of-war, which he established in the manner of the lords of Italy,'[8] and to do so, he had to obtain the consent of the 'Lords of France,' who received pensions in return for the taxes that would be levied on their lands.[9] In any case, these potential contributors are included in Mathieu de Coussy's list of council members deemed favourable to the project.

As a result of the final deliberation, it was decided to implement it:

4 Mathieu de Coussy, 'Chroniques' in *Choix de Chroniques et Mémoires relatifs à l'Histoire de France* (Paris: Delagrave, 1835), pp.13–14.

5 De Coussy, 'Chroniques', p.14.

6 Gruel, *Chronique d'Arthur de Richemont*, pp.188–189.

7 Olivier de la Marche, *Mémoires* in *nouvelle collection des mémoires pour servir à l'histoire de France*, Tome Troisième (Paris: publisher not stated, 1837), p.407.

8 Denis Godefroy, *Mémoires de Philippe de Comines*, Tome premier (Bruxelles: François Foppens, 1723), Livre 6, Chapter 7, p.407.

9 Godefroy, *Mémoires de Philippe de Comines,* Tome premier, Livre 6, Chapter 7, pp.406–407.

Men-at-arms in battle, c. 1440. Illustration from 'the Chroniques de Flandres,' Bibliothèque nationale de France, Ms 2779 f. 223. (Public Domain)

Then it was decreed, both by the King and by the aforementioned members of the council, that there would be fifteen captains, each of whom would have one hundred lances under their command; and that each lance would be counted as wages for six persons, three of whom would be archers and the fourth a *coustillier*, along with the man-at-arms and his page; the man-at-arms, being the sixth, as mentioned, would receive wages of .... francs per month in royal currency, and would be placed and distributed by provinces and dioceses in various places throughout the kingdom by the good towns; and each of the said captains would know his place and his retreat, and where he and his men should be and have their rendezvous. In addition, it was ordered that they would receive and be paid their wages, both in the good towns and in the flat country, and that there would be certain clerks appointed by the bailiwicks, *sénéchaussées* and *prévôtés*, who would receive and pay the aforementioned sums, and report to the said captains in due course, as their charge might increase. These captains were elected and appointed by the King and the lords of the council, and also summoned in the presence of the King; and there, they were told and ordered to strictly observe and maintain, as much as they feared falling into the indignation of the King and the aforementioned lords, the said *ordonnances*, and that they should not allow their men to cause any damage or violence to merchants, labourers, or others, whatever their status, however dear to them it was that such damage should be returned upon them; and that they should take such men as they were sure of and could not give account for.

All this being done, they were given written instructions as to where they were to go and what they were to do. And shortly thereafter, once these captains had been provided with the men they needed, and had chosen, to the best of their ability, from among all their companies, the most skilled and best dressed, up to their limited number, it was ordered, as stated above, that all the others, namely those who were not hired, should withdraw quickly and without delay to the countries from which they came, without pillaging or robbing the poor people; otherwise, if they did not do so, provision would be made for them, and justice would be done to them as abandoned and unacknowledged people. And to better provide for this, certain royal orders were sent to the officers serving in this regard in several bailiwicks; and when these orders and commands came to their knowledge, they immediately went to various places and dispersed, without consulting each other, so that in the following fortnight, no more news was heard of them in all the King's lands.

As for the fifteen captains mentioned above, when they were seated as described above, with their people, by province, diocese, bailiwicks, *sénéchaussées* and *prévôtés* of the kingdom, they began to conduct themselves, govern and maintain themselves through the good towns, very gently and courteously, without doing any violence or harshness to the burghers and peasants thereof, nor to the merchants and labourers of the flat country, nor allowing their people to do so. If any of them did the contrary, and the complaint came to these captains, he immediately and without delay punished and chastised them with all severity; and with that, they made restitution to those who had suffered any damage, which might have been taken from them.

Now, even though the number of men if war thus paid and maintained, as has been said, amounted to about nine or ten thousand horses, they were few in number in the good cities; for there were only twenty, twenty-four, or thirty in each of Troyes, Châlons, Reims, Laon, or other similar cities, depending on their size and power; whereby they could not be powerful enough to take any control or authority over the above-mentioned burghers and *manats*. In addition, the royal officers and ordinary justices kept a close watch on them and their behaviour, to observe whether they committed any faults, for which their captains did not do their duty in punishing them.

On the other hand, there were certain being committed by the King who would often visit them in their quarters to ensure that they were being treated properly, without selling or losing their horses and harnesses; and when one of them died or was otherwise unable to serve, another was immediately appointed to take his place. There were even several who, at their own expense, followed the captains for quite some time, in the hope of attaining their rank and being

> enlisted when the opportunity arose; and even then, they often had to seek admission by great means and notable recommendations. If any business arose for the King, wherever it might be in his kingdom, he would immediately send each of his messengers to the said captains, or to some of them; and immediately, without delay, within a few days they would set out and go to him, or to the places where he wanted them to be. In this way, he found himself provided with a good number of combatants, well prepared, quite suddenly, with the help of his princes, his knights, and his nobility. [10]

Thomas Basin also presented the contents of this *ordonnance*. Basin wrote in Latin, but here is the translation:

> King Charles, together with his principal military commanders and the most eminent counsellors of his kingdom, decided to reduce and organise his forces into a fixed and defined number. These would be divided and distributed under the command of certain military leaders who had shown greater diligence and courage in military affairs, and who would receive regular pay so that they would always be ready, with their weapons and horses, to carry out the King's orders. It was therefore decided that fifteen hundred lances would be chosen from among those who, being older, taller, in better physical condition, and having better horses and weapons than the others, were considered to be stronger and more vigorous. Each lance was to have two archers and a squire, mounted and armed, with two grooms to look after the horses of the armed men; thus, each lance was to have six horses and no more. These fifteen hundred lances were entrusted to fifteen captains or military commanders, each of whom was to have one hundred lances under his command. This number was considered sufficient both for the defence of the kingdom and for the reconquest of the lands still held by the enemy. Indeed, it was more than enough for all these purposes, especially when one considers the corresponding reduction in taxes, for, as we have often pointed out, most of the kingdom was exhausted and depopulated, miserable and uncultivated. And the fact that sufficient force was available for the above-mentioned purposes was subsequently clearly demonstrated, for thanks to it, thus restored to order and military discipline, all the possessions that the English held in Normandy and Aquitaine were then recovered, and they themselves were henceforth driven out and routed without much difficulty, as we shall recount in due course.
>
> … However, once organised in this manner into defined units and under the command of certain militia leaders from across the

10 De Coussy, 'Chroniques,' pp.14–16.

> kingdom, it was divided among the various provinces so that each part of the kingdom had its own contingent, in which, depending on the capacity and resources of the location, accommodation with the necessary furnishings was provided for a hundred lances, or more or less. When this arrangement and the number of soldiers were initially established, the shortage was so great, and the poverty and misery of the people so severe, that royal revenues and taxes in most provinces of France were almost entirely exhausted. At that time, in order to ensure the payment of the soldiers, it was necessary to tax not in cash, but in a fixed quantity of wheat and basic necessities, both for the soldiers and their horses. Thus, one or more parishes, if they were very poor, provided a lance with the tax in grain, according to the extent of their means. Gradually, however, as the parishes began to prosper, it was decided that the soldiers would receive a salary from the royal taxes that had been established for the payment of these lances. These military rents were converted into a sum of money, and each month, twenty sous tournois were assessed for one lance and its two archers.[11]

Finally, Gilles (or Jacques) le Bouvier, successor to Jean Chartier, summarises the deliberations of the *ordonnance* and its implementation as follows:

> After which, the King ordered in the city of Nancy that all the men-at-arms who had been in Germany and before Metz should present themselves for inspection, and that the best and most capable among them should be selected and retained, fifteen hundred lancers and four thousand five hundred archers; and that the rest should be ordered to return to their homes and their countries; and he removed and dismissed all the captains, or most of them, and ordered that only fifteen captains remain, each of whom would have one hundred lancers under his command, and the archers, who would be housed by the towns of this Kingdom, and fed and paid from the people's goods, with a strict and severe warning to these men-at-arms and archers not to be so bold as to cause any trouble or take anything from any man in the fields or in the town. Another account tells of this in a different way, namely that it was first deliberated and resolved that fifteen hundred men-at-arms would be retained, as many coustilliers, and three thousand archers, over all of whom captains were appointed and put in charge, and an *ordonnance* was made for them to be lodged and fed by the towns of the Kingdom, and each of them was assigned a certain quantity of provisions, to be delivered to them and their horses by the people. But since then,

11 Thomas Basin, *Histoire des règnes de Charles VII et de Louis XI* (Paris: Renouard, 1855), Chapter III, pp.165–168.

> this *ordonnance* was changed, and it was said that each man-at-arms *garni* [who was him, his page and squire] would be paid for two archers and one *coustillier*, at thirty francs per month, which would be delivered to them each quarter of the year. And in order to cover this expense, a tax was imposed, which was called the *taille des gens d'armes* [tax on men-at-arms].[12]

It should be noted here that le Bouvier distinguishes between two *ordonnances*. The second *ordonnance* to which he refers is that of 26 May 1445, which is discussed below, as the first *ordonnance* does not yet refer to the valet or *coustillier des archers*.

Thus, at the beginning of 1445, the *ordonnance*, which has since disappeared, was produced. The *Révérend Père* Daniel wrote in 1721 that he had not found this *ordonnance* in the collection of royal *ordonnances* compiled by Pierre Rebuffe, *Jurisconsulte*.[13] This *ordonnance* is believed to have been issued between 9 January and 15 March 1445, probably after the

A man-at-arms of the *compagnies d'ordonnance*, c. 1445. Drawing from Viollet-le-Duc, *Encyclopédie médiévale*. (Public Domain)

12 Godefroy, *Histoire de Charles VII roy de France*, p.427.

13 R. P. Gabriel Daniel, *Histoire de la milice françoise et des changements qui s'y sont faits depuis le début de la monarchie dans les Gaules jusqu'à la fin du règne de Louis le Grand* (Paris: Jean-Baptiste Coignard, 1721), Tome I, p.212.

Peace of Metz of 28 February.[14] We do not have the original, which has been lost, but it has been reconstructed from several documents: the descriptions by chroniclers Mathieu de Coussy and Thomas Basin reproduced above, an order issued on 26 May 1445, in Louppy-le-Château, which supplements the lost order, and an interesting copy found in the Historical Archives of the City of Barcelona, brought to light by an article by Stéphane Péquignot in 2015.[15] The latter document is a copy of the order attached to a letter dated 23 March 1445, sent by one Étienne Petit. He wrote that he gave Ramon Belhoms 'a copy of the order that the King [Charles VII] issued concerning the soldiers that the King wishes to keep and house in his kingdom.'[16] This is the text, Catalan version of the 'copy of the order' on the men-of-war of the King of France Charles VII obtained by Étienne Petit. This copy is undated, the original having been made between 1 March 1 and 15 March 1445, and the copy made before 8 April 1445:

> To put the men-of-war in place and ensure that the kingdom is free from pillaging, the King orders that 15 or 16 captains be appointed to govern the said men-of-war, who will be in charge of them.
>
> Firstly, the King wishes and orders that all companies of men-of-war be cleared of baggage, and that all said men-of-war be reduced to a total of 1,500 lances and 3,000 archers. And each man-at-arms shall have three horses and a *coustillier* [*consetller*, in the Catalan copy of the *ordonnance*] and a page and two archers who shall have three horses. For a total of combatants, the said 1,500 lances and archers, 6,000 combatants, which at three horses per lance and three horses for two archers, amounts to a total of 8,000 horses.
>
> The following are the names of those whom the King wished to be at the head of the said gendarmes

First le connétable Arthur III de Richemont	100 lances and 200 archers
Monsieur le *Maréchal* (André de Laval) de Lohéac	100 lances and 200 archers
Monsieur le Sénéchal (Pierre de Brézé, *Sénéchal* d'Anjou)	100 lances and 200 archers
Monsieur Regnault de Dresnay	100 lances and 200 archers
Monsieur (Louis) de Beauveau	100 lances and 200 archers

14 Contamine, *Guerre, État et société à la fin du Moyen âge*, Tome 2, p.278.

15 Stéphane Péquignot, 'De la France à Barcelone. Une version catalane de "l'ordonnance perdue" de Charles VII sur les gens d'armes (1445)', *Revue Historique*, 4:276 (2015), p.794.

16 Péquignot, 'De la France à Barcelone. Une version catalane de "l'ordonnance perdue"', p.798.

Floquet (Robert de Floques, Bailli d'Évreux)	100 lances and 200 archers
Pierre Louvain, vicomte de Berzy	100 lances and 200 archers
Monsieur le *Maréchal* (Philippe de Culant, seigneur) de Jalognes	100 lances and 200 archers
Monsieur (Charles de) Culant	100 lances and 200 archers
Le cadet d'Albret (Charles II d'Albret)	100 lances and 200 archers
Monsieur (Jean V) de Bueil	100 lances and 200 archers
Poton (de Xaintrailles)	100 lances and 200 archers
Joachim (Rouault, *Maréchal de France*)	100 lances and 200 archers
Monsieur (Jean) d'Estouteville (seigneur de Torcy et Blainville)	70 lances and 140 archers
Robin Pettylow et Robert Conningham (*capitaine de la garde écossaise*)	70 lances and 140 archers
Monsieur Martin Garayt (Garcia?)	25 lances and 50 archers
Monsieur Theaude (de Valpergue, Italian)	25 lances and 50 archers
Monsieur Guy d'Alsigny	20 lances and 40 archers
Idem. at two who will hold from the King	20 lances and 40 archers

The said number of men-of-war thus amounts to 1,500 lancers, 3,000 archers, and ~~1,500~~ *coustilliers*, who shall be lodged and provided for as follows. Namely, the King will lodge the said men-at-arms throughout the country under his command, except for Languedoc, and they will be provided with provisions worth four francs per lance and two francs per archer per month.

Firstly, in the lowlands of Auvergne	100 lances and 200 archers
Item, in the highlands of Auvergne	100 lances and 200 archers
Item, in Rouergue or Quercy	100 lances and 200 archers
Item, in Armagnac and Comminges	100 lances and 200 archers
Item, in Bourbonnais, Forez, Beaujolais and Lyonnais	100 lances and 200 archers
Item, Gévaudan and Vivarais and Velay	150 lances and 200 archers
Item, in Berry	100 lances and 200 archers

Item, in Poitou and Saintonge and Angoumois	150 lances and 300 archers
Item, in Touraine below and beyond the Loire River and county Blois	100 lances and 200 archers
Item, around the river Loire	100 lances and 200 archers
Item, in Nivernais, County of Gien, Joigny, Estampes, Montargis, Niort, Duchy of Nemours and all the Beauce, from Chartres to Vendôme, and the Duchy of Orléans on Beauce's part	100 lances and 200 archers
Item, in Ile-de-France, Brie and Champagne	100 lances and 200 archers
Item, in Upper and Lower Limousin	100 lances and 200 archers

For the sum of 1,400 lances housed in the above country.

In Montbéliard, Bar, and Lorraine, which are not included in this number, it seems that the King must now have them leave the country and tell each of the captains of the said men-at-arms and archers where they will be lodged, so that each may diligently convey them to the country where they are to be lodged in order to protect them from pillaging and also to divide their lodgings. And that the King should now appoint people in each country to instruct the said captains' men to make their said lodgings, and also to advise on the matter of provisions, so that when the said gendarmes come to the country where they are to be lodged, they may find provisions for a month, so that they do not cause damage to the fields.

Item, the said men-at-arms and archers shall lodge in the country which the King shall order them to, and each captain of one hundred lancers and two hundred archers shall appoint ten men of good character from among their company, who shall be in charge of nine lancers each and the archers, and shall have a chamberlain, and shall be lodged by tens of lances and archers in the villages and places of the country where they are ordered to be, and shall have justice.

Item, regarding provisions, the King shall write to the estates of each county, namely to the 12 representatives of the church, nobles, and others, who shall assemble with the elected representatives and decide on the manner of their provisions and lodging, how said provisions shall be paid for, or whether said provisions shall be delivered by the castellany, and that it be now determined what provisions are reasonable per month for one hundred lancers and 200 archers, which is the number of men and horses, namely 600 men and 600 horses. And that diligence be made to ascertain and, as soon as the quantity of provisions necessary has been ascertained, that it be immediately transmitted throughout the country so that the said men-of-war arms may be supplied as soon as they arrive at their lodgings.

Item, it shall be ordered that the said men-of-war shall be lodged where they are ordered to be lodged, that they shall not be permitted to go on cavalcades or to forage in the town where they are lodged without the authorisation of their head of chamber, who shall be required to report this to the authorities of the town where they are lodged. The authorities shall record in writing the names of those who have departed, the day they left, and the day they returned. It shall also be noted who has been robbed or plundered by the country.

Item, the King orders the captains to keep their men in such order and justice that trade and work may be carried out, so that everyone may be safe in the fields. And for those who do otherwise, the King shall punish them so severely that all others may take heed.

Item, that the King shall have *montres* carried out every month and shall also be informed every day whether the men are present, and that a review shall be carried out every month and a full *montre* every three months, or every two months when payment in cash is made to the said men-at-arms.

Item, it seems that it is better to pay the said men-of-war every two months, and following a montre, so that the number of said men-of-war who will be there and what clothing they are wearing can be counted.

(Archives Historiques de la Ville de Barcelone, Conseil de Cent, 1B X-15, n° 43r°-n° 44v°).[17]

This *ordonnance* was subsequently supplemented by the *ordonnance* of Louppy-le-Château dated 26 May 1445. This new *ordonnance* (see Appendix V) specifies the provisions for housing men-at-arms specifically in Poitou. This *ordonnance* specifies that for each man-at-arms there should be one *coustillier*, one page, and three horses, and for the two archers, one page or *valet de guerre* and three horses. Finally, this *ordonnance* stipulates that 190 lances and archers will be housed in Poitou, including 100 lances commanded by Pierre de Brézé, Seneschal of Poitou, 60 lances commanded by the *Maréchal de* Lohéac, who will be stationed in lower Poitou 60 lances and 30 lances commanded by Floquet, plus the archers, for a total of 1,140 men.[18]

Analysis of these various documents reveals the shortcut created by chroniclers regarding the basic unit named the lance. Mathieu de Coussy

17 Péquignot, 'De la France à Barcelone. Une version catalane de "l'ordonnance perdue"', pp.825–828. See Appendix IV for the original version in old Catalan.

18 Bessey, *Construire l'armée française*, Tome I, pp.102–105.

reports that 'there would be fifteen captains, each with a hundred lances under their command; and that each lance would be counted as wages for six people, three of whom would be archers and the fourth a *coustillier*, with the man-at-arms and his page; the man-at-arms accompanied, him being the sixth.'[19] Thomas Basin makes the same mistake when he writes that 'each lance must have two archers and a mounted and armed squire'[20] and the same is true of Olivier de la Marche, who wrote his memoirs decades after the *ordonnance* was promulgated:

> At that time, King Charles assembled his council to consider and seek advice on the men-of-war (who were destroying his kingdom on all sides), and to bring said men-of-war into line and order, and to maintain them without losing them, and to remove from him those whom he greatly doubted, and it was advised that he should put under fifteen hundred lances, chosen and elected, and divide them among certain captains to lead and govern them, and that each lance would have two archers and an armed *coustillier*, and that a tax would be levied in the kingdom of France, by which this company would be paid.[21]

Some modern historians have taken the same shortcut. In reality, the *ordonnance* issued at the beginning of 1445 did not include archers in the composition of the lance. The copy of the lost *ordonnance* explicitly states:

> All the said men-of-war shall be reduced to 1,500 lances and 3,000 archers. And each man-at-arms shall have three horses and a *coustillier* and a page and two archers who shall have three horses. For a total of combatants, the said 1,500 lances and archers, 6,000 combatants, who have three horses per lance and three horses for two archers, amount to a total of 8,000 horses.[22]

Similarly, the *ordonnance* of 26 May 1445 specifies that only 'a certain number of men-at-arms and archers would remain, namely, for each man-at-arms: a squire, a page, and three horses, and for each archer: a page or a military servant and three horses.'[23]

As we can see, there is a systematic separation between men-at-arms and archers. Indeed, when these companies are listed, the number of lances is clearly distinguished from the number of archers. For example, in the

19 Coussy, 'Chroniques,' p.13.

20 Basin, *Histoire des règnes de Charles VII et de Louis XI*, Livre IV, Chapter III, p.166.

21 De la Marche, *Mémoires*, p.407.

22 Péquignot, 'De la France à Barcelone. Une version catalane de "l'ordonnance perdue"', p.825.

23 Bessey, *Construire l'armée française*, Tome I, p.103.

copy of the *ordonnance* above, 'Constable Arthur III de Richemont, 100 lances and 200 archers.' Similarly, in 'Chroniques de Normandie' Gilles le Bouvier recounts the arrival of Charles VII in Rouen on 19 October 1446:

> And after several words spoken between them for the good of the said city, the first to enter was Messire Pierre de Brézé, Seneschal of Poitou, with a hundred lances and archers. After him entered the Lord of Manny, with a hundred lances and the archers of Robert de Floques, bailiff of Évreux. And the hundred lances and archers of the said Count of Dunois and the other batailles went to lodge in the villages around the city.[24]

In this passage, lances and archers are once again clearly differentiated.

In other words, the *ordonnance* of early 1445 did not yet constitute a unit, the '*lance fournie*', of six men including a man-at-arms, a *coustillier*, two archers, and two pages, but it maintained the distinction between the lance, which now consisted of three men (a man-at-arms, a *coustillier*, and a page), and the men-of-trait, consisting of two archers and a page for each lance. The unit referred to by Mathieu de Coussy and historians, the '*lance fournie*,' appeared at the end of 1445. The term appears for the first time in the *Lettres du Roi Charles VII, par lesquelles il institue dans la sénéchaussée de la Marche cinq commissaires à l'effet de percevoir, d'après un nouveau mode, un aide pour la solde des gens d'armes*, letters dated 4 December 1445, which specify the provisions for collecting the aid that will enable the payment of the men-of-war's wages. Initially, this *ordonnance* recalls the context and the King's desire to restore peace to his kingdom:

> Charles, by the Grace of God, King of France .... taking pity and compassion on our poor people who, in times past, have suffered so much from the wars that have raged for so long in our kingdom, and from the pillaging that has taken place in our kingdom during those wars, leading to its great destruction and depopulation, we have recently put an end to said pillaging, which we had been unable to do until now, and we have also organised and equipped men-at-arms and lodged them throughout our lands of Languedoc, where they are now, and after the truce we made and took last year with our nephew of England, with the intention of achieving the final peace that we have always sought and desired, among other things, the passage of our said nephew of England has been arranged, which he must make this coming season across the sea and come to France to agree with us and negotiate and conclude, at the pleasure of our lord, on the said matter of peace between the Kingdoms of France

24 Gilles (Jacques) le Bouvier, *Les chroniques de Normandie* (Rouen: A. Hellot, 1881), p.129.

> and England. And because this matter is so important and weighty, as everyone knows and understands, and because it will be to our honour to be accompanied by lords of our blood, nobles and barons of our kingdom, in great numbers, during the said truce, which is still in force, and until we see whether we shall have peace or war, we need to maintain our said men-of-war in our said countries, as they are at present or by other means better ordered and of less burden to our people; for this reason, it is and will be convenient for us that the above-mentioned matters and other affairs of ours involve very great and unbearable burdens and expenses, which we cannot reasonably provide for without the help of all our loyal subjects, we have decided, desired, and ordered, and after mature deliberation with the lords of our blood and other members of our Grand Council, both to maintain the armed forces in our said countries without pillaging, and also to provide and obtain some finances for the said agreement and other said affairs for this present year, we desire, order, mandate and commit that the said men-at-arms who are from the country and jurisdiction of the county of Marche shall henceforth be paid according to the *ordonnance* we have now made, beginning on the 1st day of January next, in the manner that follows[25].

This *ordonnance* therefore confirms, here for the county of Marche, that the companies that will be housed in this country will be paid for by the taxpayers of the country concerned. The *ordonnance* of 26 May 1445 stipulated that companies would be supplied in kind. However, the *ordonnance* of 4 December, as well as a later *ordonnance* dated 26 November 1446 concerning Limousin, authorised the country to pay for supplies for soldiers in cash or in kind. The following passage from the *ordonnance* of 4 December, which specifies the rates, is important because it refers to the '*lance fournie* with six men and six horses.' This is the first reference to this unit:

> That is to say, for the man-at-arms, ten pounds sterling, and for the archers and the squire, another ten *livres tournois* with twenty *sous tournois*, for the lance, for the captain's status; which is in total, per month, for a *lance fournie* with six men and six horses, twenty-one *livres tournois* in silver, and for the remaining ten *livres tournois* for the payment of the said *lance fournie*, they shall pay, deliver, and furnish each month the following provisions: namely, a load of three-quarters of wheat and rye in equal parts; each load weighing two hundred and fifty pounds Paris weight; three cartloads of suitable wood; six loads of oats, each weighing two hundred and fifty pounds

25 Auguste Valet de Viriville, 'Notices et extraits de chartes et de manuscrits appartenant au British Museum de Londres', *Bibliothèque de l'École des Chartes* (1847), 8, pp.127–131.

> of the said weight, and two cartloads of hay and straw, two parts hay and one part straw; each cartload weighing one thousand pounds of the said weight; or they shall pay and provide, at their discretion, the people of the said country to the said men-of-war with provisions in the manner they have done until now, and in addition four *livres tournois* per month per man-at-arms, the third and for two archers and their cook or servant another four *livres tournois* with twenty *sols tournois* per month per lance for the captain's expenses for the number of men-at-arms who are lodged in the said country; among which, taking one of these courses by the people of the said country, the said men-of-war shall always be bound to pay their hosts moderate and reasonable expenses. And we want all kinds of people to be liable for this, except for people of the church, nobles living nobly, and others who were exempted by our latest *ordonnances*, and with this, by virtue of the said agreement and our other affairs, impose and levy, to the said country and jurisdiction of the March, with the reasonable expenses declared below and in addition to the fact and payment of the said men-of-war, the sum of five thousand *livres tournois*; five hundred *livres tournois* for expenses.
>
> This sum is in lieu of the aid of two hundred thousand *livres tournois* that we were forced to provide in our country of Languedoc, as we did last year. But considering the poverty of our people and the burden they bear from the said men-of-war, we have moderated the said country, for its portion of the said aid, to the said sum of five thousand *livres tournois* and five hundred *livres tournois* for the said expenses. …

The *ordonnance* then goes on to list the persons who will be taxed and those who will be exempt, and specifies the methods of collection, with collectors being appointed by letters of commission. Finally, it concludes with the methods of payment:

> And shall pay the men-of-war monthly, beginning on the first day of January; and shall pay the said assistant in two instalments: the first on the first day of April, and the second on the first day of September. And this shall be done by each party, without any dispute, you, commissioners (the soldiers and aid being paid first), shall do and administer to the parties in good reason and justice.
>
> And because these presents may have to be dealt with and worked on in various places and in many ways, we desire and are pleased that, in view of these, made under the royal seal, full faith be added as to this original present, by which we strictly command and order all our justiciars, officers, vassals, and subjects that, in doing and executing the aforementioned matters, they give your clerks and deputies in this regard all obedience, comfort, and assistance, as required and as the case may require.

> Given at Razillé near Chinon on the fourth day of December in the year of grace 1445 and the 23rd year of our reign.
> Signed by the King in his council, J. de la Lorre.[26]

Another *ordonnance*, probably also enacted in December 1445, specified that 'the three means of livelihood of men-of-war, primarily held.'[27] This *ordonnance* specifies that the subjects of Charles VII will be required to pay, support, and house the soldiers 'beginning on the first day of January 1446.'[28] The requirements will thus be supplied to a '*lance fournie* of six men.'

Finally, the first article of the *ordonnance* of 5 January 1446, concerning the maintenance of 160 men-at-arms and 320 archers in the Auvergne region[29] also uses this designation when it specifies that 15 *livres tournois* will be paid in wages and salaries for 'the man-at-arms, third of the three and the horses, and as much for two archers and their squire, with one franc for the rank of captain, which is in total 31 francs per month, for a *lance fournie* with six persons and six horses.'[30] The second article specifies that

> For the conduct of our other affairs, we shall be equally content if, instead of the said fifteen francs for each pay, they pay, if they see fit, only ten francs in cash, that is to say, for the man-at-arms, 10 francs, and for the archers and their squires, another ten francs, with one franc for the captain's position, which is in total for one month, per *lance fournie* with 6 men and 6 horses, 21 francs, and that for the remaining ten francs for the payment of the said lance fournie, as stated, they may at their leisure deliver and pay for each month the following provisions, namely: a load of three quarters of wheat, half wheat and half rye, each load weighing 200 pounds according to Paris weights, three cartloads of suitable wood, six bushels of oats in the customary manner and two cartloads of hay and straw, two parts hay and one part straw, each cartload weighing 10 quintals according to Paris weights.[31]

It can be noted from the *ordonnance* issued in early 1445 that the *coustillier* now clearly forms part of the lance, joining the man-at-arms and the page, which did not seem to be the case previously. From January 1446 onwards, he is of course included in the *lance fournie*, alongside the page, the archers, and the valet.

---

26 Vallet de Viriville, 'Notices et extraits de chartes et de manuscrits appartenant au British Museum de Londres', pp.127–131.

27 Bessey, *Construire l'armée française*, Tome I, pp.112–113.

28 Bessey, *Construire l'armée française*, Tome I, p.112.

29 Bessey, *Construire l'armée française*, Tome I, pp.106–111.

30 Bessey, *Construire l'armée française*, Tome I, p.108. 'third of the three' would today be written as 'first of the three'.

31 Bessey, *Construire l'armée française*, Tome I, p.108.

But what this *ordonnance* heralds above all is the creation of a real standing army. The significance of this decision and this legislative act should not be downplayed. Charles VII had to overcome considerable resistance when promulgating this *ordonnance*. Although he wrote in 1471–1472, Thomas Basin repeatedly expressed his opposition in his *Histoire de Charles VII*. – Chapters 5 and 6 of Book IV are devoted to this subject. The chronicler exclaims, 'what a grave and pernicious burden this continuous service in the paid cavalry has brought, and will continue to bring as long as it lasts'[32] and 'that the King's natural militia, without such a large standing force, could suffice for the defence of the kingdom,'[33] even though, writing after the events that ended the Hundred Years' War, he emphasises in Chapter 6 that a standing army will prevent any new English desire to resume hostilities. Basin mainly criticises the financial burden placed on the people to maintain this army. He further emphasises this heavy and unfair taxation imposed by the royal power in the last chapter of his chronicle devoted to Charles VI.[34] The Archbishop of Reims, Jean Jouvenel (or Juvénal) des Ursins, is also highly critical of the consequences of permanent troops becoming idle.[35]

A man-at-arms of a *compagnie d'ordonnance*, c. 1450. Drawing from Viollet-le-Duc, *Encyclopédie médiévale*. (Public Domain)

Based on the *ordonnance* of 2 November 1439, ordering that a certain number of captains of men-at-arms and archers be appointed by the King, and that each of these captains 'be given a certain number of men-of-war,'[36] the *ordonnance* of early 1445 details the arrangement: there will be 15 or 16 captains, whose companies of men-of-war will be 'cleansed of baggage,' for a total of 1,500 lances and 3,000 archers, or 6,000 fighting men and 8,000 horses.

The various *ordonnances* issued in 1445 and 1446 thus served several purposes: the

32 Basin, *Histoire des règnes de Charles VII et de Louis XI,* Livre IV, Chapter V, p.170.

33 Basin, *Histoire des règnes de Charles VII et de Louis XI,* Livre IV, Chapter VI, p.174.

34 Basin, *Histoire des règnes de Charles VII et de Louis XI,* Livre V, Chapter XXVI, p.324.

35 Philippe Contamine, 'La Guerre de Cent Ans: le XVe siècle. Du "Roi de Bourges" au "Très Victorieux Roi de France"', in A. Corvisier (ed.), *Histoire militaire de la France: 1, Des origines à 1715* (Paris: Presses Universitaires de France, 1992), pp.171–208.

36 Vilevault, *Ordonnances des rois de France de la troisième race, treizième volume*, pp.306–307.

establishment of companies led by captains appointed by the King, whose basic unit was the lance, which quickly became the lance fournie; the distribution of these companies throughout the various countries of the kingdom, the maintenance and control of these companies in the countries where they were stationed, and their financing and subsistence.

Captains and Distribution of *Compagnies d'Ordonnance*

For 1445, the names of these captains were recorded by Philippe Contamine. The table below compares this list with the Catalan copy of the 1445 *ordonnance*:

Philippe Contamine[37]	Copy of the Ordonnance of 1445
Philippe de Culant: 100 lances	*Le Connétable* de Richemont: 100 lances and 200 archers
André de Laval-Lohéac: 60 lances	Philippe de Culant, *Maréchal*: 100 lances and 200 archers
Charles, duc de Bourbon: 100 lances	*Le maréchal de* Lohéac: 100 lances and 200 archers
Poton de Xaintrailles: 100 lances	Poton de Xaintrailles: 100 lances and 200 archers
Jean d'Estouteville, seigneur de Torcy: 100	Jean d'Estouteville (Totavilla): 70 lances and 140 archers
Joachim Rouault: 100 lances	Joachim Rouault: 70 lances and 140 archers
Robert de Floques: 100 lances	Robert de Floques: 100 lances and 200 archers
Arnaud-Amanieu d'Albret, seigneur d'Orval:[38] 100 lances	Le cadet d'Albret: 100 lances and 200 archers
Pierre Louvain, vicomte de Berzy: 100 lances	Pierre Louvain: 100 lances and 200 archers
Pierre de Brézé, seigneur de la Varenne: 100 lances	Pierre de Brézé, *Sénéchal*: 100 lances and 200 archers

37 Contamine, *Guerre, État et société à la fin du Moyen Âge,* Tome 2, p.399.

38 This is the son of Charles II d'Albret who was a companion of Joan of Arc and who was a member of the Royal Council.

Charles de Culant: 100 lances	Charles de Culant:[39] 100 lances and 200 archers
Jean de Bueil: 80 lances	Jean de Bueil: 100 lances and 200 archers
Robert Coningham: 40 lances	R. Pettylow & R. Coningham: 70 lances and 140 archers
Galéas Jambe: 10 lances	
Étienne de Lespinasse: 20 lances	
Tristan l'Hermite: 21 lances	
Robin Pettylow: undetermined	
Regnault du Dresnay: undetermined	Regnault de Dresnay: 100 lances and 200 archers
Olivier de Coëtivy: undetermined	
Boniface de Valpergue: undetermined	Théaude de Valpergue:[40] 25 lances and 50 archers
Martin Garcie: undetermined	Martin Garayt: 25 lances and 50 archers
Geoffroy de Couvran: undetermined	
Guillaume de Rosnyvinen: undetermined	'The two who stand with the king': 20 lances and 40 archers
Olivier de Broons: undetermined	Louis de Beauveau : 100 lances and 200 archers
Nicole et Cristye Chamber: Scottish Men-at-Arms and Archers of the Bodyguard	Guy d'Alsigny : 20 lances and 40 archers

Philippe Contamine lists 26 names of captains, whereas the copy of the *ordonnance* lists only 21. These differences stem from the fact that the Catalan copy of the *ordonnance* dates from 8 April 1445, while Contamine's list is a reconstruction that does not specify a date, given that the 1445 *ordonnance* was probably promulgated between 9 January and 15 March, most likely in the first half of March.[41] The total is indeed 1,500 lancers and 3,000 archers, as specified in the copy of the *ordonnance* and by Mathieu de Coussy.

39 Charles de Culant, brother of Philippe de Culant, *Maréchal de France*.

40 Théaude ou Théodore de Valpergue, brother of Boniface de Valpergue given in the Contamine list.

41 Péquignot, 'De la France à Barcelone. Une version catalane de "l'ordonnance perdue"', p.814.

The reform of 1445 was preceded by a draft *ordonnance* in 1443 or 1444.[42] An initial list of captains had been drawn up: Blain Loup, Lord of Beauvoir, and Antoine de Chabannes (100 lances in total), the Bastard of Culant (100 lances), Pierre Aubert (100 lances), Jean de Blanchefort (100 lances), Boniface de Valpergue (100 lances), Robin Pettylow and Montgomery (100 lances together), Joachim Rouault (100 lances), Étienne de Lespinasse (100 lances), Ponchon de Rivière (100 lances), Olivier de Coëtivy (100 lances), Olivier de Broons (100 lances), Mathelin Lescouet and Adam de la Rivière (100 lances together), 'the Spaniards' (100 lances), Pierre Louvain, Guillemin Lombart and Raffile (sharing 100 lances for the bodyguard).[43] The captains planned for this initial project numbered 19 and shared 14 companies of 100 lances, including the bodyguard, for a total of 1,400 lances.

Many captains were thus dismissed under the implementation of the new *ordonnance*: Antoine de Chabannes, Pierre Michel, Geoffroy de Saint-Belin, Christophe de Coëtivy, Amaury d'Estissac, Jean and François d'Apchier, Jean de Blanchefort, Thugdual le Bourgeois and Mathelon Lescouet, two Bretons, the Gascons Dimanche de Court, Gaston Lérigot, the elder and younger Estrac, and the Castilians Jean de Salazar, Conques, and Gonzalès to name a few.[44] These two lists also show differences from the 1444 draft, demonstrating the difficulty of the selection process. Many captains were thus dismissed because they were former *écorcheurs*, bastards, or because they had shown indiscipline, as in the case of Jean de Salazar.[45] However, some captains of *écorcheurs* escaped this purge – such is the case of Robert de Floques, who was captain of the *écorcheurs* from 1420 to 1441, and Pierre Louvain.

Sallet with a visor, *c.* 1445. Drawing from Viollet-le-Duc, *Encyclopédie médiévale*. (Public Domain)

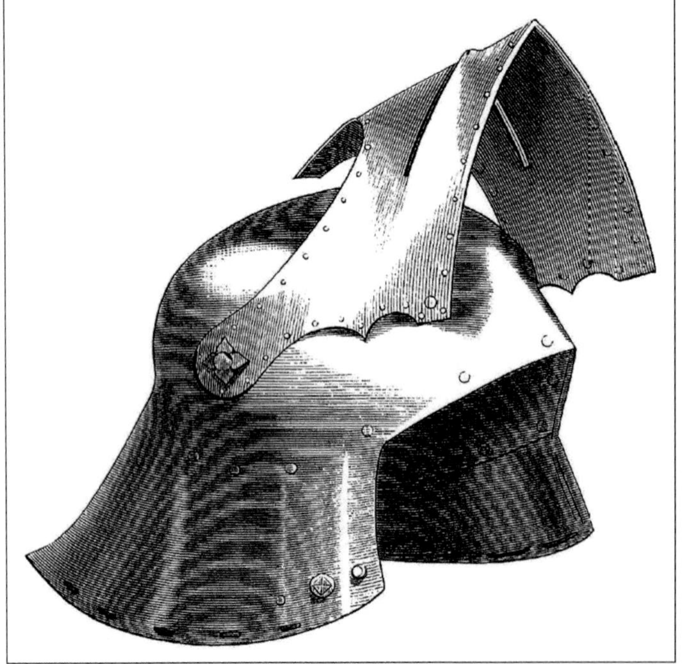

Philippe Contamine suggested a list of captains for the years 1446 and 1447 based on available archival documents. These captains are the two *Maréchals de France*, Philippe de Culant, who would command 113 lances, and André de Laval-Lohéac, with 60 lances; Charles, Duke of Bourbon, Poton de Xaintrailles, Jean d'Estouteville, Lord of Torcy, Joachim Rouault, Robert de Flocques, Arnaud-Amanieu d'Albret, Lord of Orval, Pierre Louvain, Viscount

42 Contamine, *Guerre, État et société à la fin du Moyen Âge,* Tome 2, p.399.
43 Contamine, *Guerre, État et société à la fin du Moyen Âge,* Tome 2, p.596.
44 Contamine, *Guerre, État et société à la fin du Moyen Âge,* Tome 2, p.399.
45 Contamine, *Guerre, État et société à la fin du Moyen Âge,* Tome 2, p.399.

of Berzy, Pierre de Brézé, Lord of La Varenne, Regnault du Dresnay, and Geoffroy de Couvran, these 10 captains commanding 100 lances each; Jean de Bueil with 80 lances, the sire de Beauvau with 80 lances, Charles de Culant, brother of the *Maréchal*, with 70 lances, Robert Coningham with 40 lances, Robin Pettylow with 40 lances, Boniface de Valpergue with 30 lances, Martin Garcie with 30 lances, Tristan l'Hermite with 21 lances, Adam de la Rivière with 20 lances, Étienne de Lespinasse with 20 lances, and Galéas Jambe with 10 lances; and finally Olivier de Coëtivy, Guillaume de Rosnyvinen, Olivier de Broons, as well as the two captains of the King's bodyguard, the Scotsmen Nicole and Cristye Chamber, with an undetermined number of men-at-arms and archers for each.[46]

Some of these captains' names can be found in chronicles, such as Thomas Basin *Histoire de Charles VII*. For example, during the reconquest of Normandy in 1449 and 1450, Robert de Floques, known as Floquet, Captain of Évreux, led 100 lances during the capture of Conches in July 1449.[47] Pierre de Brézé, Poton de Xaintrailles, Philippe de Culant, Lord of Jalognes, and Jean d'Estouteville, Lord of Torcy, were present in Lisieux in September 1449.[48] Jean d'Estouteville, Lord of Torcy, with 100 lances and a total of 'four hundred armed men,' and Amanieu d'Albret, Count of Orval, with another 100 lances, joined Lisieux later, in October.[49] Pierre de Brézé and Floquet, among others, fought at Formigny on 15 April 1450.[50] The same would be true for the reconquest of Guyenne from 1451 to 1453, with, for example, Amanieu d'Albret, Count of Orval, who fought around Bordeaux in June 1451.[51] Gilles le Bouvier reports that Jacques de Chabanne, *Grand Maître d'Hôtel du Roi*, and Joachim Rouault were at the head of 200 lances, while Pierre de Beauvau and Geoffroy de Saint-Belin commanded 160 lances in May 1451.[52] Bouvier cites, among others, Joachim Rouault, Théodore de Valpergue, the *Maréchals de* Lohéac and de Jalognes, Poton de Xaintrailles, the Lord of Pannesac, seneschal of Toulouse under the Count of Dunois, for the entry into Bordeaux in July 1451.[53] At the end of 1452, Charles VII sent 600 lances to the Vendée, commanded by the *Maréchals de France* Philippe de Culant and André de Lohéac, Amanieu d'Albret, Count of Orval, Joachim Rouault, and 'other captains.'[54] At the siege, and then at the Battle of Castillon in mid-

46 Contamine, *Guerre, État et société à la fin du Moyen Âge*, Tome 2, p.399.
47 Basin, *Histoire des règnes de Charles VII et de Louis XI*, Livre IV, Chapter XV, p.205.
48 Basin, *Histoire des règnes de Charles VII et de Louis XI*, Livre IV, Chapter XVII, p.216.
49 Basin, *Histoire des règnes de Charles VII et de Louis XI*, Livre IV, Chapter XX, pp.228–229.
50 Basin, *Histoire des règnes de Charles VII et de Louis XI*, Livre IV, Chapter XXIII, p.236.
51 Basin, *Histoire des règnes de Charles VII et de Louis XI*, Livre IV, Chapter I, p.249.
52 Chartier, *Histoire de Charles VII, Roy de France*, p.459.
53 Godefroy, *Histoire de Charles VII Roy de France par Jean Chartier*, pp.462–463.
54 Godefroy, *Histoire de Charles VII Roy de France par Jean Chartier*, p.468.

July 1453, were, among others, the companies of the *Maréchals de* Culant and de Lohéac, Jacques de Chabanne, and Jean de Bueil.[55] Other captains were appointed much later, such as Jacques de Clermont, squire, who was 'appointed captain of one hundred lances and archers' on 5 January 1450, according to Jean Chartier[56].

An interesting consequence of this process of selecting captains in 1445 is reported by Olivier de la Marche:

> And it was at this time that trimming horses sold for such high prices in France: and there was talk of selling a horse of renown for five hundred, a thousand, or twelve hundred réaux. The reason for this high price was that there was talk of issuing an *ordonnance* on the men-of-war of France, dividing them into companies under commanders, and selecting and electing them by name and nickname. And it seemed to every gentleman that if he showed himself on a good horse, he would be better known and respected. [57]

These companies would be distributed throughout the kingdom, outside Languedoc, in order to be supplied with provisions and paid four francs per lance and two francs per archer per month. The copy of the 1445 *ordonnance* gives us their distribution by host area:

> The lowlands of Auvergne, 100 lances and 200 archers
> The upper Auvergne region the same number.
> Rouergue and Quercy together for the same number.
> Armagnac and Comminges likewise.
> Bourbonnais, Forez, Beaujolais, and Lyonnais likewise.
> Gévaudan, Vivarais, and Velay together for a total of 150 lances and 200 archers.
> Berry for 100 lances and 200 archers.
> Poitou, Saintonge, and Angoumois for a total of 150 lances and 300 archers.
> Touraine and the County of Blois for 100 lances and 200 archers.
> Both banks of the Loire River for the same number.
> Nivernais, the Counties of Gien, Joigny, Estampes, Montargis, and Niort, the Duchy of Nemours, and all of Beauce, as well as the Duchy of Orléans for its part located in Beauce, the same number.
> Ile-de-France, Brie, and Champagne for the same number.
> Limousin for the same.
> A total of 1,400 lances housed and paid for in these countries.

55 Godefroy, *Histoire de Charles VII Roy de France par Jean Chartier*, p.468.
56 Godefroy, *Histoire de Charles VII Roy de France par Jean Chartier*, p.190.
57 De la Marche, *Mémoires*, p.407.

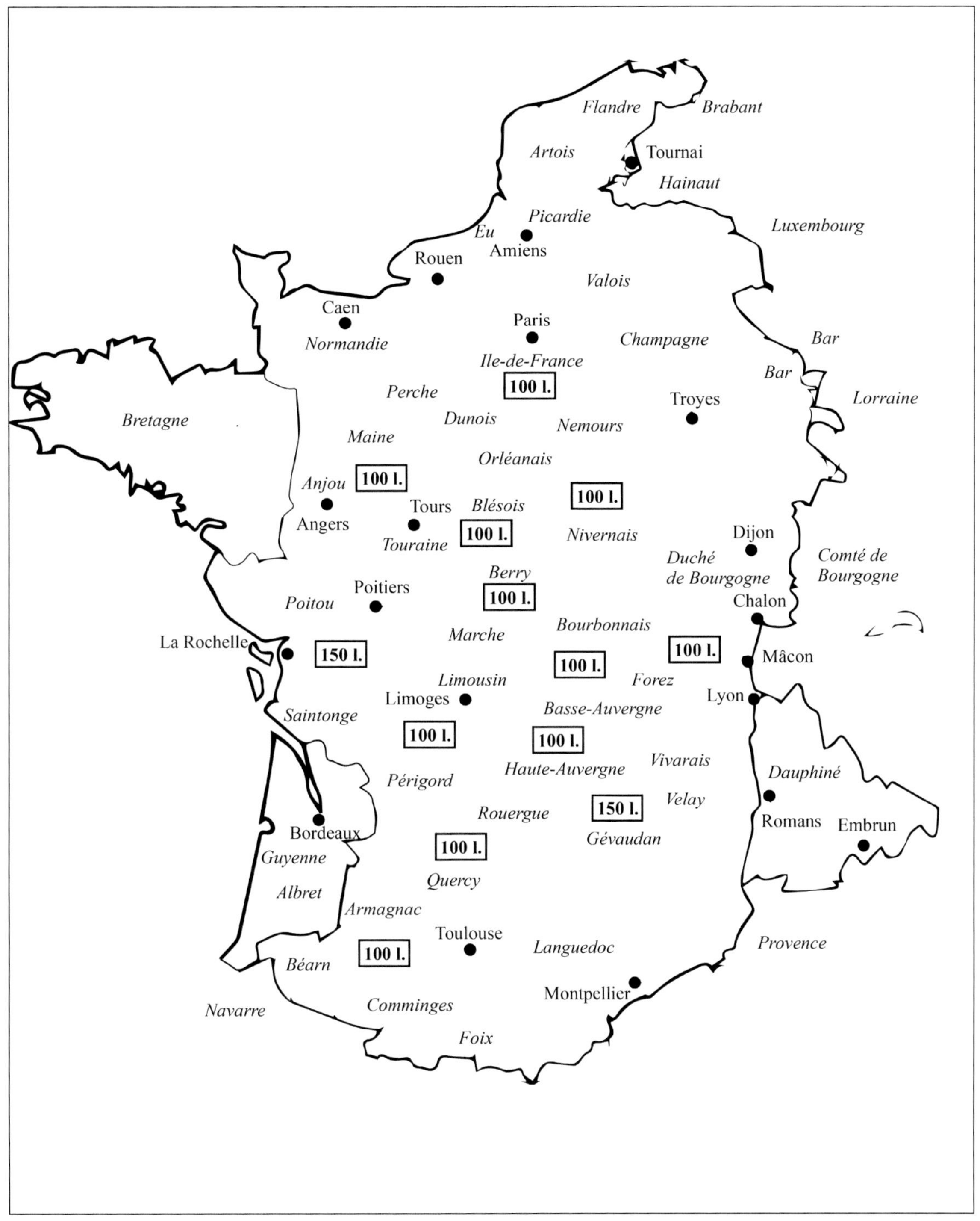

Distribution of the *compagnies d'ordonnance* within the Kingdom of France in 1445. (Artwork by the author)

The King thus dispersed his companies throughout the country to prevent companies of *écorcheurs* from devastating them or imposing the *patis* on communities, to the detriment of public finances. The remaining 100 lances and 200 archers, for a total of 1,500 lances and 3,000 archers, represented the company assigned to guard King Charles VII.

Philippe Contamine gives the following breakdown of companies with the names of their captains in January 1446, but he is unclear about his source: he cites the *ordonnance* issued in Chinon on 5 January 1446[58] but this *ordonnance* only concerns Auvergne (see below). The text to which he refers breaks down the companies as follows:

> *Maréchal de* Lafayette will inspect 30 men-at-arms and 60 archers stationed in Quercy and Rouergue under Boniface de Valpergue; 80 men-at-arms and 160 archers stationed in Rouergue under the Lord of Bueil; 40 men-at-arms and 80 archers stationed in Gévaudan and Vivarais under Robin Pettylow; 30 men-at-arms and 60 archers stationed in Velay under Martin Garcie; 40 men-at-arms and 80 archers stationed in the upper Auvergne region under Robert Coningham; 100 men-at-arms and 200 archers lodged in the lower Auvergne under Arnaud-Amanieu d'Albret, Lord of Orval; 20 men-at-arms and 40 archers lodged in the lower Auvergne under Adam de la Rivière; 100 men-at-arms and 200 archers stationed in Bourbonnais, Lyonnais, Forez, Beaujolais, and Charlieu under Geoffroy de Couvran; 60 men-at-arms and 120 archers stationed in Poitou under André de Laval, Lord of Lohéac; 100 men-at-arms and 200 archers stationed in Poitou under Pierre de Brézé, Lord of La Varenne; 30 men-at-arms and 60 archers stationed in Poitou under Robert de Floques, bailiff of Évreux; 70 men-at-arms and 140 archers stationed in Saintonge under the same; 91 men-at-arms and 182 archers stationed in the upper and lower Limousin under *Maréchal* Philippe de Culant; 22 lancers and 44 archers stationed in Combraille under the same; 70 lancers and 180 archers stationed in Berry, on the lands of the Lord of Albret, under Charles, Lord of Culant; 80 men-at-arms and 160 archers stationed in Anjou under the Lord of Beauvau.
>
> *Maréchal de* Culant will inspect 100 men-at-arms and 200 archers stationed in Touraine, Blois, and Orléans under Regnault du Dresnay; 100 men-at-arms and 200 archers in Langres, Troyes, Châlons-sur-Marne, and Reims under Jean d'Estouteville, Lord of Blainville; 100 men-at-arms and 200 archers stationed in Nivernais, Donzois, Gien, Joigny, and Vézelay under Poton, Lord of Xaintrailles; 100 men-at-arms and 100 archers stationed in Ile-de-France, Brie,

58 Philippe Contamine, 'La Guerre de Cent Ans: le XVe siècle. Du "Roi de Bourges" au "Très Victorieux Roi de France"', in A. Corvisier (ed.), *Histoire militaire de la France: 1, Des origines à 1715* (Paris: Presses Universitaires de France, 1992), pp.171–208.

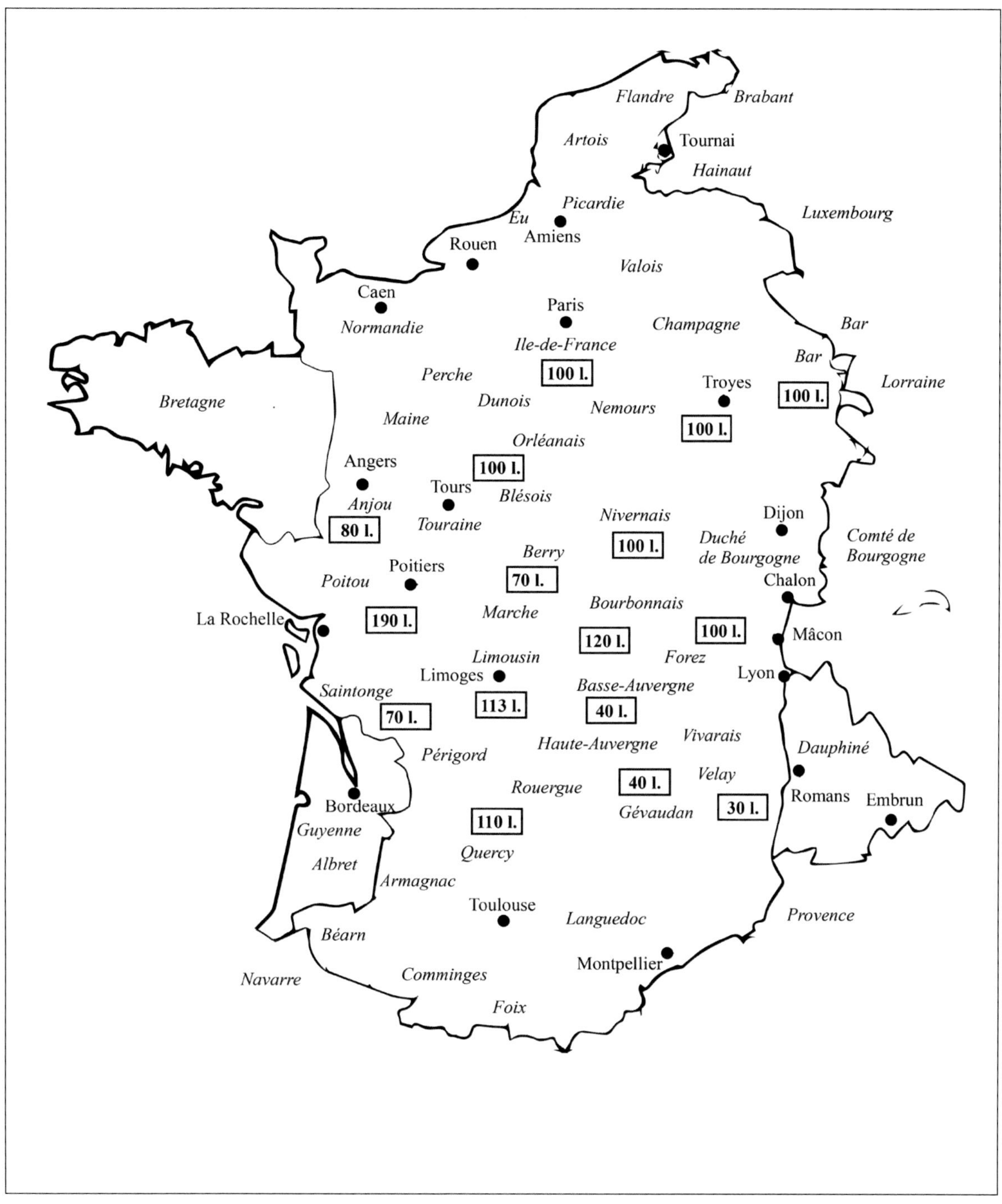

Distribution of the *compagnies d'ordonnance* within the Kingdom of France in 1446. (Artwork by the author)

> Valois, and Soissonnais under Pierre de Louvain; 100 men-at-arms and 200 archers lodged in Lorraine and Barrois, the name of their captain being omitted (perhaps Joachim Rouault).

That makes a total of 1,463 lances and 2,866 archers. The number of men-at-arms is consistent with the 1,500 lances planned when we add the 20 to 40 men-at-arms from the King's bodyguard. The number of archers is less consistent and comes from Pierre de Louvain's '100 men-at-arms and 100 archers,' which may be a transcription error.

The actual accommodation of the *ordonnance* companies therefore appears to vary in order to meet different needs. Thus, while the *ordonnance* of early 1445 provided for 150 lances in Poitou, Saintonge, and Angoumois, the *ordonnance* of 26 May 1445 now provided for 190 in Poitou alone, including 100 under Brézé for upper Poitou, 60 under Lohéac for lower Poitou, and 30 under Floquet, probably also housed in lower Poitou.[59] Similarly, the *ordonnance* of 5 January 1446 provided for the lodging of 160 lances in Auvergne, whereas the *ordonnance* of early 1445 provided for 200.[60]

From the King's Household to the Bodyguard Companies

The *Maison du Roi* (King's Household) is an ancient institution. It was already in existence in the thirteenth century under the name of *Hôtel*. The King's sergeants-at-arms were its main component at that time. Under Saint Louis, there were 25 crossbowmen in the *Hôtel*, but their numbers were increased in times of war. In 1285, Philippe III le Hardi had around fifty valets from the King's *Hôtel* in his service. The *Hôtel* also included knights: Saint Louis had 363 at the beginning of his crusade in 1270, and Philippe III le Hardi's *Hôtel* probably had around a thousand in 1285.

The *ordonnance* of 1445 provides for 1,500 lances, 1,400 of which are stationed in the kingdom's provinces. The remaining 100, provided for in the 1444 draft, represent the bodyguard and other small units probably also devoted to the protection of the King.[61] The draft *ordonnance* of 1444 already provided for the formation of a company of 100 lances and 200 archers intended for bodyguard duties, but this measure does not appear to have been implemented. The Catalan copy of the *ordonnance* of 1445 lists 20 lances and 40 archers commanded by a certain Guy d'Alsigny

59 Bessey, *Construire l'armée française*, Tome I, p.103.
60 Bessey, *Construire l'armée française*, Tome I, p.107.
61 Péquignot, 'De la France à Barcelone. Une version catalane de "l'ordonnance perdue"', p.816.

and 20 lances and 40 archers 'who will stand alongside the King.'[62] These 20 lances were ordered in 1446 by the two Scottish captains mentioned by Philippe Contamine, along with an unknown number of other lances: Nicole and Cristye Chamber.[63] According to Philippe Contamine, a company of Scottish bodyguards had existed since 1424, commanded by Martin d'Arblay in 1425 and 1426.[64] In November 1437, the King's *Archers du Corps* were dressed in 'very noble clothing.'[65] This company of Scottish guards had 26 men-at-arms and 71 archers in 1446. In 1459, this company had 31 men-at-arms and 78 archers, divided into two detachments: one consisting of the men-at-arms and 51 archers, the other consisting of 25 archers. From 1447 onwards, two other groups were added: one consisting of 20 archers and four *cranequiniers* (mounted crossbowmen), probably of German origin, and the other consisting of 24 French archers. Thus, during the last 15 years of Charles VII's reign, the bodyguard consisted of 26 to 31 men-at-arms and 124 to 126 men-of-trait.[66]

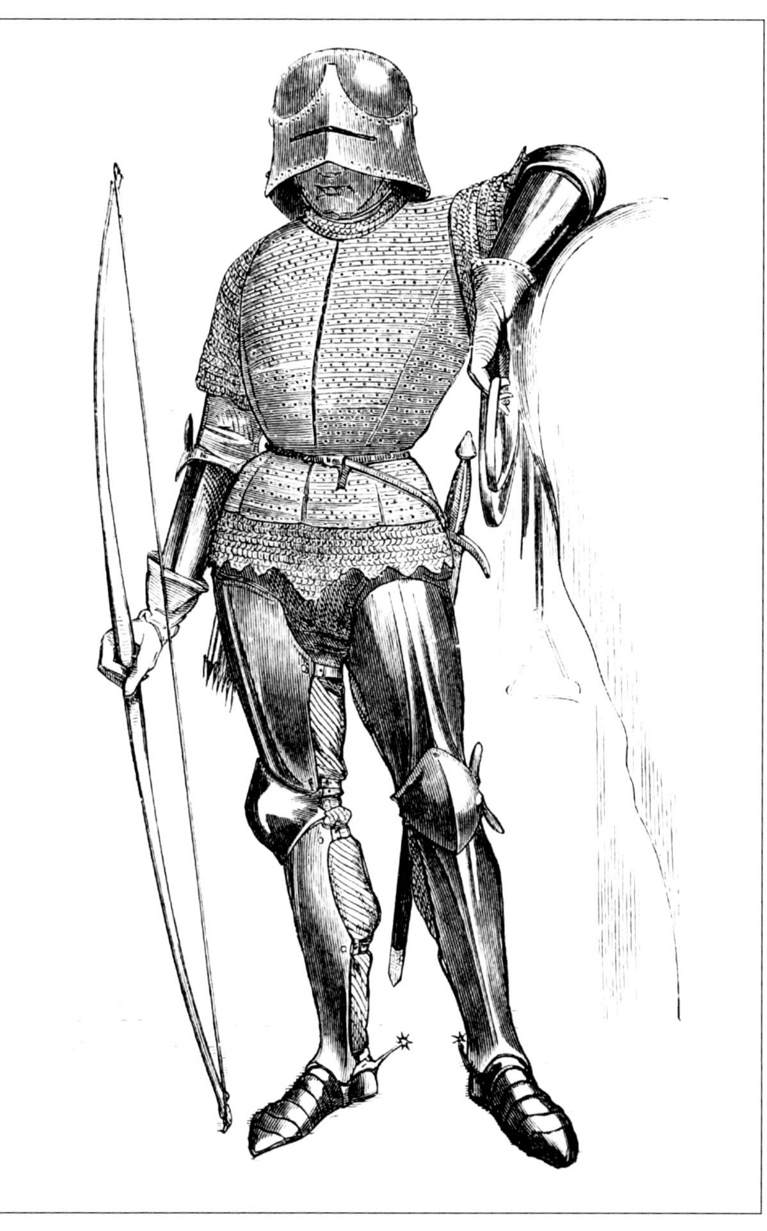

Archer of a *compagnie d'ordonnance*, c. 1450 Drawing from Viollet-le-Duc, *Encyclopédie médiévale.* (Public Domain)

62 Péquignot, 'De la France à Barcelone. Une version catalane de "l'ordonnance perdue"', p.826.
63 Contamine, *Guerre, État et société à la fin du Moyen Âge*, Tome 2, p.399.
64 Contamine, *Guerre, État et société à la fin du Moyen Âge*, Tome 2, p.247.
65 Godefroy, *Histoire de Charles VII Roy de France par Jean Chartier*, p.398.
66 Contamine, *Guerre, État et société à la fin du Moyen Âge*, Tome 2, p.256.

Implementation of the 1445 *Ordonnance*

The provisions of the *ordonnance* appear to have been swiftly implemented. Thus, in early 1445, Guillaume Gruel reported the following facts for the company of the Constable of Richemont:

> Then, at that time, the Lord Constable led the men-of-war through Burgundy, even though the *Maréchal de* Burgundy had also, to fetch the King's men who were in Montbéliard. And when they had come, my lord inspected them and dismissed those who were to be dismissed, and put the good men in *ordonnance*, and the bad men and all their baggage were sent away; and they had a letter of safe conduct from my lord. And thus was found at that time the *ordonnance* of living among the men-of-war. And this was, it seems to me, thanks to God; for never did any man who was dismissed say that it was wrong; and the captains were appointed, who have remained ever since. Thus was the pillaging of the people, which had lasted a long time, removed, and my lord was very happy about this, for it was one of the things he desired most, and had always tried to bring about, but the King would not hear of it until that hour.[67]

It is difficult to pinpoint this event. We know that Charles VII passed through Montbéliard in January 1445 and that at that time Louis de Bueil's company was lodged in Montbéliard.[68]

Once the order was promulgated, regulations for housing, supplying and paying the soldiers were sent to the seneschals. Such as the one dated 26 May 1445 already cited, sent to the Seneschal of Limousin and the Bishop of Poitiers, or those also cited above concerning the county of la Marche or of Auvergne.

Philippe Contamine studied the distribution of *compagnies d'ordonnance* within the country where they were based, to analyse the burden they place on communities, focusing on the election of Laon:

> From 1 January 1446 onwards, at the very least, the election of Laon had to pay for, feed and house 18 lances [i.e. 108 men and 108 horses] belonging to Pierre de Louvain's *ordonnance* company. All were stationed in a walled town: six lances in Laon, three in Bruyères, three in Crépy, three in Ribemont and three in Vervins. In Laon, accommodation was apparently provided by professional hoteliers: the hosts of the *Trois Rois*, the *Plat d'étain*, the *Chaudron*, the *Porcelets* and the *Barbe d'étoupe*. Elsewhere, it may have been

67 Gruel, *Chronique d'Arthur de Richemont*, pp.188–189.

68 Contamine, *Charles VII*, pp.345–346

> private individuals ['in their hotels and homes'] and even, in Ribaumont, the abbey.[69]

As we can see, these provisions made it possible to replace the practices and depredations of irregular companies, particularly the *patis*, with a regulated and more coordinated system.

As for the actual number of lances and companies, the figure of 1,500 lances, originally planned, seems to have been effectively implemented. This is notably what Thomas Basin[70] and Gilles le Bouvier assert, and what Mathieu de Coussy suggests when he mentions 15 captains. Philippe Contamine specifies that this figure would increase to 1,800 lances from 1449 on, for the conquest of Normandy and Guyenne. Upon the death of Charles VII in 1461, the figure was 1,729 lances for 34 companies, only 8 of which had 100 lances according to Contamine,[71] 23 companies according to Jean-François Lassalmonie, with a twenty-fourth company being created later, in 1464.[72] Philippe de Commynes confirms the order of magnitude when he states that 'King Charles VII raised, at the time of his death, eighteen hundred thousand francs in all from his kingdom, and held about seventeen hundred men-at-arms of *ordonnance* for all men-at-arms, ... forty-seven thousand francs, some four or five thousand men-at-arms, foot soldiers, both for the camp and for dead pay, more than twenty-five thousand.'[73]

Grande (Large) and *Petite* (Small) *Ordonnance*

In addition to the companies that would soon be known as '*grande ordonnance*', there were also '*petite ordonnance*' companies, created in 1450. This term referred to garrison units responsible for guarding royal fortresses on the coasts, borders and in reconquered provinces, such as Normandy in 1451 and Guyenne in 1454. These companies were composed of men-at-arms with their page and two archers, all veterans. The *petite ordonnance* companies, composed of 'men-of-war on *morte paye* (dead pay)', therefore had no *coustilliers* or valets for the archers. They were thus formed of lances of four men and four horses. Horses were deemed unnecessary and were

69 Philippe Contamine, 'La Guerre de Cent Ans: le XVe siècle. Du "Roi de Bourges" au "Très Victorieux Roi de France"', in A. Corvisier (ed.), *Histoire militaire de la France: 1, Des origines à 1715* (Paris: Presses Universitaires de France, 1992), pp.171–208.

70 Basin, *Histoire des règnes de Charles VII et de Louis XI,* Chapter III, p.165.

71 Contamine, *Guerre, État et société à la fin du Moyen Âge*, Tome 2, p.283.

72 Jean-François Lassalmonie, 'L'abbé Legrand et le compte du trésorier des guerres pour 1464: les compagnies d'ordonnance à la veille du bien public' in *Journal des Savants* (2001) 1: p.49.

73 Godefroy, *Mémoires de Philippe de Comines, Tome premier*, Livre 6, Chapter 7, p.407.

abolished at the end of 1452, which also led to a reduction in pay. They were then paid two-thirds of their former pay, which earned them the name *petite paye* (small pay) or morte paye (dead pay).[74] Charles VII's order of 21 April 1451, reprinted in the appendix, thus orders the payment of 600 lances and 450 small pay.[75]

---

74 Contamine, *Guerre, État et société à la fin du Moyen Âge*, Tome 2, p.277.

75 Bibliothèque nationale de France, ms. Fr. 25712, n°247; Gruel, *Chronique de Richemont*, pp.279–280.

8

The *Francs-Archers* and Artillery in the Standing Army

The *ordonnances* of 1445 created permanent mounted troop companies. These cannot be limited to the role of cavalry, as the archers formed a mounted infantry and were therefore highly mobile, with the aim of fighting in coordination with the men-at-arms, particularly when the latter dismounted to fight on foot. The King of France therefore lacked a real infantry capable of fighting independently, equally suited to fighting in pitched battles, besieging or defending towns or strongholds.

This second stage was brought about by the *ordonnance* of 28 April 1448, which established the *francs-archers*.

Franc-archer, c. 1445–1455. Drawing from Viollet-le-Duc, Encyclopédie médiévale. (Public Domain)

The *Ordonnance* of 1448 Establishing the *Francs-archers*

In his chronicles, Thomas Basin recounts how the institution of the *francs-archers* was created. As mentioned elsewhere Basin wrote in Latin, this is a modern translation:

> In addition to this force of fifteen hundred lances, another infantry militia composed of archers was created throughout the kingdom, called the *francs-archers*. Thus, in every town, village or hamlet, one man in fifty had to be chosen from among those who seemed fit to serve in this militia because of their stature, strength and physique. He had to be armed and dressed in military uniform at the expense of the fifty houses, and his weapons, bow and quiver had to be renewed and repaired whenever necessary. In fact, they received no pay, except when they were called upon to leave their parish for a royal expedition; but, keeping their weapons always ready, they remained at home, busy cultivating their fields or practising a trade or craft. However, so that they would not be subject to heavier

> military service than others without honour or advantage, they were exempt from royal taxes and duties. For this reason, and because the taxes were heavy and burdensome, it was easy to find many people willing to enlist voluntarily in his army; indeed, they often fought among themselves for the privilege of such immunity in order to secure their military service. Such a love of liberty is so innate in the soul of almost all men that any man of noble spirit will not hesitate to expose himself to the risk of death to defend it; although we do not wish to decide lightly which of these servitudes is the heaviest or most burdensome for a wise man: the payment of taxes or this kind of military service. Thus, in the French militia, about a year after the conclusion of a truce with the English, order is positive: at first, indeed, not only useful, but indispensable and absolutely necessary, for a militia, however numerous, is useless without order and discipline, but rather becomes the very breeding ground for brigandage, all crimes and total dissolution.[1]

The *ordonnance* in question is that of 28 April 1448. Here are its provisions (I have not reproduced the usual preliminaries):

> We have wanted and order .... that in each parish of our said kingdom there shall be an archer who shall be and remain continually dressed in sufficient and suitable clothing, with a sallet, dagger, sword with *trousse* [a specified number of arrows], jack or brigandine *huque*, and shall be called *francs-archers*. These shall be elected and chosen by you in the said election, the most skilled and capable in the art and practice of archery that can be found in each parish, without regard or favour to wealth or to any requests that may be made to us in this regard. And they shall be required to maintain themselves in the aforementioned clothing and to shoot the bow and go in their said clothing on all holidays and non-working days so that they may be more skilled and accustomed to the said exercise to serve us whenever we summon them. And we shall pay them four francs per man per month for the time they serve us. And so that the said archers may have more resources and be more eager to take up and maintain the said status and clothing.[2]

This *ordonnance* was followed three years later, on 9 November 1451, by an instruction comprising 23 articles detailing the process. Four additional articles were added in 1459. These three documents are reprinted in the appendices.

1 Basin, *Histoire des règnes de Charles VII et de Louis XI*, pp.168–170.

2 Bessey, *Construire l'armée française*, Tome I, pp.114–116.

The *francs-archers* of Compiègne, *c.* 1450. Drawing from Bonnault d'Houët, *Les francs-archers de Compiègne*. (Public Domain)

According to Bonnault d'Houët, Charles VII was inspired by Charles V in generalising the oaths of archers and crossbowmen still in force in certain towns.[3] The principle behind this *ordonnance* was to grant tax exemption, hence the name *francs-archers* (archers free of tax), to volunteers with a particular skill or competence in exchange for a service, in this case military service. The *francs-archers* were then chosen by the elected representatives on the basis of aides and taxes, i.e. representatives of the elections appointed by the King, most often simple commissioners. The chosen archers and crossbowmen then had to take an oath to the King's agents, who recorded their names, nicknames and places of residence on a *rôle* (roll). This service was paid at the rate of four *livres tournois* per month.

The implementation seems to have been relatively quick since, for the election in Senlis, the bailiff and the captain of the town met on 19 July 1448 to select and distribute the *francs-archers*. The town of Senlis was then required to provide 6 *francs-archers* out of the 14 planned for the diocese. For the election in Compiègne, the town had to present the same number, i.e. six *francs-archers*.[4]. We even know the names of those from the latter town: Mathieu Lombart, Guillaume Pouillet, Jehan Bernart, Nicolas Darel or Colard, Jehan Lebel, Pierre Boulenois and Thomas Waliquier, who appear in the town's registers from 10 March 1449 onwards.[5]

The number of *francs-archers* recruited in 1449 appears to have been 4,000. According to Chartier, the King left Rouen that year with a company

3 Baron de Bonnault d'Houët, *Les francs archers de Compiègne 1448–1524* (Compiègne: Publication de la Société Historique de Compiègne, 1897), p.12.
4 De Bonnault d'Houët, *Les francs archers de Compiègne 1448–1524*, p.14.
5 De Bonnault d'Houët, *Les francs archers de Compiègne 1448–1524*, p.16.

'estimated to number around six thousand combatants, including four thousand *francs-archers*.'[6] The following year, in June 1450, the Count of Clermont's army numbered 1,200 lances, 4,000 to 5,000 'archers *guisarmiers*' and *coustilliers* on horseback, and 2,000 *francs-archers* on foot, while the Count of Dunois's army numbered 500 lances, 2,500 mounted *guisarmiers* and *coustilliers*, and 2,000 *francs-archers*.[7] A little later, for the Siege of Caen, the royal army had more than 1,000 lances, 2,000 mounted archers, 1,000 mounted *guisarmiers* and *coustilliers*, and 3,000 to 3,500 foot *francs-archers*.[8] At that time, archers were often used for sieges, in support of the artillery. Thus, in July 1450, after the surrender of Falaise, Charles de Culant, Lord of Blainville, and Jean Bureau, 'with 1,500 *francs-archers* and several other men-of-war in their company, laid siege to the town and castle of Donfront.'[9]

Franc-archer c. 1450, wearing a brigandine and armed with a war hammer. Drawing from Viollet-le-Duc, *Encyclopédie médiévale*. (Public Domain)

The nine articles added in November 1451 were addressed specifically to the captains of the *francs-archers*, requiring them to take an oath before the bailiff or seneschal and granting them an annual salary of 120 *livres tournois*. We do not know how many captains there were, but one name is known to us: Captain Yvon de Carnazet, Lord of Lardi, who was appointed head of the *francs-archers* in the Paris region.[10] Furthermore, Article 19 now required that there be one *franc-archer* for every 50 households, rather than one *franc-archer* per parish. Finally, Article 20 ordered *francs-archers* who have sold or given away their clothing and equipment to replace it at their own expense. Four further articles were added in 1459 to prevent abuse and clarify certain provisions. Article 26 specifies that *francs-archers* may only use their clothing and equipment for shooting, including on public holidays. Finally, Article 27 announces the delivery of brigandines instead of jacks.

6 Godefroy, *Histoire de Charles VII Roy de France par Jean Chartier*, p.188.
7 Godefroy, *Histoire de Charles VII Roy de France par Jean Chartier*, p.206.
8 Godefroy, *Histoire de Charles VII Roy de France par Jean Chartier*, p.207.
9 Godefroy, *Histoire de Charles VII Roy de France par Jean Chartier*, p.212.
10 De Bonnault d'Houët, *Les francs archers de Compiègne 1448–1524*, p.23.

The Artillery of the Bureau Brothers

Under Charles V, artillery underwent technical and quantitative developments. It was during the siege of Saint-Sauveur-le-Vicomte in 1375 that artillery played an important role for the first time: more than 32 cannon, manufactured by foundry workers and gunners under the direction of 'master gunners', were brought from Paris, Caen and Saint-Lô. Three years later, Milet de Lyons, who was then 'master of large cannons', was appointed 'general master of the King's artillery'.[11] Previously, the royal artillery services had been under the authority of the master crossbowman of France. But every large town now had one or even several masters of artillery. The same was true of the provinces and bailiwicks.[12]

In 1411, a conflict of jurisdiction arose between the *maréchals de France* and the King's master of artillery, a conflict that contributed to a significant weakening of his authority and constituted a decisive step in the process of marginalising this office. By *ordonnance* of 22 April 1411, Charles VI transferred 'knowledge' of archers and gunners to the *maréchals*, to whom he also conferred the right to inspect them during montres and reviews. This decision reveals the subordinate position still occupied by the master of artillery at the beginning of the fifteenth century, who was dependent on other military officers of the kingdom. The rivalries between the *maréchals* and the master of the crossbowmen thus reflect the gradual rise in power of the gunners and, more broadly, of artillery in the military organisation of the French monarchy.[13] This decision granted 'Jehan le Maingre' (i.e. Jean II Le Meingre), known as Boucicaut, *maréchal*, responsibility for inspections, reviews and payment of wages to the gunners. This order is presented in the Appendix II.

Gunners and culveriners thus continued to grow in importance within the King's standing army. Charles VII had access to effective artillery thanks to the brothers Jean and Gaspard Bureau. The Bureau brothers reorganised the field artillery by developing the use of cannon. From 1437 onwards, Jean Bureau was present in the royal army that besieged Montereau: 'And there one could see spears being thrust, bombards, cannon and culverins being fired...'[14] Both brothers personally commanded the artillery during the reconquest of Normandy and Guyenne. The two brothers distinguished themselves in particular during the Siege of Meaux in 1439. Gaspard thus became temporary master of artillery by royal letters in 1442, then grand

---

11 Philippe Contamine, 'La Guerre de Cent Ans: le XIVe siècle. La France au rythme de la guerre', in A. Corvisier (ed.), *Histoire militaire de la France: 1, Des origines à 1715* (Paris: Presses Universitaires de France, 1992), pp.125-152.

12 Édouard Perroy, 'L'artillerie de Louis XI dans la campagne de l'Artois (1477)' in *Revue du Nord* (1943), 103, p.175.

13 Bessey, *Construire l'armée française*, Tome I, p.86.

14 Godefroy, *Histoire de Charles VII Roy de France par Jean Chartier*, pp.395–396.

master of artillery on 27 December 1444. His brother Jean was appointed treasurer general of France in 1443. Thus, for the Siege of Harfleur in 1449:

> Sixteen large bombards were assembled in front of the city, which the King himself came to fire and throw against the city.... The governor of this artillery and mines was Master Jean Bureau, Treasurer of France, who was very subtle and ingenious in this matter, and in many other things. With him was Gaspard Bureau, his brother, who was master of the King's artillery.[15]

In 1450, this artillery consisted of 'large bombards, large cannons, *veuglaires*, serpentines, crapaudines, culverins and ribaudequins,' and was 'well stocked with powder, mantels and all other things needed to make approaches and take towns and castles, and with a large quantity of carts to transport them, and experienced drivers to operate them, who were paid and bribed on a daily basis.'[16] The reconquest of Normandy was a campaign marked mainly by sieges, and the Bureau brothers excelled at this game: 'it was a marvellous thing to see the boulevards, approaches, ditches, trenches and mines that the aforementioned [i.e. the Bureau brothers] had built in front of all the towns and castles that were besieged during this war. For in truth, there was no place or city that was surrendered by agreement.'[17]

The Bureau brothers contributed significantly to the decisive victory at Castillon in 1453 by transporting their 300 pieces of artillery down the Dordogne River from the foundries of Périgord and making perfect use of the terrain, which they seemed to know well.

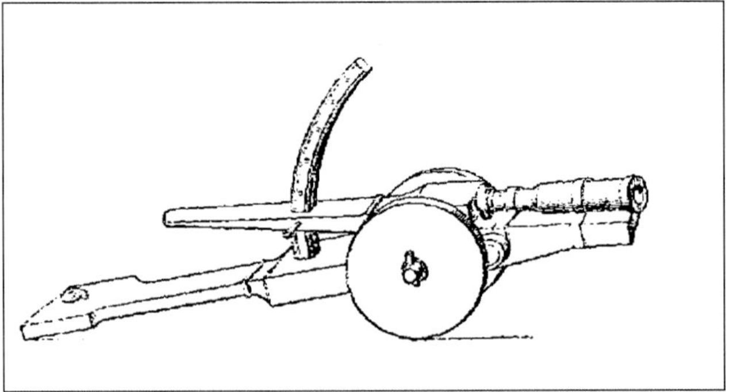

Cannon around 1450, illustration from Lieutenant-Colonel Belhomme, *Histoire de l'infanterie de France*, Tome 1 (Paris: Henri-Charles Lavauzelle, 1893). (Public Domain)

15 Godefroy, *Histoire de Charles VII Roy de France par Jean Chartier*, pp.188–189.

16 Godefroy, *Histoire de Charles VII Roy de France par Jean Chartier*, p.216.

17 Godefroy, *Histoire de Charles VII Roy de France par Jean Chartier*, p.217.

9

Compagnies d'Ordonnance, *Francs-Archers* and Artillery under Louis XI

Louis XI succeeded to the throne on the death of his father on 22 July 1461. Taking advantage of a succession crisis in Aragon, his first action was to take possession of Roussillon and Cerdagne on the French-Spanish border. Four years later, he had to face a revolt by his great feudal lords, who had united within the *Ligue du Bien Public*.

The *Compagnies d'Ordonnance* Under Louis XI

In 1464, there were 24 *compagnies*, including 14 companies of 100 lances, giving a total of 1,876 or 1,886 lances. The captains of 100 lances were: the Count of Maine; Poncet de Rivière; Bertrand de la Tour, Count of Boulogne and Auvergne; the Bastard of Armagnac, Count of Comminges; Jean de Gargueselles, Grand Squire; Joachim Rouault, *Maréchal de France*; Louis, Lord of Crussol, *Grand Panetier de France* of France; Tristan l'Hermite, Provost Marshal of France; Jean Salazar, Lord of Saint-Just; the Count of Dunois; Antoine de Châteauneuf, Lord of Lau; Jean Deteuil, Lord of Laborde; Jean de Montauban, Admiral of France; and Robert de Floques, known as Floquet. The other companies were commanded by: Geoffroy de Saint-Belin, Bailiff of Chaumont (86 or 96 lances); Gaston de Lion, Seneschal of Saintonge (50 lances); Estevenot de Tauleresse, Bailiff of Montferrand (30 lances); Louis, Bastard of Bourbon, Lord of Roussillon (20 lances); Regnault de Chastelet, Squire and King's Cutler (20 lances); Thomas, squire and bailiff of Caen (50 lances); Robert de Coningham (50 lances); Guillaume Chenu, Lord of Portneau (70 lances); Jean, Lord of Pont and Rostrenen, bailiff of Cotentin (70 lances); Jean du Fou, the King's chief first *échanson*, i.e. cupbearer (30 lances).[1] From that year onwards, six commissioners were appointed to carry out the *montres*. This *ordonnance* is reprinted in the Appendix IX.[2]

On 6 March 1465, as his great vassals were forming a coalition against him, Louis XI asked the Duke of Bourbon to join him and to raise 100 lances in his country through the Bastard of Bourbon.[3] On 8 April, Louis XI estimated that he had around 1,000 lances of the *ordonnances* at his disposal, and he hoped to have 600 more within a week.[4] He also believed that the countries of Savoy and Dauphiné could muster an additional 1,000 lances.[5] However, these figures probably included the *ban* and *arrière-ban* of these countries, notably 400 lances of the Dauphiné's men-of-war, in addition to the permanent companies, as the King wrote to his chancellor on 10 May.[6] On 1 May, the King left 900 men-at-arms on the marches of Anjou, Maine and Normandy and took 1,200 with him to Bourbonnais.[7] The royal troops, commanded by the Count of Maine and Pierre de Brézé, Count of Évreux and Seneschal of Normandy, took all of the strongholds of the Bastard of Orléans, one by one. Louis XI then launched an army of 400 lances and a body of *francs-archers* against the possessions of René d'Anjou and a vanguard of 200 lances, comprising the companies of Philippe de Melun (replacing Louis de Crussol, who had fallen into disgrace) and Jean Salazar, against the Dukes of Berry and Bourbon. The Count of Maine, assisted by Pierre de Brézé, was put in charge of guarding the Breton border, while Joachim Rouault, *Maréchal de France*, was sent to Picardy with his 100 lances. On 18 April, the King garrisoned the Breton border with 1,000 lances. He claimed to have 800 lances with him and now hoped to receive reinforcements of 1,000 to 1,200 lances from Dauphiné and Savoy, not counting 'the *francs-archers* and nobles from all countries.'[8] The King also hoped for reinforcements from Jean V, Count of Armagnac (300 lances), Jacques d'Armagnac, Duke of Nemours (200 lances) and Charles II, Count of Albret, but none of them proved loyal. It was from his former Dauphiné lands that the King would receive the strongest support, with 2,000 men of the nobility commanded by Robin Malortie. On 8 March, Louis XI had

1 Jean de Reilhac, Secrétaire, Maître des comptes, Général des finances et ambassadeur des rois Charles VII, Louis XI & Charles VIII, *Documents pour servir à l'histoire de ces règnes de 1455 à 1499*, Tome premier (Paris: H. Champion, 1886), pp.158–164.

2 De Reilhac, *Documents pour servir à l'histoire de ces règnes de 1455 à 1499*, Tome premier, pp.164–168.

3 Joseph Vaesen et Étienne Charavay, *Lettres de Louis XI, Roi de France, Tome II* (Paris: Renouard, 1885), p.233.

4 M. Champollion Figeac, *Documents inédits historiques tirés des collections manuscrites de la bibliothèque royale*, Tome second (Paris: Didot Frères, 1843), p.222.

5 Vaesen et Charavay, *Lettres de Louis XI, Roi de France*, Tome II, pp.264–265.

6 Vaesen et Charavay, *Lettres de Louis XI, Roi de France*, Tome II, pp.289–291.

7 Champollion Figeac, *Documents inédits historiques*, Tome second, p.240.

8 Champollion Figeac, *Documents inédits historiques*, Tome second, p.228.

written to Soffrey Alleman instructing him to arm and equip 200 lances supplied by the nobility to join and serve him, and that these men-of-war should be 'mounted and armed with white armour' and bring 'as many men and as good clothing as they can.'[9] Reinforcements of 4,000 Milanese soldiers were also expected, but they would have to cross Savoy and would not reach the Alps until July. On 26 June, the Count of Comminges led 400 lances back to Bourges to cut off the Duke of Bourbon and the Count of Armagnac.[10] But here again, we do not know whether these were *compagnies d'ordonnance* or the *ban*.

On 18 May, Louis XI wrote to the Count of Eu to raise as many soldiers as he could, who would be paid once the montre and review had been carried out and the men were 'found to be sufficiently clothed.'[11] On the same day, he wrote to his chancellor to raise the *ban* and *arrière-ban*.[12] This was because the war of the *Ligue du Bien Public* was disrupting the military companies. Thus, on 26 May 1465, Louis XI wrote to Poncet de Rivière, captain of 100 lances, informing him that he had been warned that:

> You do not have all your men, which is a great fault on your part, if this is the case; for you know that I pay for the entire number and would be greatly disappointed. And for this reason, on pain of being removed from your position, make sure that, if you have any to spare, you put them there; for you are in a country where you can find good men, both men-at-arms and archers, and do not fail in this, for I assure you that if I know that you or any other captain are short of men, you will never serve me in this position. See to it in such a way that no one but you has to remedy the situation; for you could not do anything that would displease me more than this.[13]

The harsh tone of this letter is notable and may have been one of the reasons that prompted Poncet de Rivière to contact the *Ligue du Bien Public*. He was stripped of his command after the war.

The episode involving the *Ligue du Bien Public* thus disrupted the royal army, with several captains of *compagnies d'ordonnance* choosing the opposing side and taking their men with them. A total of 450 lances chose to side with the Duke of Brittany: the captains concerned were André de Laval, Lord of Lohéac, commanding 100 lances; Odet d'Aydie, Lord of Lescun, commanding 100 lances; Christophe, Lord of Coëtivy, commanding 90 lances; Geoffroy de Couvran at the head of 40 lances; Jean,

9 E. Pilot de Thorey, *Catalogue des actes du dauphin Louis II devenu le roi de France Louis XI*, Tome deuxième (Grenoble: Imprimerie de Maisonville, V. Truc, successeur, 1899), pp.71–72.

10 Vaesen et Charavay, *Lettres de Louis XI, Roi de France*, Tome II, p.319.

11 Vaesen et Charavay, *Lettres de Louis XI, Roi de France*, Tome II, p.297.

12 Vaesen et Charavay, *Lettres de Louis XI, Roi de France*, Tome II, p.301.

13 Vaesen et Charavay, *Lettres de Louis XI, Roi de France*, Tome II, pp.306–307.

Lord of Pont, commanding 40 lances; Olivier de Broons at the head of 40 lances; and Gilles, Lord of La Hunaudaye, at the head of 40 lances. The companies of Jean de Bueil, Antoine de Chabannes, Count of Dammartin, Pierre d'Amboise, Lord of Chaumont, and the Lord of Urfé would reinforce this army. Although these defections reduced the size of the royal standing army, these lances were not among the 1,700 lances recorded by Jean de Reilhac in 1464. They were therefore no longer paid for by the royal treasury.

To face the League, the Count of Maine had 300 lances and 700 to 800 men-at-arms, according to Commynes.[14] Louis XI promised him reinforcements of 1,100 lances and 6,000 to 8,000 *francs-archers*.[15] Letters from the King dating from this period provide us with the names of a few captains: they include the Count of Maine, who defected on the day of the Battle of Montlhéry, Louis de Crussol (100 lances), Jean Salazar (100 lances), *Maréchal* Joachim Rouault (100 lances), Poncet de Rivière (100 lances), the Bastard of Armagnac, Count of Comminges (100 lances) and Louis, Bastard of Bourbon (20 lances).

After the Battle of Montlhéry (16 July 1465), Louis XI claimed that he still had 1,500 to 1,600 lances of *grande ordonnance* 'without our cousins the Count of Nevers, the Count of Eu, the baillis of Vermandois and Senlis, the Lord of Roye, the Lord of Haincourt, and others, who joined us, numbering 300 lances and more.'[16] The total would therefore be around 1,900 lances of *grande ordonnance*, a figure confirmed by Olivier de la Marche.[17] On 24 November 1465, following the Treaty of Conflans, the loss of Normandy meant that Louis XI lost the recruitment of 600 lances, or 3,600 combatants, not counting the *morte payes*. The King then asked the Dauphiné to raise and pay for an additional 100 lances, at 31 francs per lance per month, a figure that included the captain's pay.[18] According to Philippe Contamine, the number of lances rose to 1,765 in 1466 and then to 2,065 in 1468, a figure that fell to 1,990 lances in 1470. In 1473, this figure rose again to 2,094 lances, to which Louis XI added 415 extraordinary lances. These were special lances organised on the Italian model: in these lances, the archers, who were fewer in number, were replaced by 12 *génétaires* (based on the Spanish *jinetes*) and about 20 *coustilliers*. In 1475, the total number temporarily increased by 1,000 lances. The total number of lances then rose to 2,846 lances divided into 40 companies at the beginning of 1476, then to 4,142 lances at the beginning of 1478. This figure fell back to 3,177 lances in 35 companies at the beginning of 1479, of which about 20 would fight at Guinegatte. At the beginning of 1482, Louis XI was paying nearly 4,000

14 Godefroy, *Mémoires de Philippe de Comines*, Tome premier, p.17.

15 Christian Delabos & Philippe Gaillard, *Montlhéry, 16 juillet 1465* (Annecy: Historic'One Editions, 2003), pp.42–43.

16 Vaesen et Charavay, *Lettres de Louis XI, Roi de France*, Tome II, pp.341–342.

17 De la Marche, *Mémoires*, p.502.

18 De Reilhac, *Documents pour servir à l'histoire de ces règnes de 1455 à 1499*, Tome premier, pp.212–215.

lances. At the death of Louis XI, 3,992 lances divided into 43 companies were financed by the state. However, only 2,092 lances remained on 30 May 1484, when Charles VIII was crowned.[19] The figure of 4,000 lances represents 24,000 combatants, an impressive number for the time. Added to the 16,000 *francs-archers* who could be quickly mobilised, Louis XI then had 40,000 trained men-of-war at his disposal.

Men-at-arms and archers of the *ordonnance*, 1471. The *huques* of the archers on the left are two-coloured: red on the left and green on the right with a white cross in the centre. The one worn by the man-at-arms in the centre is blue with a fleur-de-lis. Illustration from a French manuscript, Bibliothèque nationale de France, Ms 2609 f. 718. (Public Domain)

A *compagnie d'ordonnance* could, of course, be dissolved, either by force of circumstance or by royal decree. In such cases, the members of the company were then distributed among other companies. This is what happened on 28 May 1472 to the company of Odet d'Aydie the Younger, younger brother of his namesake Odet d'Aydie, Lord of Lescun, who was in the service of Louis XI's enemies. A new *Ligue du Bien Public* had been formed in August 1471 between Duke Charles of France, then Duke of Guyenne, the Duke of Brittany and the Count of Foix. A few days after the capture of La Rochelle on 23 May and the death of Charles of France on 24 May, which led to the return of Guyenne to the crown, Louis XI asked Antoine de Chabannes:

19 Contamine, *Guerre, État et société à la fin du Moyen Âge*, Tome 2, pp.280–282

> My Lord Grand Master, I beg you to remove Odet's men-of-war, and leave him none if you can, and let the Seneschal of Guyenne take them until his company is full. And if there are still more, put them in a band and send them to me first, and I will find them a captain and pay all those who wish to remain there.[20]

It seems that under Louis XI, men-at-arms and archers tended to increase the number of horses they owned. Indeed, at the beginning of 1463, the King wrote to the *Maréchal de* Comminges that 'the lance provided retains only six horses.'[21] At the same time, he wrote the same instruction to the Lord of Montglat, thus showing the importance he attached to this matter: 'And ensure that only six horses are left with the lance provided, in accordance with the order made for this purpose, and that all the baggage is brought over here.'[22] Ten years later, in January 1473, Jean de Troyes stated that Louis XI reduced the number of horses per lance to six, which suggests that at the beginning of his reign, all or some of the lances in the kingdom may have had a higher number: 'namely three horses for the lance for the gendarme,[23] his page and the *coutillier*, and two horses for the two archers, and one horse for the valet.'[24]

Finally, the political instability that marred the first decade of Louis XI's reign reignited the very problems that had led to the formation of the *compagnies d'ordonnance*, as shown in this letter from the King to the people of Lyon, written on 29 May 1470:

> Dear and beloved, since our accession to the throne, we have always desired and continue to desire above all else to relieve our people and remove and abolish many great evils and abuses, plunder and robbery which they have endured until now against our will and desire, and which has been and is the greatest displeasure that can befall us, and we have often deliberated and undertaken to give order and good provision to the said evils and exactions, and even on the spot, the livelihood and government of the men-of-war under our command, we, on account of the troubles, divisions and other great affairs that have arisen in our kingdom, have been so occupied that until now we have been unable to attend to them properly or to remedy them as we have desired and desire with all our heart. And because, with the help of Our Lord and our good and loyal subjects, we now see the affairs of ourselves and our said kingdom well disposed, we have concluded

20 Vaesen et Charavay, *Lettres de Louis XI, Roi de France*, Tome IV, p.329.

21 Vaesen et Charavay, *Lettres de Louis XI, Roi de France*, Tome II, p.92.

22 Vaesen et Charavay, *Lettres de Louis XI, Roi de France*, Tome II, p.94.

23 Jean de Troyes actually used the word 'gendarme' and not 'homme d'arme' (man-at-arm).

24 M. Petitot, *Collection complète des mémoires relatifs à l'histoire de France: Tome XIII, les chroniques de jean de Troyes* (Paris: Foucault, 1820), p.441.

and deliberated to put such good order, police and government or affairs of our said kingdom, both in the lives and government of our said people of war and otherwise, that the said evils, pillaging and robberies will cease, and that our said subjects will live in peace and tranquillity. And for this purpose, we have, with the advice and deliberation of several lords of our blood, captains and warlords, and people of our great council, made certain *ordonnances*, which, so that no one may claim ignorance, we have sent and published throughout all the sénéchaussées, bailiwicks, good towns, and other places of our said kingdom. And with this, so that the said evils, pillaging and exactions may be repaired and that the said men-of-war may be lodged in closed towns and live according to the contents of our said *ordonnances*, we are presently sending the *maréchals de* France, captains and other notable men in the countries and places where the said men-of-war have been and are lodged, of which things we have been pleased to inform you, so that you may know more and more the good and great will that we have had and have for the good and relief of you and our said kingdom and our said subjects, and that, if the said men-of-war have committed any faults, plunder and exactions, that you inform the said commissioners and our officers of the places where the said cases have been committed, so that they may be dealt with as is reasonable. And if it should happen that our said commissioners or officers should wish to delay or postpone matters out of favour or otherwise, we expressly desire and command you to inform us of this with all diligence, and we shall deal with it in such a manner that everyone will take example from it.[25]

Armour for a man-at-arms, c. 1470–1490. Collection of the Musée de l'Armée, Paris. (Photo by the author)

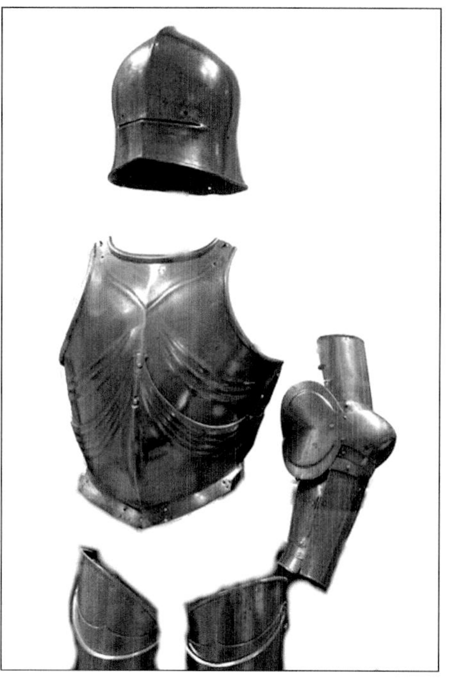

However, the depredations did not cease, as the King wrote a similar letter to the inhabitants of Reims on 22 January 1473.[26]

The *Francs-Archers* Under Louis XI

In 1465, the institution of *francs-archers* remained in accordance with the *ordonnances* established by Charles VII. Thus, on 13 July 1465, Louis XI asked the *bailli* of Troyes to ensure that all *francs-archers*, 'like all other non-nobles who are fit for war and equipped for battle, and who can be used against our rebels and disobedient subjects, whether they be people from

25 Vaesen et Charavay, *Lettres de Louis XI, Roi de France*, Tome IV, pp.119–121.
26 Vaesen et Charavay, *Lettres de Louis XI, Roi de France*, Tome IV, pp.101–102.

good towns or flat countries, be brought into our service.'[27] It was from the following year that the institution began to evolve.

The *ordonnance* of 1466 (see Appendix XI) established four captain generals of the francs-archers.[28] These four captain generals were: Aymar du Puyfieu, known as Cadorat, Bailli of Mante; Pierre Aubert, Lord of La Grange and Bailli of Melun; Ruffec de Balsac, Seneschal of Beaucaire; and Pierre Comberel, Lord of L'Isle. Each of these captain generals now had 4,000 *francs-archers* under his command, making a total of 16,000. These captain generals were distributed throughout the territory, the kingdom being divided into four parts, and received 800 *livres* in wages. They commanded a total of 28 captains, each of whom was in charge of 500 *francs-archers*. From this number of 28, we can deduce that each captain general also has 500 *francs-archers* directly under his command to reach a total of 16,000. In 1465, according to Philippe de Commynes, Louis XI brought 4,000 of his *francs-archers* from Normandy to defend Paris.[29]

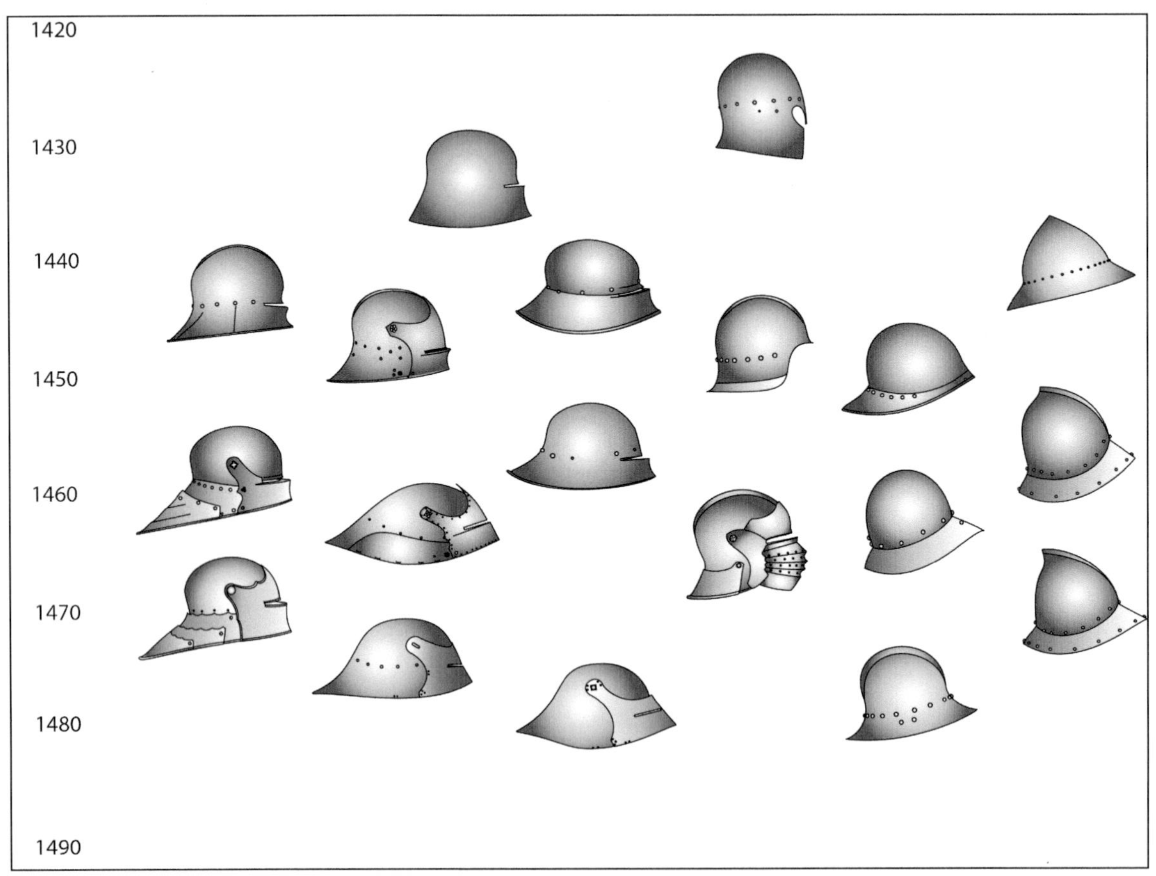

Évolution of the sallet helmet between 1420 and 1490. (Artwork by the author)

27 De Reilhac, *Documents pour servir à l'histoire de ces règnes de 1455 à 1499*, Tome premier, p.199.

28 Bessey, *Construire l'armée française*, Tome I, pp.125–130.

29 Godefroy, *Mémoires de Philippe de Comines*, Tome premier, p.48.

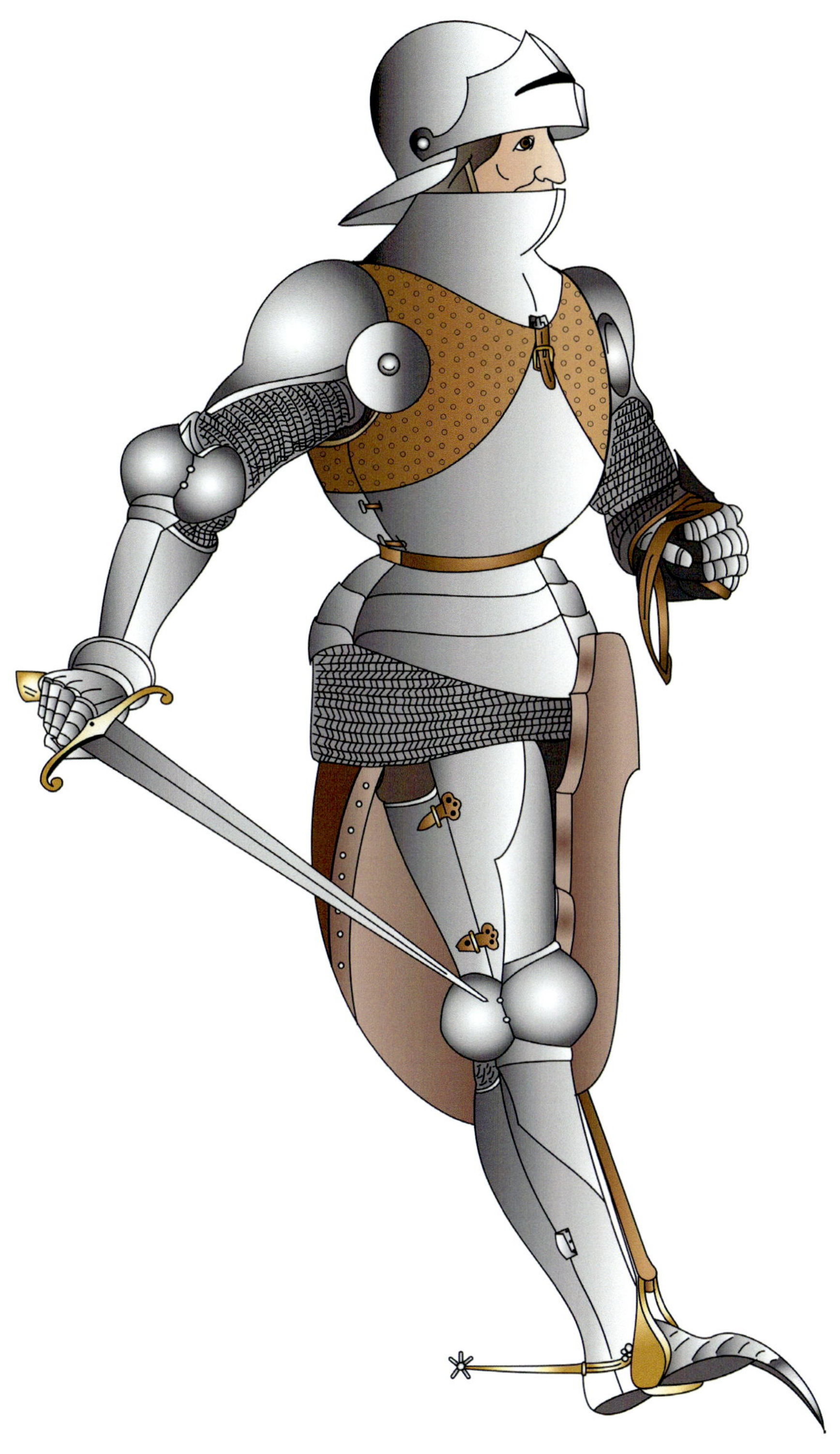

Plate A. Mounted man-at-arms, *c*. 1445–1455, reconstructed after Viollet-le-Duc. (Artwork by the author)

See Colour Plate Commentaries for further information.

Plate B. Two men-at-arms of a *compagnie d'ordonnance*.
(Artwork by the author)
See Colour Plate Commentaries for further information.

Plate C. Two men-at-arms of a *compagnie d'ordonnance*.
(Artwork by the author)
See Colour Plate Commentaries for further information.

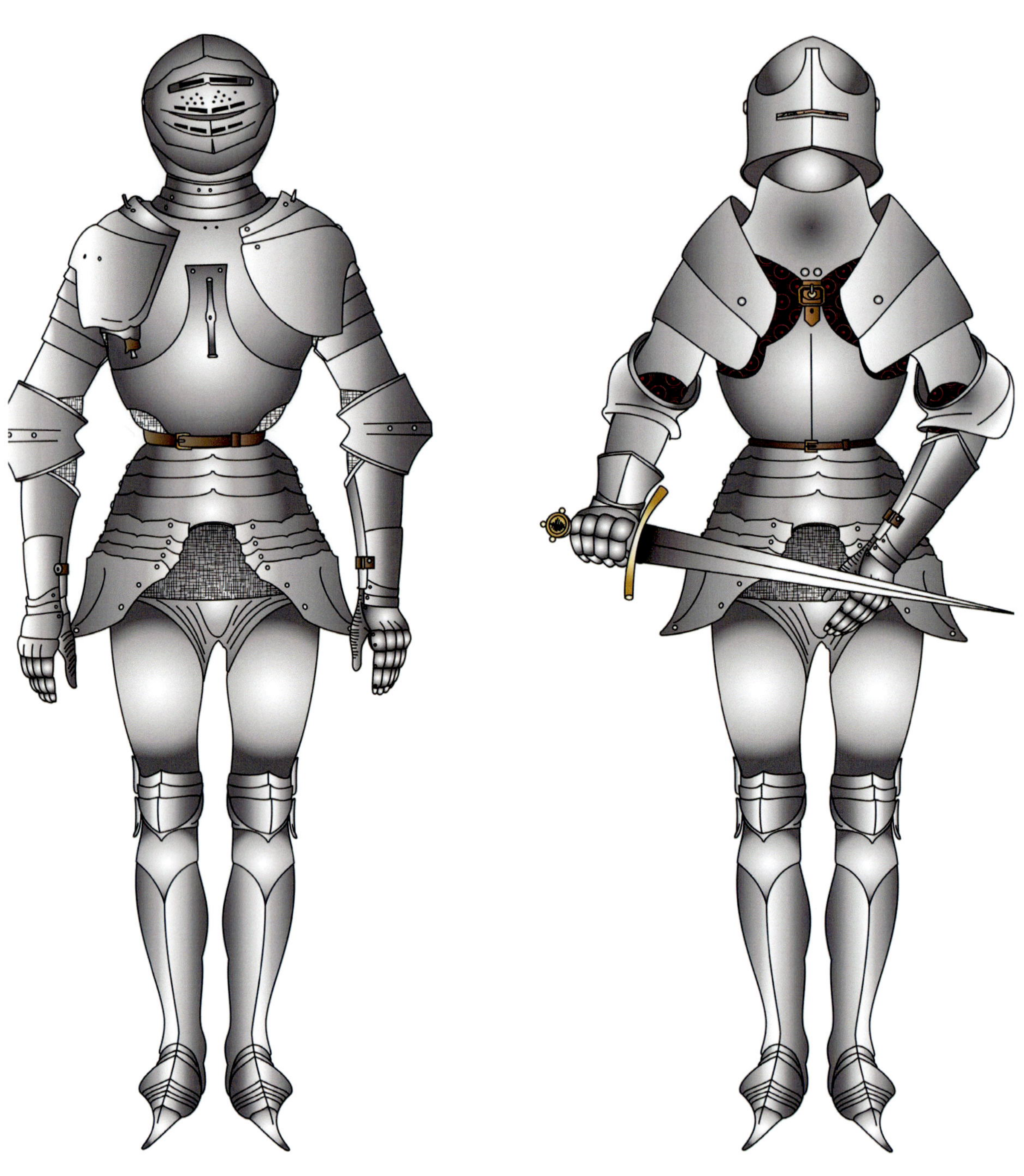

Plate D. Two complete armours for men-at-arms, shown in front view.
(Artwork by the author)
See Colour Plate Commentaries for further information.

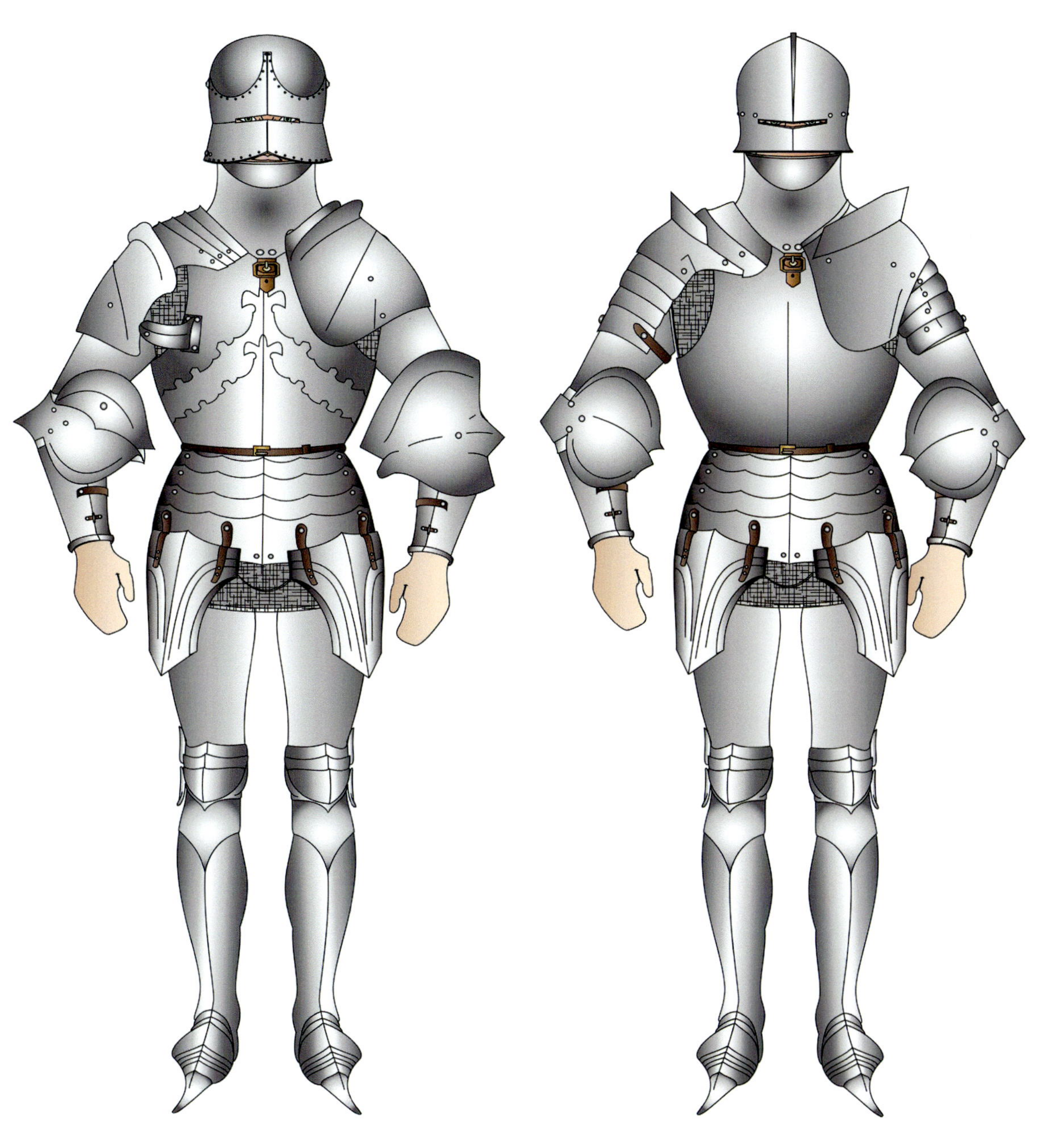

Plate E. Two further complete armours, dated *c.* 1470–1480.
(Artwork by the author)
See Colour Plate Commentaries for further information.

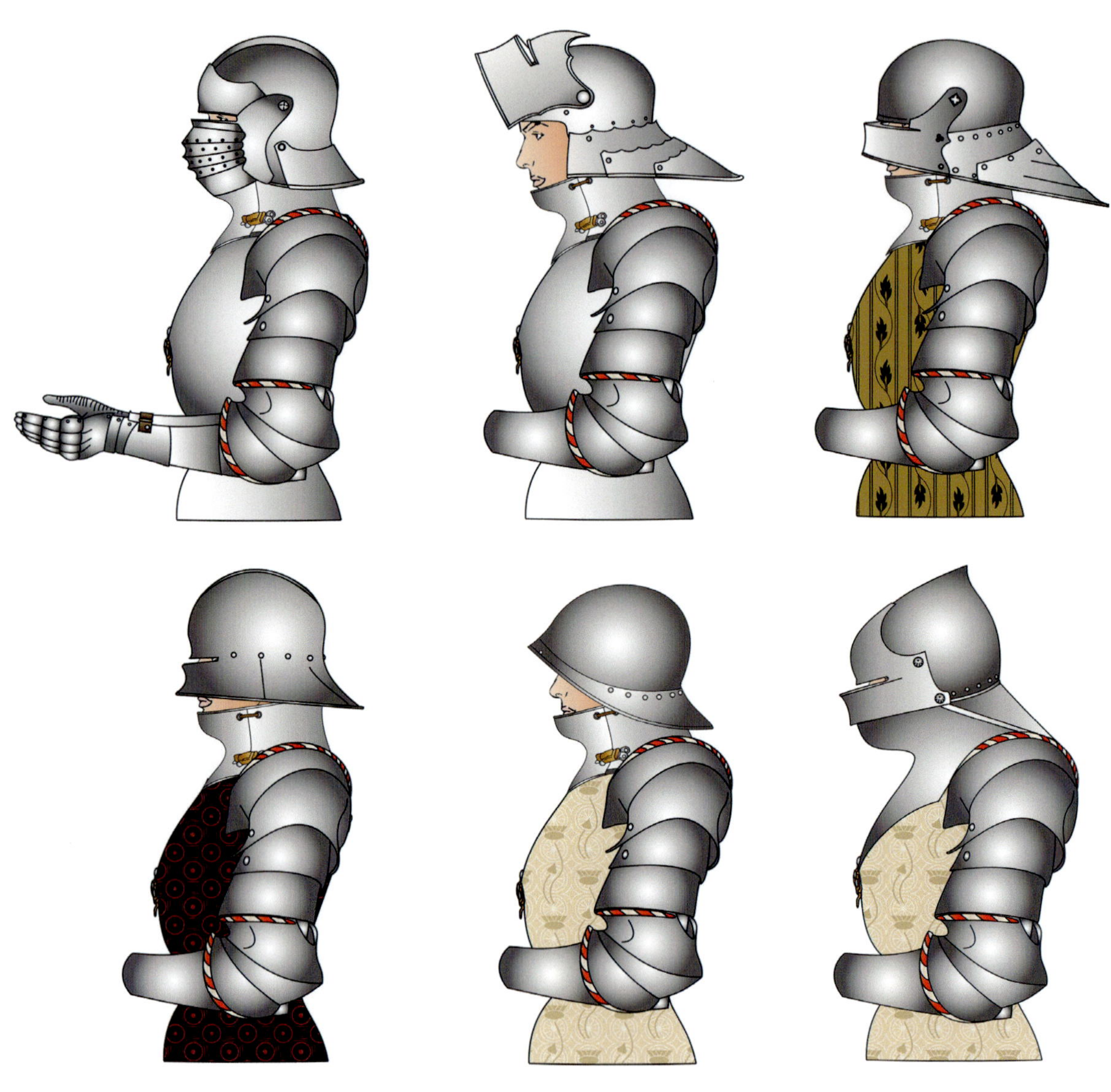

Plate F. Busts of men-at-arms wearing breastplates and brigandines.
(Artwork by the author)
See Colour Plate Commentaries for further information.

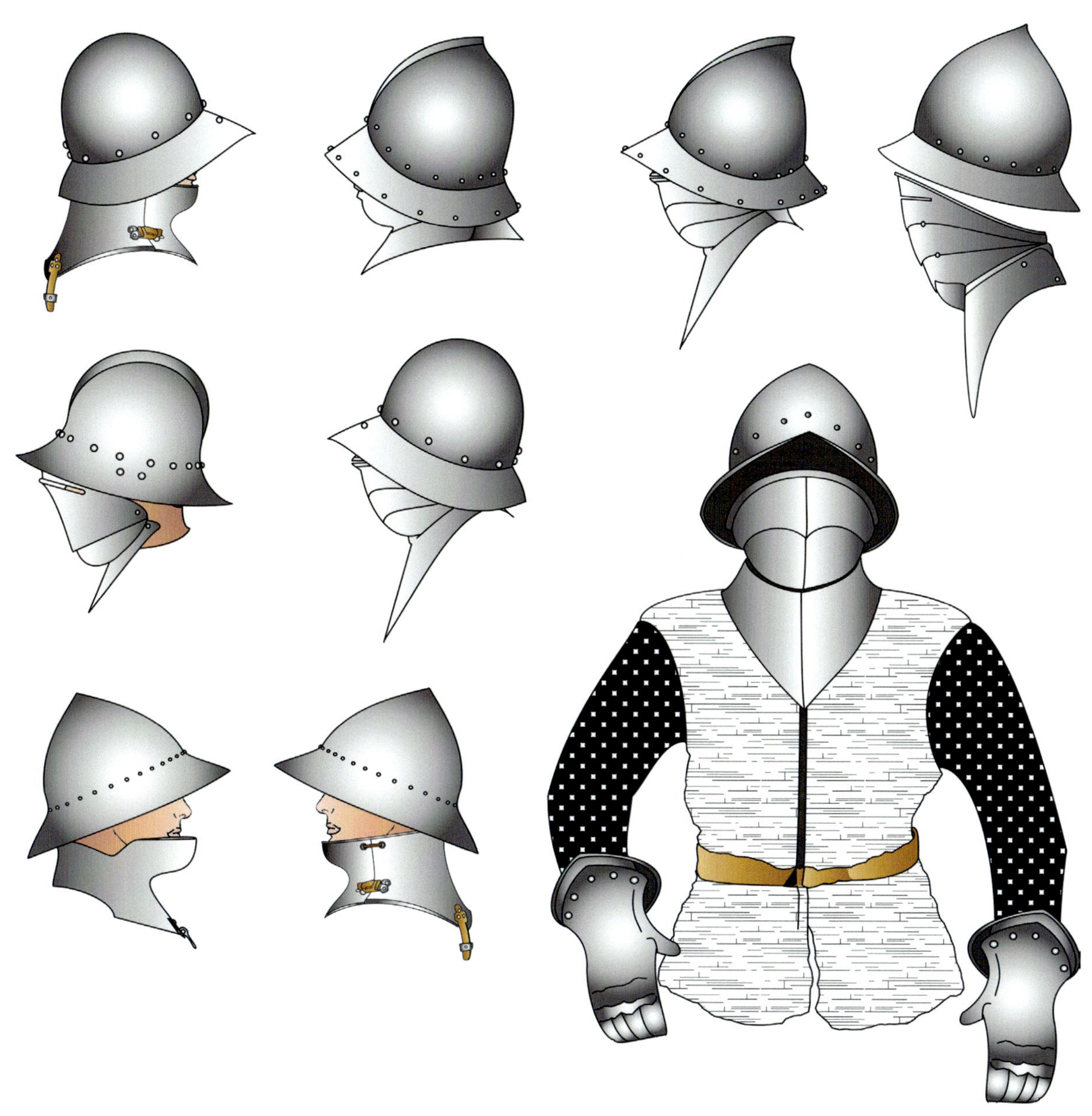

Plate G. Chapels and *capacetes* in the fifteenth century.
(Artwork by the author)
See Colour Plate Commentaries for further information.

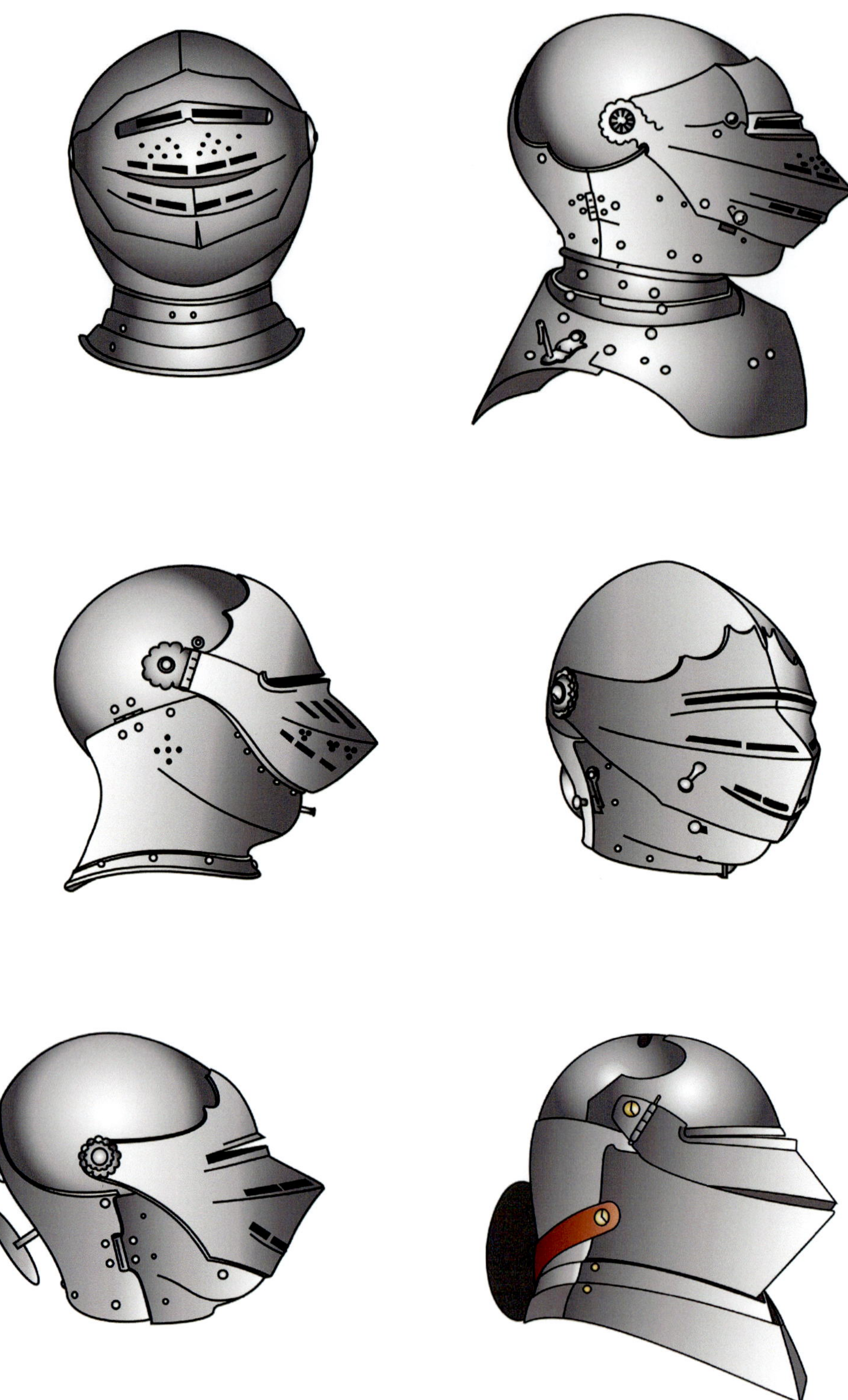

Plate H. Armet helmet styles.
(Artwork by the author)
See Colour Plate Commentaries for further information.

Plate I. Archers during the reigns of Charles VII and Louis XI.
(Artwork by the author)
See Colour Plate Commentaries for further information.

Plate J. Archers *d'ordonnance* during the reigns of Charles VII and Louis XI.
(Artwork by the author)
See Colour Plate Commentaries for further information.

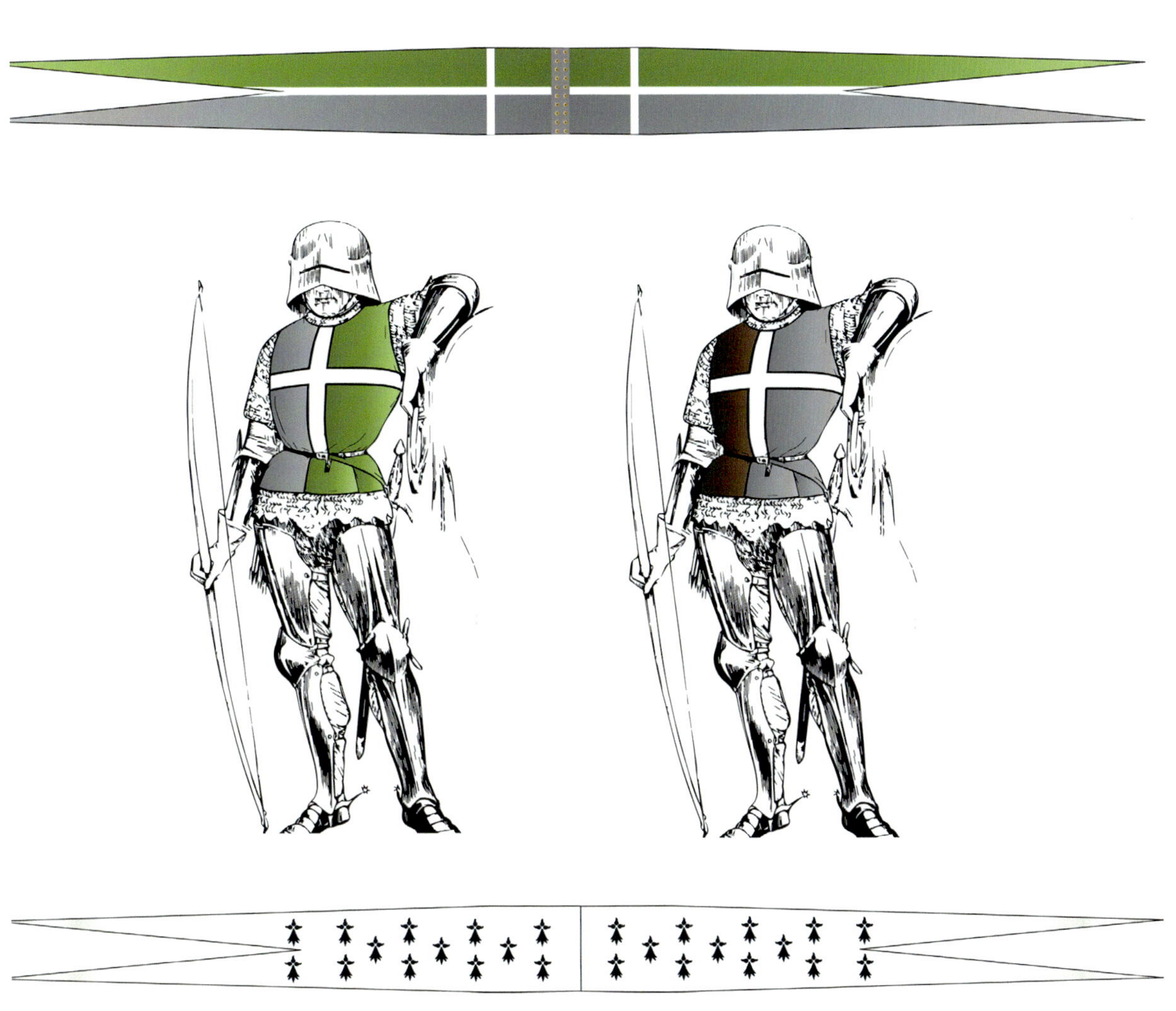

Plate K. Archers during the reign of Charles VII.
(Artwork by the author)
See Colour Plate Commentaries for further information.

Plate L. Pennants.
(Artwork by the author)
See Colour Plate Commentaries for further information.

The archers were now equipped with jacks, sallets, gauntlets, swords and daggers in addition to their main weaponry, although those who had brigandines were of course allowed to keep them. The main weaponry consisted of bows, crossbows, *vouges* or spears. The crossbow remains very popular, especially for sieges. Thus, on 22 August 1472, Louis XI asked Antoine de Chabannes, his grand master, to send 80 to 100 crossbowmen, 'the best you can find', in addition to artillery and provisions, to the *Bailli* of Caux.[30]

A few years later, the *ordonnance* of 12 January 1474 (see Appendix XIII), addressed complaints about the excesses and malpractices committed by the *francs-archers* or their captains. The brigandine reappeared in their equipment, along with a new weapon, the pike, which replaced the spear, and several articles were devoted to the hocqueton. Finally, a new *ordonnance* dated 30 March 1475 was intended to 'give orders and regulations on the maintenance of the said *francs-archers* and remove all pillaging that might occur and protect our subjects from undue charges.' This *ordonnance* notably granted the *francs-archers*, to 'help them carry their weapons and clothing .... an iron-bound cart drawn by three horses' for 15 *francs-archers*. These carts were initially 'provided and paid for out of the treasury' and were then maintained 'at the expense of the inhabitants who made up the said fifteen *francs-archers*' (see Appendix XIV).

According to Jean de Troyes, it was in 1480, probably following the Battle of Guinegatte in 1479, that the King 'had all the *francs-archers* in the kingdom of France dismissed, and in their place wanted the Swiss pikemen to be and remain there to serve in his wars. And he had all the cutlers make a large quantity of pikes, halberds, and large daggers with wide blades.'[31] Thus he transformed his *francs-archers* into pikemen and halberdiers.

The King's Household Under Louis XI

In 1465, Louis XI's personal guard consisted of 25 archers from the corps and 75 archers from the guard, two units each commanded by a captain. In 1463, these archers were dressed in 'one hundred red, green and white cloth jackets .... embroidered with the lord's badge.'[32] On 4 September 1474, Louis XI created the company of gentlemen of the King's Household. This was a company of 100 lances, consisting of men-at-arms and twice as many archers, dedicated to guarding his person. This company was notably present in July 1475 to face the English in the vicinity of Eu.[33] On 10 June 1475, Louis Mallet de Graville was appointed to lead these 100

30 Vaesen et Charavay, *Lettres de Louis XI, Roi de France*, Tome V, p.47.

31 Petitot, *Collection complète des mémoires relatifs à l'histoire de France*, Tome XIII, p.343.

32 Archives Nationales, KK 65 ff. 100–112.

33 Vaesen et Charavay, *Lettres de Louis XI, Roi de France*, Tome V, p.370.

Men-of-war c. 1480. Illustration by Jean Colombe, master illuminator to Charles VII. Bibliothèque nationale de France, Ms 091 f. 171r. (Public Domain)

men-at-arms and their archers assigned to guard the body of the King.[34] According to Philippe Contamine, from 1474 onwards, Louis XI could count on 160 gentlemen of the *hôtel*, 40 crossbowmen and 400 archers. On 8 January 1477, the King split this company into two units: the company of 100 gentlemen of the *Maison du Roi* and the company of 200 archers of his guard. Under Charles VIII, this second company became the Archers of the Bodyguard. Commynes recounts the dispatch of the company of the King's gentlemen to Burgundy in 1478: 'And the King sent me there with the pensioners of his household; it was the first time he had given a leader to the said pensioners; and since then he has continued this practice to this day.'[35]

Artillery Under Louis XI

Like his father, Louis XI seemed to value his artillery. Thus, on 30 September 1467, he reminded the Chamber of Accounts to pay what was owed to his master of artillery:

> We have written and sent several requests to proceed with the ratification of our letters of donation and receipt that we have granted to our beloved and loyal Gaspard Bureau, knight, master of our artillery, for all that he may owe us both for the said artillery and for the buildings and other revenue and expenditure charges that he had from our late beloved lord and father and from us since our accession to the crown; which you have nevertheless deferred until now and are still deferring, as we have been told, until you are certified in truth of our will, on which you have recently, through our beloved and loyal counsellor and chamberlain, the *sire de* Precigny, president of our Chamber of Accounts, sent the statement of accounts of the said Gaspard Bureau concerning the said artillery, by which statement it appears that he owes us the clear sum of twenty-eight thousand seven hundred and four *livres* sixteen sous *parisis*, not including the sum of eleven thousand nine hundred and thirty-eight *livres*, four *sous* and one *denier maille parisis* that you have deducted

34 Contamine, *Guerre, État et société à la fin du Moyen Âge*, Tome 2, pp.320–333.
35 Godefroy, *Mémoires de Philippe de Comines*, Tome premier, p.391.

> from the names and for the wages of him and his controller, for which he is in arrears, nor other sums that he must receive in the last three of the said accounts; and without including what he may owe us both for the artillery equipment and for the aforementioned buildings and other work he has carried out, as stated.[36]

Under his reign, the artillery was expanded, particularly between 1470 and 1474. Upon the death of Gaspard Bureau, shortly after 1469, the position of master of artillery passed to Gobert Cadiot and then, on 15 August 1473, to Guillaume Bournel. In 1477, three artillery bands were mobilised for operations in Picardy, Artois and Hainaut. These bands appear to have been created recently: the *grande bande*, about which little is known, was present in front of Arras, then Le Quesnoy and Avesnes. It had 10 cannon: a very large bombard pulled by 41 horses, three large bombards, two medium-sized ones and four *courteaulx*. A total of 175 horses were needed to move all the pieces.[37]

The second band is better known. It was under the command of Giraud de Samain, who had earned his spurs under Charles VII at Formigny. This band had 30 pieces, of a more modest calibre than the *grande bande*: a large cannon called *le doyen* (the dean), which required 11 horses to move, 2 serpentines, 4 large culverins, 12 medium culverins and 11 'pers', which were old light pieces, a twelfth one having been lost at the Battle of Montlhéry. Moving the entire band required waggons pulled by 121 horses. Surprisingly, this band had a permanent staff of 29 gunners, including its captain, which seems small. These were probably only the gun commanders, with temporary personnel, notably labourers, and the cartage added to this permanently paid staff. The pay of these gunners varied from 23 *livres* to 180 *livres* per year, depending on their experience and probably their speciality.[38]

The third band was named Rousselet after its first leader, Thomas Bachelier, known as Le Rousselet. This band had 25 pieces: 7 serpentines, 10 culverins and 8 falcons, which together required a cartage of 165 horses to move them.[39]

A fourth band was created in 1477 for the conquest of Burgundy: the 'Burgundy band', commanded by Jean Barrabin. To form it, cannon and gunners were recruited from the towns of Troyes and Langres, supplemented by foreign gunners and new serpentines. In the spring of 1477, this band was composed of 17 gunners and two bombardiers plus 17 workers.[40] Thus, even before 1477, the organisation of artillery into different bands had become widespread.

36 Vaesen et Charavay, *Lettres de Louis XI, Roi de France,* Tome III, pp.171–172.
37 Perroy, 'L'artillerie de Louis XI dans la campagne de l'Artois (1477)', pp.186–187.
38 Perroy, 'L'artillerie de Louis XI dans la campagne de l'Artois (1477)', pp.190–192.
39 Perroy, 'L'artillerie de Louis XI dans la campagne de l'Artois (1477)', pp.193–194.
40 Perroy, 'L'artillerie de Louis XI dans la campagne de l'Artois (1477)', pp.195–196.

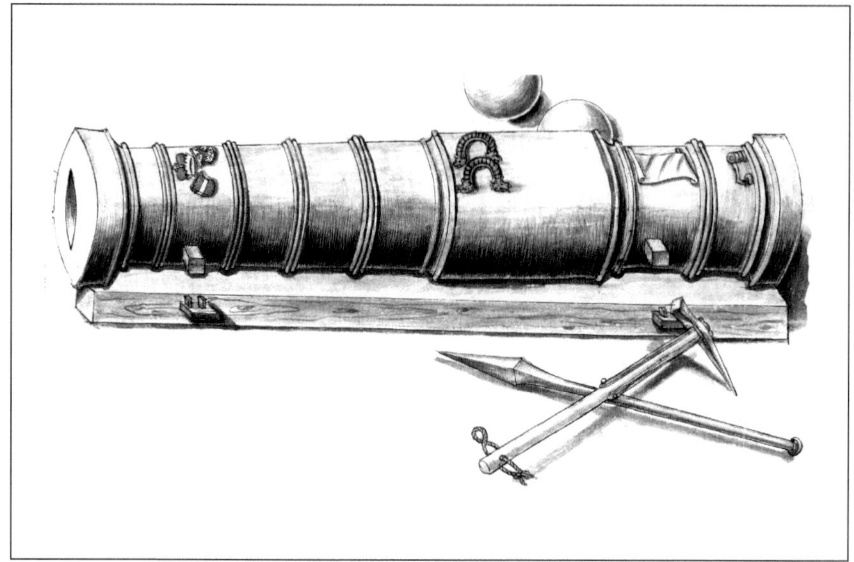

German bombard *c.* 1493–1500. From the *Inventory of the Arsenal of Maximillian I*, collection of Wien, Österreichische Nationalbibliothek, Cod. 10824. (Public Domain)

Although artillery could destroy significant portions of fortifications, it had its limitations: slow firing speed, rapid wear and tear on equipment, massive consumption of ammunition, and the inability to achieve victory without effective infantry support. Despite intensive bombardment and repeated assault attempts, the stronghold held out. To function, these artillery units required heavy logistical organisation: transfers of gunpowder, cannonballs and artillery pieces from different arsenals, transport by both river and land, and redistribution of equipment after campaigns. Thus, although artillery appeared to be a weapon that was fully integrated into the royal army, it was also a heavy weapon to handle, still lacking in operational effectiveness and very costly. For example, a King's gunner was paid 4 pounds per month in 1458, with this rate rising to 15 pounds per month, or 180 pounds per year, the following year.[41]

41 De Reilhac, *Documents pour servir à l'histoire de ces règnes de 1455 à 1499*, Tome premier, p.71.

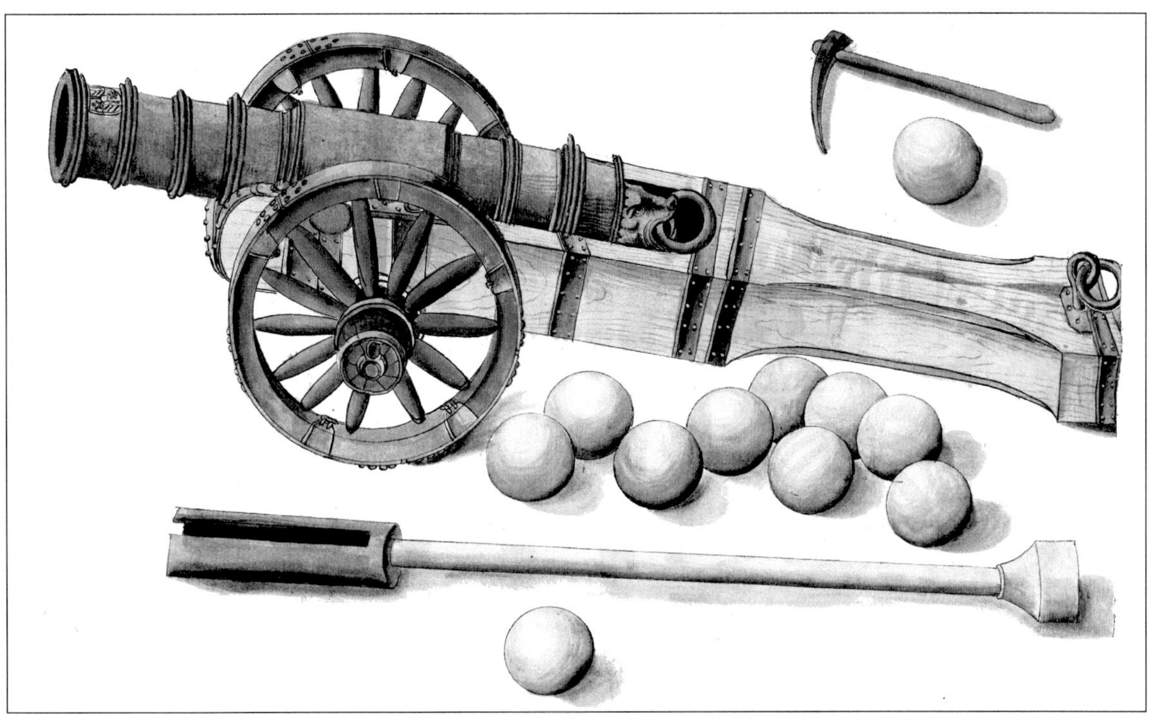

German cannon *c.* 1493–1500. From the 'Inventory of the Arsenal of Maximillian I'. (Public Domain)

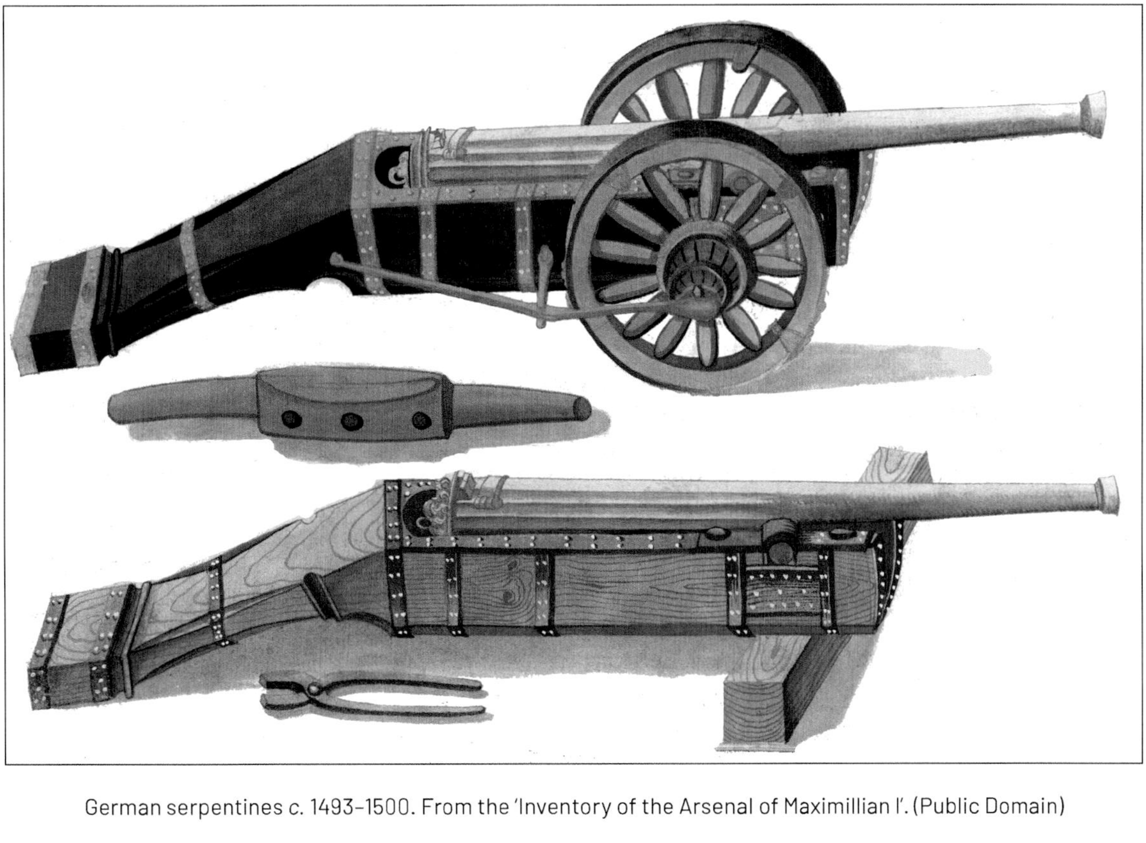

German serpentines *c.* 1493–1500. From the 'Inventory of the Arsenal of Maximillian I'. (Public Domain)

10

Appearance and Equipment of the *Compagnies d'Ordonnance*

Although the ordinances of Charles VII's reign do not explicitly describe the equipment of the men in the *compagnies d'ordonnance*, there are a few sources that seem to give us a clear idea of this equipment: the military uniform of 1446, written by an anonymous author, and chronicles such as those of Chartier and le Bouvier.

Protection, Armament and Appearance of the Men-At-Arms of the *Compagnies d'Ordonnance*

According to the *Costume militaire*, written in 1445 or 1446,[1] when going to war, men-at-arms generally wore armour. According to Viollet-le-Duc, the term armour referred not only to the horse's clothing but also to the equipment of the man-at-arms.[2] Around 1220, it became customary to protect the mount with a caparison.[3] In the fourteenth century, this caparison often only covered the rump. In France, steel plate protection for horses did not appear until the end of the fifteenth century.[4]

The complete white armour consists of a closed breastplate, forearm guards, upper arm guards, leg armour, gauntlets, a visored helmet called a sallet, and a small chin guard covering only the chin, according to the anonymous author of the 1446 *Costume militaire*. However, there are differences, especially in the head, arm and leg protection. The arms are protected by articulated pieces, often from Italy, which follow the movements

---

1 René de Belleval, *Du costume militaire des Français en 1446* (Paris: Auguste Aubry, 1866), pp.1–4.

2 George Bernage, *Encyclopédie médiévale d'après Viollet-le-Duc* (Bibliothèque de l'image, 1996), p.351.

3 Bernage, *Encyclopédie médiévale d'après Viollet-le-Duc*, p.356.

4 Bernage, *Encyclopédie médiévale d'après Viollet-le-Duc*, p.364.

of the body without hindering movement. The left arm, which received the impact of the lance, is more heavily covered than the right, to withstand the shock and avoid injury to the elbow. The legs are also enclosed in jointed armour, with large knee pads, sometimes supplemented with mail on the feet.

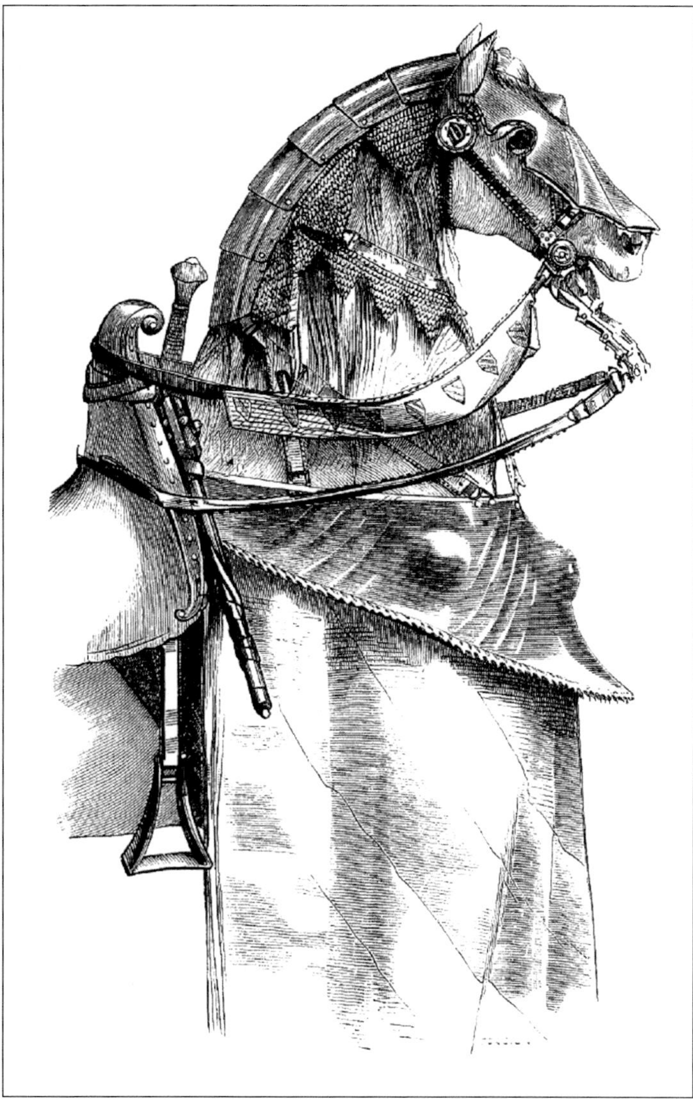

Horse armour c. 1450, comprising a chanfron, a neck bard and a breast barding. Drawing taken from Viollet-le-Duc, *Encyclopédie médiévale*. (Public Domain)

According to this anonymous author, there are three types of head protection: *bicoques*, *chapeaux de Montauban* and sallets. *Bicoques* are similar to the old bascinets: oval in shape, they covered the head and opened at the ears using hinges. *Chapeaux de Montauban* are round helmets with a wide brim and sometimes a central comb, resembling hats. Sallets, which appeared at the beginning of the fifteenth century, quickly became the most common form of head protection and, according to the anonymous author, the best: they covered the back of the neck, temples, ears and cheeks, and had a small visor that protected the eyes and nose. Sallets without visors or with fixed visors became the most common head protection for infantrymen during the first half of the fifteenth century. Two leather straps fastened under the chin allowed the sallet to fit securely on the head. According to Viollet-le-Duc, the fixed-visor sallets worn by men-at-arms stayed on the head better than those worn by infantrymen because they enveloped the skull more effectively.[5] Probably shortly before 1440, more comfortable sallets with movable visors appeared.

5 Bernage, *Encyclopédie médiévale d'après Viollet-le-Duc*, p.428.

The forearm guards were made up of either several articulated pieces 'in the Milanese style' or three pieces covering the hand, arm and sometimes the elbow. The left arm is more heavily protected, sometimes with a heart-shaped guard protecting the elbow. The pieces are fastened with laces. Leg protection is closed at the front and back, with large guards at the knees and sometimes a little mail at the instep.

This appearance and equipment is confirmed by Jean Chartier. This chronicler describes the men-at-arms who made up the *compagnies d'ordonnance* in 1450 as follows:

> The King .... had all these men-at-arms and archers dressed in good, sturdy clothing; that is to say, the men-at-arms were all armed with good breastplates, greaves, swords, sallets, most of which were trimmed with silver, and lances carried by the pages of each of the men-at-arms, mounted on three good horses, namely for himself, his page and his squire; the squire was armed with a helmet, jacket, coat or hauberk, brigandine, axe or guisarme.[6]

This description is similar to that of Gilles le Bouvier, known as Berry, the first Herald of France:

Man-at-arms of a *compagnie d'ordonnance* c. 1446. Drawing taken from Viollet-le-Duc, *Encyclopédie médiévale.* (Public Domain)

6 Godefroy, *Histoire de Charles VII Roy de France par Jean Chartier*, pp.215–216.

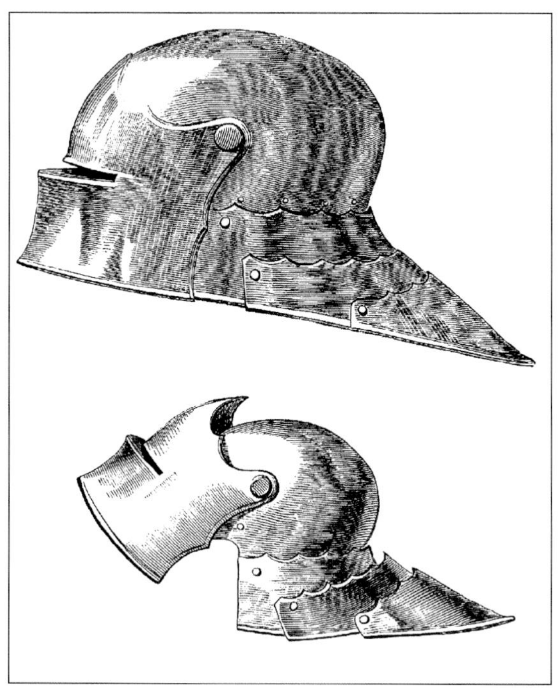

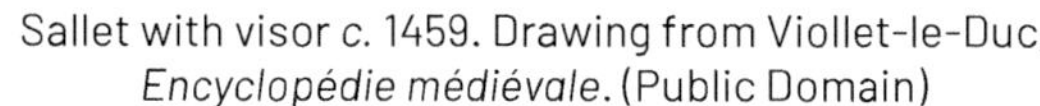

Sallet with visor *c.* 1459. Drawing from Viollet-le-Duc, *Encyclopédie médiévale*. (Public Domain)

Arm guards, *c.* 1446. Drawing from Viollet-le-Duc, *Encyclopédie médiévale*. (Public Domain)

> The men-at-arms, each mounted on three horses for themselves, their valet and a page, all armed with breastplates, leg armour and sallets, daggers and swords trimmed with silver, and lances carried by each page, while the valet was armed with a sallet, brigandine, jack or haubergeon, and axe or guisarme.[7]

As offensive weapons, men-at-arms carried short, heavy swords, used for thrusting and cutting, along with long daggers.[8] The fifteenth-century lance measured 5 metres in length. The iron point had been lengthened and from the mid-fourteenth century onwards was more firmly attached to the shaft. To manage such a weapon, a handle fitted with a collar made of small steel balls was added to prevent the wood from slipping in the hand.[9] 'To charge with a late fourteenth century lance, the man-at-arms would stand on the stirrups, brace himself against the top of the saddle's *troussequin*, lean his

7 Gilles (Jacques) le Bouvier, *Les chroniques de Normandie*, pp.165–166.

8 De Belleval, *Du costume militaire des Français en 1446*, pp.1–4.

9 Bernage, *Encyclopédie médiévale d'après Viollet-le-Duc*, pp.394–395.

body forward and bend his right arm sharply.'[10] Due to their bulkiness, lances were only carried during combat, as shown in this letter from Louis XI to Antoine de Chabannes:

> My Lord Grand Master, I have received your letters, and as for what you write to me about the long lances, it seems to me that your opinion and that of the master of the said lances is good, namely not to distribute them for the time being, and I wish that this be done and that they be carried in waggons, like lead mallets and other artillery items.[11]

Gunner in haubergeon, *c.* 1470–1480. He is armed with a *trait à poudre*. Drawing taken from Viollet-le-Duc, *Encyclopédie médiévale*. (Public Domain)

The jack (or *jacque*) was a padded garment made of several layers of cotton, linen, wool or felt. Louis XI regulated its manufacture, requiring it to be made of deer skin and 25 to 30 layers thick. The brigandine provided better protection as it consisted of metal plates riveted onto a leather or fabric garment. The brigandine was then covered with leather or fabric, which could be velvet or silk for the wealthiest of its owners. The rivet heads protruding from the fabric formed an elegant decoration. Lighter and more flexible than a cuirass, but just as resistant, this protection was also frequently worn by men-at-arms.[12] Men-at-arms also often wore a corselet over the brigandine. This former consisted of a breastplate protecting the stomach and a gorget protecting the throat, laced together.[13] The haubergeon was a small hauberk, i.e. a mail tunic.

10 Bernage, *Encyclopédie médiévale d'après Viollet-le-Duc*, p.396.

11 Vaesen et Charavay, *Lettres de Louis XI, Roi de France*, Tome III, p.266.

12 The *cotte de maille* (chainmail), or hauberk, was a long garment made of chainmail; the word 'cotte' refers to a long shirt.

13 Bernage, *Encyclopédie médiévale d'après Viollet-le-Duc*, p.258.

A man-at-arms wearing well polished armour was referred to as 'armed in white'. Thus, for the entry of Charles VII into Rouen in 1449, Jean Chartier reports that Pierre de Fontenil, squire to the King, was 'armed all in white, mounted on a large warhorse covered and harnessed in azure velvet with large silver-gilt decorations', while Poton de Xaintrailles, the King's Grand Squire, was also 'armed entirely in white and mounted on a steed, similarly covered and harnessed in azure velvet with large silver-gilt decorations, like Fontenil, who wore the King's great ceremonial sword in a sash.'[14] For his part, the Count of Nevers was 'armed all in white, mounted on a steed covered in green velvet, embroidered with gold thread, followed by three pages dressed in purple and black, with their robes lined with white satin; the harnesses of their horses were also purple and black; and in addition, he was accompanied by 12 gentlemen also armed all in white, mounted on horses covered in purple satin and each blanket bearing a white cross, except for one of them whose horse's blanket was green satin.'[15] The Count of Clermont was 'likewise armed all in white, mounted on a steed covered in black velvet, and his pages dressed in his livery.'[16]

Although these passages describe the entourage of nobles during a parade, they show the luxury with which warhorses could be harnessed and equipped on such occasions. Lances could also be covered in velvet. Thus, on the same occasion, one of the pages of the Count of Saint-Paul carried 'a lance covered in vermilion velvet' and the other page a lance 'of patterned velvet covered in equally patterned gold cloth.'[17] The lances of the men-at-arms could bear a pennant: thus, the Lord of Culant, Grand Master of the King's Household, was at the head of the battle with five to six hundred lances, each bearing a pennant 'of vermilion satin.'[18] Culant himself was 'fully armed, wearing a hat on his head, and mounted on a steed richly covered with blue and red striped velvet, over which were attached large white silver leaves.' He was followed by the King's Standard, carried by Roger Blosset, described as 'crimson satin, with Saint Michael in the field of the said standard, which was also strewn with golden suns.'[19] The chronicler Jean de Troyes states that on 20 April 1474, a large parade was held in Paris, bringing together between 80,000 and 100,000 men (a figure that seems excessive), all dressed 'in red livery with beautiful white crosses.'[20] The entire army, including men-at-arms, archers, *coustilliers, francs-archers* and others, seems to have been dressed in these standardised hocquetons.

---

14 Godefroy, *Histoire de Charles VII Roy de France par Jean Chartier*, p.180.
15 Godefroy, *Histoire de Charles VII Roy de France par Jean Chartier*, p.181.
16 Godefroy, *Histoire de Charles VII Roy de France par Jean Chartier*, p.182.
17 Godefroy, *Histoire de Charles VII Roy de France par Jean Chartier*, p.181.
18 Godefroy, *Histoire de Charles VII Roy de France par Jean Chartier*, p.182.
19 Godefroy, *Histoire de Charles VII Roy de France par Jean Chartier*, p.182.
20 Petitot, *Collection complète des mémoires relatifs à l'histoire de France*, Tome XIII, p.444.

Horse Harness comprising a chanfron, a neck barding and a breast barding, *c.* 1460–1490. *Croupière* bards were rare in the French army at the time. Drawing taken from Viollet-le-Duc, *Encyclopédie médiévale*. (Public Domain)

Archers of the *Compagnies d'Ordonnance* and Mounted Crossbowmen

According to the 1446 *Costume militaire*, archers often wore leg and head protection, with sturdy padded jacks or brigandines: like men-at-arms: 'archers wear leg armour, sallets, thick jacks lined with thick canvas or brigandines, bows in their hands and *trousse* at their sides; and they do not use crossbows as commonly as in other places, except to guard positions'. *Trousse* refers to a quantity of arrows and not their container; it was of 24 arrows for the English and 18 arrows for the *francs-archers*. The archers' offensive weapons were long, sharp two-handed swords and yew bows with large arrows fitted with double-edged barbed points.[21]

This equipment is confirmed by Jean Chartier, who offers us this description: 'And each of the said men-at-arms had two mounted archers, armed mostly with brigandines, leg armour and sallets, most of which were

21 Belleval, *Du costume militaire des Français en 1446*, p.4.

also trimmed with silver, or at least had jacks or good haubergeons.'[22] A description almost identical to that of Gilles le Bouvier, from which it seems to be inspired: 'and each of the said men-at-arms had for a lance two mounted archers armed mostly with brigandines, leg armour and sallets, many of which were trimmed with silver, and at least all had jacks or good haubergeons.'[23]

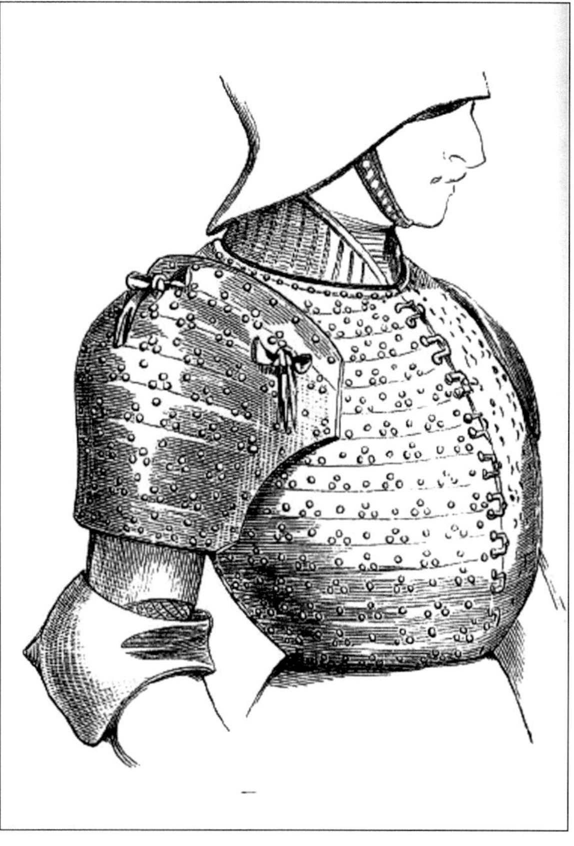

Brigandine and shoulder pad, *c.* 1460. Drawing taken from Viollet-le-Duc, *Encyclopédie médiévale.* (Public Domain)

The archers of the *compagnies d'ordonnance* also wore 'jackets' in the colours of the company captain. Jean Chartier wrote that at the entry into Rouen in 1449, 'the first were all the King's Archers, dressed in vermilion, or red and white and green jackets, studded with goldwork.'[24] These were certainly the King's Archers, but the same was true of the nearly six hundred archers from the companies of other lords: 'well mounted, all wearing brigandines and jackets of various colours and styles, leg armour, swords and daggers, sallets or head harness covered or trimmed with rich silver.'[25]

Archers of the *ordonnance* were not necessarily armed with bows. They could also be armed with crossbows. However, there were only a small number of these, and from 1464 onwards, personal approval from the King was required to replace archers with crossbowmen. The *ordonnance* of 6 June 1464 (see Appendix X) specifies that archers or crossbowmen in companies *à la petite paye* (on low pay) would receive only five pounds per month, while only archers are mentioned for companies *à la grande paye* (on high pay). It also specifies that the commissioner must ensure that 'no crossbowman takes the place of an archer.'[26]

These reminders reveal a very different reality. Jean de Troyes recounts the arrival in Paris of two hundred mounted archers under Captain Mignon in August 1465, 'among whom were several *cranequiniers* (i.e. mounted crossbowmen), *vougiers* and *couleuvriniers à main*.'[27] We cannot be sure that this was a *compagnie d'ordonnance*, but this passage shows that the term archer encompassed a wide variety of weapons. We also see archers equipped

22 Godefroy, *Histoire de Charles VII Roy de France par Jean Chartier*, p.216.

23 Le Bouvier, *Les chroniques de Normandie*, pp.165–166.

24 Godefroy, *Histoire de Charles VII Roy de France par Jean Chartier*, p.180.

25 Godefroy, *Histoire de Charles VII Roy de France par Jean Chartier*, p.180.

26 De Reilhac, *Documents pour servir à l'histoire de ces règnes de 1455 à 1499*, Tome premier, pp.164–168.

27 J. A. C. Buchon, *Choix de chroniques et mémoires relatifs à l'histoire de France* (Paris: Delagrave, 1835), p.260.

Archer of a *compagnie d'ordonnance*, c. 1465. Drawing taken from Viollet-le-Duc, *Encyclopédie médiévale*. (Public Domain)

with demi-lances at least as early as 1465. According to Jean de Troyes, that year an archer from the Count of Eu's company took aim at a Breton archer in brigandine armour and 'pierced him through the body with a demi-lance.'[28] An extract from the accounts of Olivier Baud, treasurer at war in 1465, confirms this heterogeneity of equipment in a roll covering the period from 19 November 1464 to 1 January 1465, even though this document concerns Brittany on the eve of its participation in the *Ligue du Bien Public*:

> Jehan du Rouvré, man-at-arms, an archer in brigandine armour and a *coustillier*; Mathelin de Chamballan, likewise; Olivier Rouxel and two *guisarmiers* in brigandine armour; Thomas Aguillon, man-at-arms, and an archer in brigandine armour; Guillaume le Voyer, man-at-arms, and an archer in brigandine; Jehan de la Haye, man-at-arms, and an archer...[29]

Another roll from the same extract but concerning the watch of La Guerche on 1 January 1465, lists:

> Jehan de Preauvé and two men in brigandines, from 10 October 1464; Jehan de Corsé and an archer, from 14 October; Rolland de Cyon and a *vougier* from 14 October; Jehan de la Cheneie and two archers and a *coustillier*, from 11 October; Guion Troze, an archer and a vougier from 6 October; Jehan de Champeigné, knight, an archer and *vougier*; Messire Jehan de Coismes and an archer; Artur de Pan and two archers; Jehan de la

28 Buchon, *Choix de chroniques et mémoires relatifs à l'histoire de France*, p.261.

29 Dom Gui Alexis Lobineau, *Histoire de Bretagne*, Tome II (Paris: Veuve François Muguet, 1706), p.1364.

Duchaie and two archers; Guion Painel and two archers; Jehan de Domeigné and two archers; Robert Bonenfant and two archers; Guillaume Moraut and an archer; Messire Thibaud de la Lande, a crossbowman and a *coustillier*; Messire François Ivette, an archer and crossbowman…[30]

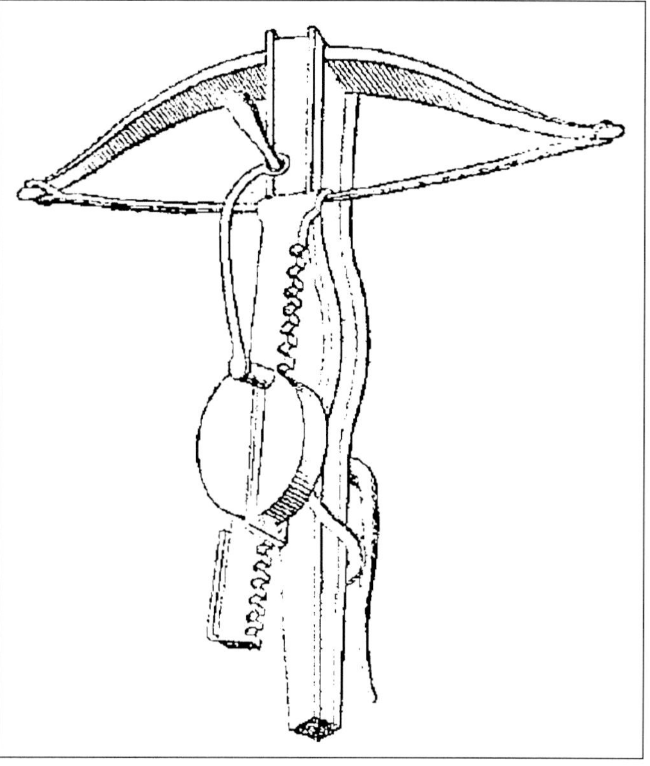

Cranequin. From Hardÿ de Périni, *Batailles Françaises*, Tome 1 (Paris: Plon-Nourrit & C., 1894), p.131. (Public Domain)

Further down these long lists, there also a *cranequinier*, confirming Jean de Troyes' account. These mounted crossbowmen appear here in the Duke of Brittany's troops and therefore perhaps reveal a local peculiarity common to Brittany and the south of France, but a reality that may not have been the case for permanent companies in territories well controlled by the King.

The weapons and protective equipment of archers is discussed in more detail below in the section concerning the equipment of the *francs-archers*.

Pages, Valets and *Coustilliers*

According to the *ordonnances*, the terms pages, valets, *coustilliers* and *guisarmiers* seem to be interchangeable. The *ordonnances* of 1445 refer to the 'pages or valets' of the archers or the '*coustilliers* or valets' of those same archers. The man-at-arms, for his part, is assisted by a page or valet and a *coustillier*. In reality, the page is a young nobleman who is not old enough to hold the position of man-at-arms and therefore to fight.

Coustilliers are rarely mentioned in the chronicles of the time. In his *Jouvencel*, Jean de Bueil refers to them in an episode taking place in 1429: 'He came and charged among them with many men, numbering forty or fifty, both lancers and archers and *coustilliers*.'[31] Le Bouvier, known as Berry, is probably referring to *coustillier*s or pages when he mentions *guisarmiers* several times. It is also possible that, for some other chroniclers, the term *guisarmiers* could have encompassed valets and *coustilliers*.

The *ordonnance* of 30 January 1455, prescribing 'the manner in which nobles must be dressed to come and serve him in arms' specifies that the

30 Lobineau, *Histoire de Bretagne*, Tome II, p.1364.

31 De Bueil, *Le Jouvencel, Tome premier*, p.214.

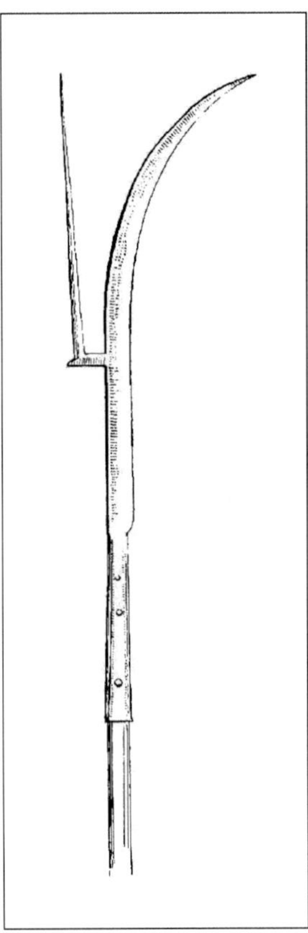

Guisarme, *c.* 1429. Drawing from Viollet-le-Duc, *Encyclopédie médiévale.* (Public Domain)

coustillier of the man-at-arms must be 'well and sufficiently mounted, as befits a *coustillier*, on a horse on which he can do his duty' and that he must be armed 'with a small corselet, small arm guard, gauntlets, sallet and gorget, *passot* sword (bastard sword) and *glaviot* (dagger).'[32] The *Costume militaire* of 1446 adds greaves for the protection of the *coustilliers* and a *langue de boeuf* (tongue of an ox) to their armament: 'The *coustilliers* .... are armoured only with haubergeons, sallets, gauntlets and leg harness, and they readily carry in their hands a kind of dart with a broad blade, called a *langue de boeuf*.'[33] They were also armed with long, narrow swords from Catalonia, according to the same source. As we have seen above, infantry were protected by sallets, brigandines, jacks or haubergeons, and armed with axes or *guisarmes*.[34]

In theory, *coustilliers* and valets, like pages, were not part of the paid fighting force: they never appeared in *montres* or during reviews. Their role was to serve men-at-arms and archers, help them get equipped, look after horses when horsemen fought on foot, and guard the camp and baggage. However, *coustilliers*, who were well armed, were commonly used as *courreurs* (runners), as we have already seen above, and could probably form a second line behind their men-at-arms, at least in the fifteenth century.

Francs-Archers

The equipment of the *francs-archers* was also relatively comprehensive. The *ordonnance* of 1448 describes their clothing and armament as 'sufficient and suitable, consisting of a sallet, dagger, sword with *trousse*, brigandine jack or huque (a kind of cape with a hood) of brigandine'. And this same *ordonnance* stipulates a little further on, in Article 5, that 'this archer shall be required to maintain himself in point of hucque of brigandine or a jack, sallet, sword, dagger, bow and *trousse* (i.e. a set of 18 arrows) or furnished crossbow, as ordered.' Finally, the first of the articles added in 1459 stipulates that brigandines supplied by the royal authority must be delivered to the *francs-archers*.

Paradoxically, we know more about the weapons and armour of the *francs-archers* than those of the *archers d'ordonnance*. Indeed, Baron de Bonnault d'Houët, in *Les francs archers de Compiègne*, published several interesting accounts of the town showing the actual equipment of the six *francs-archers*, which was paid for by the municipality. With regard to weaponry, for the six archers of the city in 1454, there were 'six *trousses* of iron-tipped arrows containing nine-twelve (i.e. 108 arrows, or 18 arrows per *trousse*) purchased by him at a price of seven *sous* per *trousse*, and four

32 Bréquigny, *Ordonnances des rois de France de la troisième race, recueillies par ordre chronologique, quatorzième volume* (Paris: Imprimerie royale, 1790), p.351.

33 De Belleval, *Du costume militaire des Français en 1446*, p.4.

34 Godefroy, *Histoire de Charles VII Roy de France par Jean Chartier*, pp.215–216.

Romanian yew bows also purchased at a price of 12 *sols* per bow.'[35] An account from 1466 mentions 28 *trousses* of arrows 'fitted with black leather *custodes*', the *custode* being the quiver.[36] Crossbows appear regularly in these accounts but are much less numerous than bows. However, an account from 1460 mentions 19 crossbow quivers covered with 'white bazenna', another mentions a jack for 'tensioning crossbows', two others mention the purchase of two Romanian yew wood crossbows, and two others mention the purchase of a crossbow of the same type.[37]

Crossbowman, *c.* 1440–1470. Drawing from Viollet-le-Duc, *Encyclopédie médiévale.* (Public Domain)

35 Bonnault d'Houët, *Les francs archers de Compiègne 1448–1524*, p.143.
36 Bonnault d'Houët, *Les francs archers de Compiègne 1448–1524*, p.150.
37 Bonnault d'Houët, *Les francs archers de Compiègne 1448–1524*, p.148.

Franc-archer, c. 1450. Drawing taken from Viollet-le-Duc, *Encyclopédie médiévale*. (Public Domain)

With regard to clothing, an account from 1456 relating to repairs to equipment provides us with interesting details about the equipment of the *francs-archers*: brigandines covered with '*gris de Rouen*' or white leather, hocquetons and hoods used to cover helmets, made of vermeil cloth, fustian to cover jackets, aiguillettes to fasten brigandines, nails for brigandines, *gorgerins* (gorget) trimmings, belts and sword hilts.[38] An account from 1464 mentions, 'expenses incurred to re-equip the city's six archers: each of them will be dressed in two hocquetons, one made of leather to be worn under the brigandine, the other made of crimson cloth crossed at the front and back, and gorgerins.'[39] Thus, like the archers of the *ordonnance*, the *francs-archers* were dressed uniformly. For Compiègne, the hocqueton and hood of the sallet were vermilion in colour.

An account from 1466 refers to a pair of gauntlets, while another mentions six sheepskins to make three hocquetons to be worn under the brigandines.[40] These were probably provisions for the winter. A later account from the period 1466–1467 mentions five leather and embroidered hocquetons to be worn under brigandines, three dozen bowstrings, three sword belts and three belts for *trousses* of arrows, a quiver for crossbow bolts, two pairs of gloves for two *vougiers*, six *brachères* for shooting (archers' wrist bracers), 18 aiguillettes for a jack, an arm guard and a gauntlet.[41] An account from 1468 mentions

38 Bonnault d'Houët, *Les francs archers de Compiègne 1448–1524*, pp.144–145.

39 Bonnault d'Houët, *Les francs archers de Compiègne 1448–1524*, p.149.

40 Bonnault d'Houët, *Les francs archers de Compiègne 1448–1524*, p.150.

41 Bonnault d'Houët, *Les francs archers de Compiègne 1448–1524*, p.153.

six pairs of gloves to be worn under the archers' gauntlets, three *trousses* of arrows, and 24 dozen laces for lacing up the jacks and hocquetons.[42]

The *francs-archers* therefore wore a sallet without a visor, forged from a single piece of metal and covered with a cloth hood of the same colour as their hocqueton. The hocqueton refers both to a garment worn over the brigandine and to a garment worn under the armour, brigandine or jack. The hocquetons worn underneath were therefore necessarily more fitted and could be replaced by a skin. In 1456, only one of the *francs-archers* of Compiègne wore a brigandine, and his *vermeil hocqueton* was lined with white cloth, probably because his hocqueton was likely to wear out more quickly on his brigandine than those protected by jacks. The brigandine was made up of overlapping iron plates, fastened with rivets, which gave it mobility. It could be lined with leather or fabric and covered with leather or fabric, or even velvet or silk. The rivet heads were visible and arranged in a regular pattern. The brigandine is thus lighter and more flexible than a cuirass, while being just as resistant. The aiguillettes, eight per brigandine, replaced buttons, which were not in use at the time. The jack replaced the brigandine for most *francs-archers*, as it was less expensive. It was made of 20 to 30 layers of old canvas and covered with leather. Less fitted than the brigandine, it provided excellent protection against injury. The *francs-archer*'s throat was also protected by a gorget and his arms by arm guards. Later, in 1479, after the Battle of Guinegatte, chronicler Jean Molinet described hundreds and thousands of bodies of *francs-archers* lying on the ground, who 'were so heavily armed that it was very difficult to kill them, for each of them had a sallet, gorget, long brigandine with a high collar, sword, dagger, *gouge*, bow and *trousse*. There was hardly a single whole lance in the entire camp; it was littered with sticks, crossbows, culverins, halberds, cranequins and harnesses...'[43]

Francs-archers in action, c. 1440–1470. Drawing taken from 'the Vigiles de Charles VII,' Bibliothèque nationale de France Ms 5054 f. 117. (Public Domain)

42 Bonnault d'Houët, *Les francs archers de Compiègne 1448–1524*, p.153.

43 J.-A. Buchon, *Chroniques de Jean Molinet* (Paris: Verdière, 1828), p.218.

Offensive weapons were therefore swords, daggers, bows or crossbows, while the *vouge* appeared later. Swords at the time were long and straight. As the plate armour of the fourteenth and fifteenth centuries was resistant to cutting blows, swords were now used for thrusting, with men-at-arms using maces or axes to fight in combat, as Viollet-le-Duc explains:

> From the day when armour became stronger and partly composed of plates, swords had to be made heavier, blades stronger, and thrusting rather than cutting became the preferred technique; hence swords with a quadrangular cross-section and a very strong point. Even when used for cutting, these swords, which were like iron bars, would damage helmets, winged visors or shoulder guards.[44]

The *vouge* is a pole weapon consisting of a single-edged blade, usually attached to the shaft by two riveted plates.[45] The *guisarme* is also a pole weapon and consisted of a long, curved iron blade with a straight point for thrusting.[46]

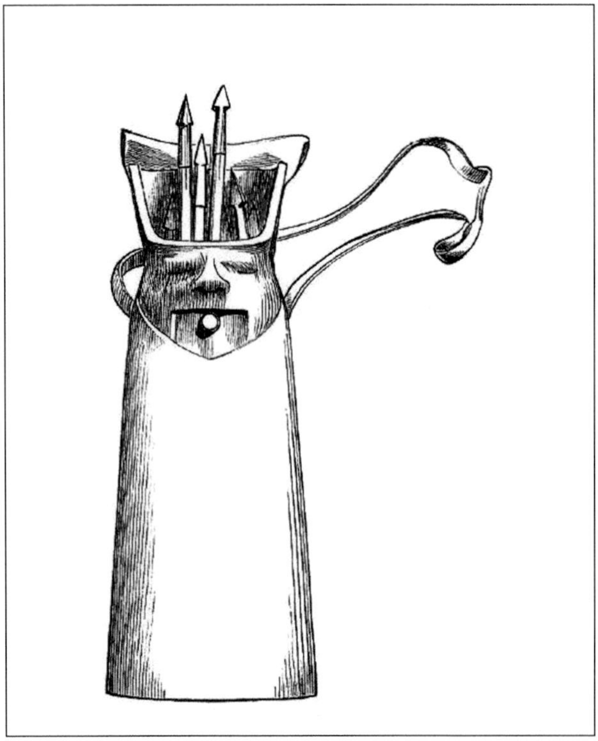

From 1466 by *ordonnance*, the *francs-archers* should be armed partly with *vouges* (surprisingly, men armed with *vouges* are called *guisarmiers*), partly with spears, partly with bows and partly with crossbows (see Appendix II). From January 1474, spears were to be replaced with pikes (see Appendix XIII).

Quiver for crossbow bolts, c. 1445–1480. Drawing from Viollet-le-Duc, *Encyclopédie médiévale*. (Public Domain)

The bow was more widespread than the crossbow in the northern half of France at the time, and its rate of fire was higher, reaching up to 12 arrows per minute with a range of two hundred paces for a trained archer. Each *franc-archer* received a *trousse* of 18 arrows with his Romanian yew bow, compared to 24 arrows for the English archer, but no quiver. The arrows were then held directly in the belt. According to Viollet-le-Duc, the French bow, measuring four feet in length, was heavy, thick and had a short range. The English bow, on the other hand, was lighter, made of yew or maple wood and measured five to six feet in length. Its range was 200 to 250 paces. The English arrow, made of pine or ash wood, measured three feet, or 95cm, while the French arrow measured

44 Bernage, *Encyclopédie médiévale d'après Viollet-le-Duc*, p.302.
45 Bernage, *Encyclopédie médiévale d'après Viollet-le-Duc*, pp.451–452.
46 Bernage, *Encyclopédie médiévale d'après Viollet-le-Duc*, p.342.

just over two feet (70cm).[47] Depictions of archers and crossbowmen during the reign of Charles VII suggest that these differences had disappeared. The bow was easier to transport and handle than the crossbow: the string was easier to remove and therefore less sensitive to humidity; overall maintenance and repairs were simpler and less expensive.

The crossbow's more accurate and powerful fire made it more of a weapon for defending strongholds or sieges. This is why the first *ordonnance* creating the *francs-archers* made no mention of the crossbow, which appeared later in the texts. Unlike archers' arrows, crossbow bolts were carried in a quiver. In the fifteenth century, there were three types of crossbows: the *à tour* or *à moufle* (muffle) crossbow, the *à pied-de-biche* (crowbar) crossbow, and the *à cry* crossbow, these names distinguishing the way the bow was cocked. Previously, the crossbow string was drawn using a stirrup into which the crossbowman placed his foot to help him pull the string.[48] The *à moufle* crossbow, which appeared around 1425, was cocked using two cranks operated by both hands, with the weapon being held during the action by a stirrup in which the foot was placed. This crank system was called a *boite à moufles* (crank box). The *pied-de-biche* crossbow, which appears to date from the end of the fifteenth century, was cocked using a lever. Lighter than the previous model, it was a weapon for cavalrymen. Finally, the *à cry* or *à cric* (jack) crossbow was the most powerful of the three. It was cocked using a crank jack, making it much less bulky than the *à moufle* crossbow[49] This crank was known as a *crénequin*, which gave rise to the term *cranequinier* to refer to the user of this type of crossbow. The crossbow bolt was then called a *vireton*.[50]

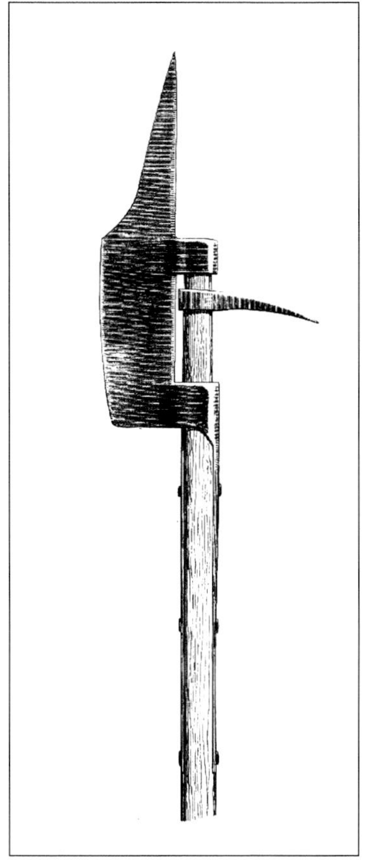

Vouge, *c.* 1450–1480. Drawing taken from Viollet-le-Duc, *Encyclopédie médiévale*. (Public Domain)

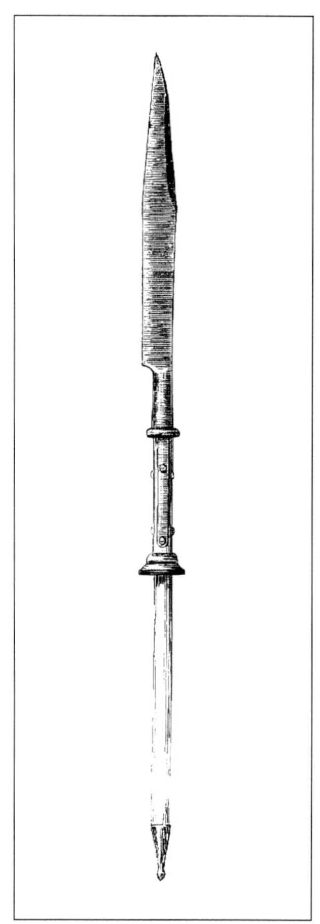

Vouge, *c.* 1450–1480. Drawing taken from Viollet-le-Duc, *Encyclopédie médiévale*. (Public Domain)

47 Bernage, *Encyclopédie médiévale d'après Viollet-le-Duc*, p.200.
48 Bernage, *Encyclopédie médiévale d'après Viollet-le-Duc*, p.191.
49 Bernage, *Encyclopédie médiévale d'après Viollet-le-Duc*, pp.192–196.
50 De Bueil, *Le Jouvencel*, Tome premier, p.108.

From 1472 onwards, *couleuvriniers* also appear in the chronicles of Jean de Troyes. During a military parade held in Paris that year, crossbowmen and *couleuvriniers* can be seen. And a hundred additional crossbowmen and *couleuvriniers* were brought in from the town of Beauvais.[51]

Couleuvrinier armed with a *trait à poudre*, c. 1475. Drawing from Viollet-le-Duc, *Encyclopédie médiévale.* (Public Domain)

51 Petitot, *Collection complète des mémoires relatifs à l'histoire de France, Tome XIII,* p.302.

11

In the King's Service

An Army with Different Components

Compagnies d'ordonnance, francs-archers, artillery, and also the *ban* and *arrière-ban* were all components that made it possible to deal with several types of threats. A month after establishing the *francs-archers* on 22 May 1448, Charles VII reorganised the service of the nobles of the *ban* and *arrière-ban* in order to secure additional leverage for the defence of the kingdom:

> Like all nobles and other people of our kingdom holding from us, in fief and sub-fief, lands and lordships, are, because of these and the privileges they enjoy and use by reason of their nobility, bound, according to the nature of their said fiefs, to serve and defend us and the public good of our said kingdom against its enemies, whenever necessary and whenever we summon them by ban and rear-ban or otherwise.[1]

The various components of this army, whether permanent like the *compagnies d'ordonnance*, rapidly mobilisable like the *francs-archers*, or locally mobilisable in times of crisis and paid only for the actual duration of their service like the *ban* and *arrière-ban*, formed different levels of response to different threats.

Thus, in 1447, while the transfer of the county of Maine from King Henry VI of England to the King of France was delayed, despite the former's commitment, Charles VII grew impatient. He called on the *compagnies d'ordonnance* stationed throughout France to gather in front of Le Mans. The institution of the *francs-archers* had not yet been created, but neighbouring

1 Bessey, *Construire l'armée française,* Tome I, p.119.

towns sent artillery and companies of crossbowmen.[2] Similarly, after the capture of Fougères by a captain in the service of England, François de Surienne, on 24 March 1449, Charles VII sent 300 lances to the Duke of Brittany. This event was the trigger for the reconquest of Normandy. Philippe Contamine estimates that the French forces mobilised for the reconquest of Normandy numbered between 15,000 and 20,000 combatants.[3] It was in this context that the Constable of Richemont assembled an army in May 1449:

> And then came Monseigneur the *Maréchal de* Lohéac, and Joachim Rouault, and Oudet de Rie, and Denisot, who, with the King's permission, came to serve the Duke [of Brittany], and there was a fine company, both from Brittany and France, and soon Saint-Aubin was fortified.... And meanwhile arrived the hundred lances of His Lordship the Constable, brought by Sir Geoffroy de Couvran and Olivier de Broon, and the matter lasted a while, and there were summonses, both from the King and from the Duke, and embassies from one side and the other.[4]

Compagnie d'ordonnance, at the time of Charles VII. Illustration dating from 1483, from 'les Vigiles du Roi Charles VII', Bibliothèque nationale de France Ms 5054. (Public Domain)

Richemont's corps was part of the Franco-Breton army of Duke François I of Brittany. This army was advancing between Mont-Saint-Michel and Cotentin. The main French army, which included the Counts of Dunois, Eu, and Saint-Pol, as well as Robert de Floques and Pierre de Brézé, the latter two captains of a hundred lances, was operating in the heart of Normandy to isolate Rouen. In 1451, Charles VII sent Amanieu d'Albret,

2 Contamine, *Charles VII*, p.376.
3 Contamine, *Charles VII*, p.386.
4 Gruel, *Chronique d'Arthur de Richemont*, pp.196–197.

Lord of Orval, to lead 300 to 400 lances to Bordeaux.[5] They were joined in June of the same year by '1,200 men-at-arms and 2,500 archers', in 12 companies.[6]

Seizures of positions would form most actions during the reconquest of Normandy. Artillery supported by *francs-archers*, who were less mobile than the *compagnies d'ordonnance*, were the most effective weapons for this type of exercise. Thus, for the Siege of Falaise in July 1449, Jean Bureau commanded the artillery and 1,500 *francs-archers*.[7] But storming strongholds was also possible when the *compagnies d'ordonnance* did not have the support of artillery. Thus, Floquet, with his hundred lances, took the town of Conches by surprise,[8] while Jean d'Estouteville, Lord of Blainville, took Tombelaine, located near Mont Saint-Michel, and then Saint-Guillaume de Mortain by assault.

The *ban* and *arrière-ban* were not only mobilised to deal with local threats. They could also prove useful, alongside the standing army, when the King had to face several threats in different parts of the kingdom. There is an interesting example under Louis XI. While the King was facing the Burgundian threat in the east and north-east,[9] on 15 April 1473 he sent an army led by Philip of Savoy to besiege the city of Perpignan, held by John II of Aragon. Louis XI called upon the Dauphiné *ban*, as well as archers and artillery, to keep his *compagnies d'ordonnance* available to deal with the Burgundian threat. Thus, on 9 March 1473, Louis XI wrote to the seneschal of Roussillon, suspected of colluding with King John of Aragon, that he was sending a 'large army' with all due haste, consisting of 300 lances, 2,000 *francs-archers* and artillery.[10] He clarified his thinking a few days later to the Lord of Lau, captain of the French garrison in Perpignan, writing that this number was sufficient to 'repel the said King John, given the little power that he is said to have.' But at the same time, he tried to reassure him by announcing that, if necessary, he would send him the army in Burgundy, commanded by the constable, comprising 1,200 to 1,500 lances and 7,000 to 8,000 archers with artillery.[11] The 300 lances referred to by the King included 200 lances from the nobility of the Dauphiné, divided into two companies of 100 lances, one commanded by Soffrey Allemand and the other by Robin Malortie.[12]

A few months later, to counter the threat of an invasion of Champagne by the Duke of Burgundy, Louis XI requested in a letter dated

5 Le Bouvier, *Les chroniques de Normandie*, p.171.
6 Le Bouvier, *Les chroniques de Normandie*, p.172.
7 Le Bouvier, *Les chroniques de Normandie*, 161.
8 Basin, *Histoire de Charles VII*, Chapter 15.
9 In November 1471, following Louis XI's breach of the Treaty of Péronne, the Bold had freed himself from the suzerainty of the King of France. In the spring of 1472, he launched an offensive in Picardy.
10 Vaesen et Charavay, *Lettres de Louis XI*, Tome V, pp.115–117.
11 Vaesen et Charavay, *Lettres de Louis XI*, Tome V, pp.122–123.
12 Vaesen et Charavay, *Lettres de Louis XI*, Tome V, pp.113–114.

21 September 1473 that 'captains and warlords, as well as a large number of my *arrière-ban* and *francs-archers*' be sent and that inspections be carried out to verify that 'all the nobles of Normandy are sufficiently mounted and armed, as befits them, and likewise the said *francs-archers*.'[13] The King of France clearly needed all the components of his army to deal with external threats.

A siege during the reign of Louis XI, *c.* 1483. Illustration dating to 1483, 'les Vigiles du Roi Charles VII,' Bibliothèque nationale de France Ms 5054. (Public Domain)

In Combat

In the years following the disasters of Agincourt and Verneuil, French captains began to imitate English tactics. Jean de Bueil, who would become captain of one of Charles VII's *compagnies d'ordonnance*, presented 'best practices' for fighting the enemy 'on foot in battle'. In Chapter 9 of the second part of his *Jouvencel*, he proposed placing men-at-arms in the centre and archers and other men-of-trait on the wings:

> To fight on foot, if you find people in a pitched battle without fortifications, their *bataille* is bound to be long; and for this reason, they must place the strength of their armed men in the centre, and their archers and other men-of-trait on the flanks, if they have any. And to protect their archers, they must have a number of men-at-arms at the ends of their wings, according to their strength. And if they are a great force in all respects, they must also have a small

13 Vaesen et Charavay, *Lettres de Louis XI*, Tome V, pp.176–177.

> *bataille* of men behind them, so that they are not attacked from behind, and to march where they see fit.[14]

But this same captain may also occasionally adopt different arrangements, placing the archers in the centre, as he recounts:

> Thus the *Jouvencel* and his entire company set off on foot with great haste and marched his banner along a hedge; and there he drew up his forces in bataille, with his banner in the middle and the largest tourbe (unit) of his warriors; and at both ends of the hedge he sent two small troops of his men-of-war, that is, on both sides, some on the right and others on the left. And between his standard and his two small troops of men-of-war were his archers, well arranged. And behind him, in a small marsh, he placed all his horses and pages, where his enemies could not reach them.[15]

For a *bataille* on horseback, his advice is different:

> The *bataille* must achieve victory after the small bataille (i.e. the vanguard), which is at the front, and the *escarmoucheurs* (skirmishers). The rearguard must be powerful and stand firm, so that everyone can regroup, unless they have to work from behind, in which case the bataille should gather them together and stand firm and act as a rearguard.... The wings are to flank the sides and charge where they see fit.[16]

Jean de Bueil advises that skirmishers, probably archers, form a front line – or vanguard – and are positioned on the flanks of the battle, while men-at-arms form the centre of the battle and the rearguard.

Another lesson now learned was the importance of gathering information and therefore reconnaissance. Jean de Bueil himself suggests, in Chapter 10 of his work, that a battle on horseback must have *escarmoucheurs* (skirmishers) and *découvreurs* (scouts),[17] a role probably assigned to *coustilliers* and archers. The author writes, in a somewhat unclear sentence, that 'the *coureurs* (runners), who had run ahead of the city, turn around, both archers and *coustilliers*.'[18] Jean Chartier also mentions the actions of these *coureurs* in his chronicles.[19] And Commynes exclaims that he had

14 De Bueil, *Le Jouvencel*, Tome premier, p.153.
15 De Bueil, *Le Jouvencel*, Tome premier, p.152.
16 De Bueil, *Le Jouvencel*, Tome premier, p.159.
17 De Bueil, *Le Jouvencel*, Tome premier, pp.158–159.
18 De Bueil, *Le Jouvencel*, Tome second, p.18.
19 Chartier, *Chroniques de Charles VII*, p.36.

'never seen so many skirmishes, however small' under Paris in 1465.[20] To illustrate these practices, let us quote Jean de Bueil, who mentions them shortly before 1430: the captain had sent 'twenty horses to beat the country' and '10 men in light armour to guard and hold the roads.'[21] These 10 men were archers, as they were commanded by Jennin the archer. The same Jean de Bueil also refers to '*fourragiers*' (foragers).[22]

In the countryside, archers played an essential role within a company: they were indispensable during sieges, thanks to their missile weapons, but, as we have seen, they were also responsible for reconnaissance and foraging. Philippe de Commynes repeatedly uses the term *chevaucheurs* (riders) to refer to these groups, probably composed mainly of archers, who roamed the countryside. They were omnipresent, as under the walls of Paris in 1465: 'The *chevaucheurs,* who had approached Paris, saw several *chevaucheur*s who had come to find out what that noise in the host was all about.'[23]

Combat around the time of Charles VII. Illustration from 1483, 'les Vigiles du Roi Charles VII,' Bibliothèque nationale de France, Ms 5054. (Public Domain)

The Battle of Formigny (15 April 1450)

It was at the Battle of Formigny that the *compagnies d'ordonnance* distinguished themselves for the first time. According to Thomas Basin, as the English were heading towards Bayeux, the French army forced them to stop at Formigny, a village three or four leagues from Bayeux. The French deployed their forces opposite the English camp 'in two parts', and the two adversaries spent much of the day observing each other from a distance.

> Then, small cannons called serpentines caused a great deal of damage to the English camp, so five hundred archers emerged and charged, quickly seizing the serpentines that were harassing them and killing or putting to flight the French who were guarding them. When they realised what was happening, a wing of French cavalry charged the English, overran them and massacred them. The others who had remained in the camp, fearing such a cavalry charge (for they themselves were mostly on foot), withdrew from the advanced camp to a nearby position which they considered safer to avoid the cavalry attack. Seeing this, and considering their initial success a favourable

20 Godefroy, *Histoire de Charles VII Roy de France par Jean Chartier,* p.56.
21 De Bueil, *Le Jouvencel, Tome premier,* p.86.
22 De Bueil, *Le Jouvencel, Tome premier,* p.106.
23 Godefroy, *Histoire de Charles VII Roy de France par Jean Chartier,* pp.57–58.

> omen, the French attacked them without delay, without giving them time to recover their composure. Although the fight was uneven, the English put up some resistance to the French before turning their backs, unable to withstand the shock of the French assault. But what struck terror into the ranks of the English and broke their morale to such an extent that they saw no other way out but to flee was the arrival of Arthur, Count of Richemont and Constable of France. He arrived from the quarters of Saint-Loup with about three hundred lances, when the battle had already begun and was almost over. At this sight, the English were dismayed and lost heart. Among those who managed to escape were Matthew Goghe, then captain of Bayeux, and Sir Robert Ver, who had come to join the English forces with many veteran men-at-arms. Thus they saved their lives, for fear had given them wings. Almost all the others, who had recently arrived from England, were killed or taken prisoner. During this battle, more than three thousand five hundred were killed and almost as many prisoners were taken to French towns and villages to be sold as slaves for a pittance.[24]

It was therefore the arrival of the Constable of Richemont that decided the outcome. Guillaume Gruel, Richemont's chronicler who took part in the battle, reports that:

> [The Constable] rode about a league and stopped to put his men in bataille; then he made his *ordonnances* and placed the Bastard of La Trimouille with 15 or 20 lances in front. He then sent out his vanguard, which included Monseigneur Jacques de Saint-Paoul, Monseigneur the *Maréchal de* Lohéac, Monseigneur de Bossac and their archers. He then ordered Messire Gilles de Saint-Simon, Messire Jehan de Malestroit and Philippe de Malestroit to command his archers. Then he ordered certain gentlemen to form a bodyguard, whose names are as follows: Regnault de Veluyre, Pierre du Pan, Yvon de Treena, Jehan Budes, Hector Meriadec, Jehan du Bois, Colinet de Lignières, and Guillaume Gruel. Then he ordered the men to form a rearguard and rode off in good order as quickly as he could. And so the first of his men arrived at Trévières, and he arrived soon after. And when he arrived, the English sent forth about four hundred men from their battle, who put to flight some 1,300 archers from the side of Monseigneur de Clermont, and gained the culverins with which they were being attacked; and had it not been for the men-of-war who held their ground, I believe they would have done great harm to our men. And when my lord arrived at a windmill there, everything was in confusion, and as soon as he could,

24 Basin, *Histoire de Charles VII*, Livre IV, Chapter 24.

> he sent part of his vanguard and those who commanded his archers. And the archers went to pass at the end of the battle of the English and those who had made the sortie on our men; our said archers killed a good hundred and twenty of them.[25]

The archers from the companies that were part of the vanguard were therefore used to outflank and attack the English from the side. Guillaume Gruel continues his account:

> Then my lord came with his archers close to the English battle, and then our people's battle and archers approached. And there came to my lord the constable, my lord de Clermont, my lord de Castres, my lord the admiral de Coëtivy, my lord the grand seneschal, Sir Jacques de Chabannes, Joachim Rouault, Sir Geoffroy de Couvran, Olivier de Broon, Oudet de Rie, Jehan de Rossnyvinen and all their battle, and joined our batailles together.[26]

The constable then suggested to Seneschal Pierre de Brézé that they go and see how the English were holding up. The seneschal asked him in response whether the attack should be made in the middle or on the wings. To which Richemont replied: 'I want to God, they will not remain there by the Grace of God.'[27] Pierre de Brézé then suggested attacking a 'taudeis' built by the English with his ensign, which the constable approved. With the enemy entrenched, the attack was carried out on foot. 'And immediately, without further ado, everyone gathered to attack, and so it was done; and the English did not stop them, and all were defeated, killed and captured, and there were well over six thousand in flight.'[28]

For his part, Gilles (Jacques) le Bouvier, in *Recouvrement de Normandie*, describes the end of the battle as follows:

> And then arrived the Lord of Richemont, Constable of France, the Lord of Laval, the *Maréchal de* Lohéac and the Lord of Sainte-Sévère, with a total of 300 lances and the archers. And when the English saw them coming, they left the field and came to the river to put it behind them, for they doubted the company of the said constable .... Then the armies of the Lord of Clermont and his company, which had 500 to 600 lances and the archers, marched forward. They charged the English, as did those of the Constable of France, who crossed the river on the main road to Formigny, near a village, at a ford and a small stone bridge. And there they fought the

25 Gruel, *Chronique d'Arthur de Richemont*, pp.205–206.
26 Gruel, *Chronique d'Arthur de Richemont*, pp.206–207.
27 Gruel, *Chronique d'Arthur de Richemont*, p.207.
28 Gruel, *Chronique d'Arthur de Richemont*, p.208.

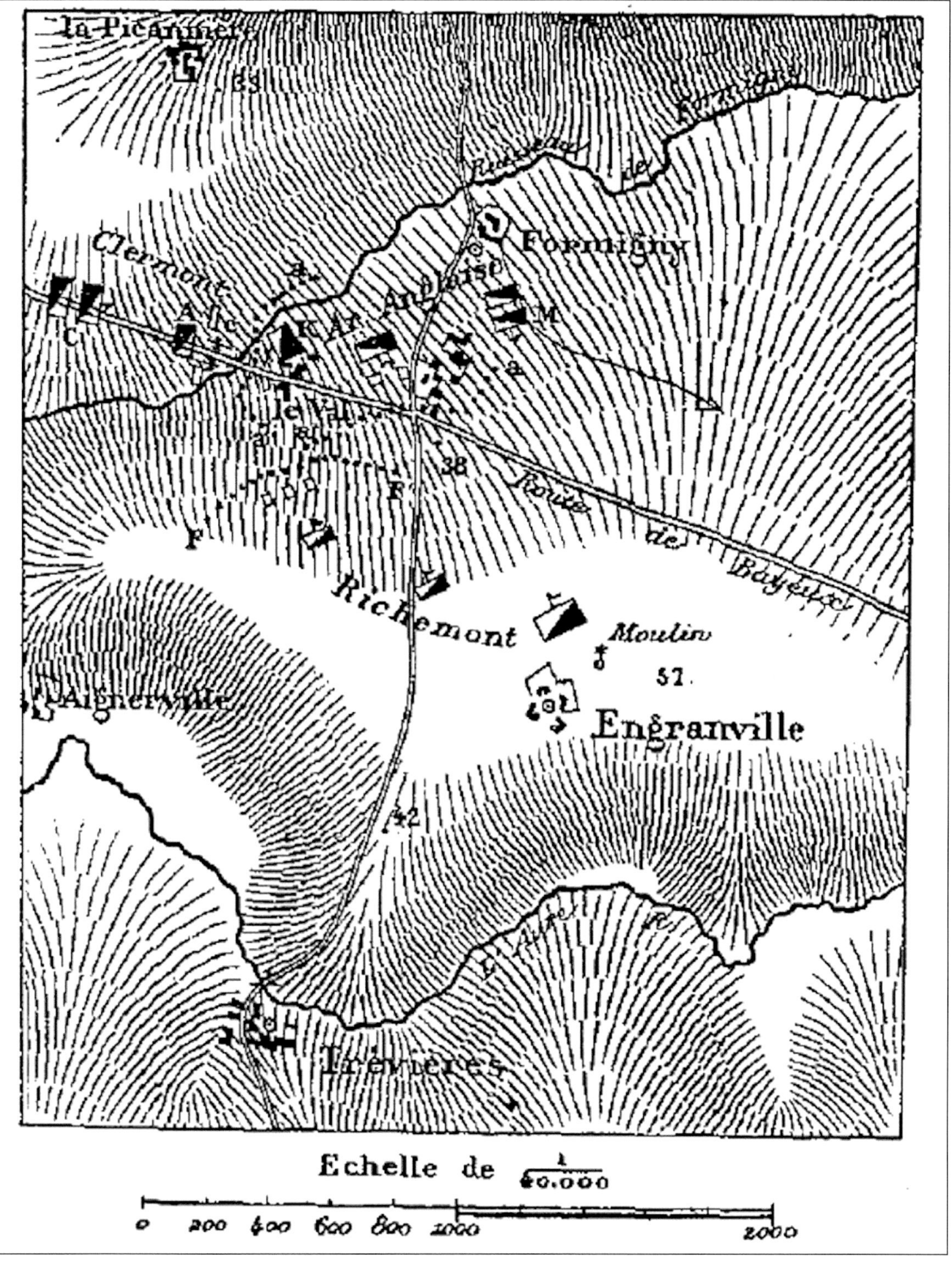

Battle of Formigny, 15 April 1450. From Hardÿ de Périni, *Batailles Françaises* (Paris: Plon-Nourrit & C., 1894), Tome 1, p.141. (Public Domain)

English on both sides very valiantly, until at last they defeated them around this river.[29]

The constable's 300 lances were therefore composed of 100 lances from his company, 100 lances from the *Maréchal de* Lohéac and 100 lances commanded by Jean de Brosse, Lord of Boussac and Sainte-Sévère. They were added to the companies commanded by the Count of Clermont, making a total of nearly 600 lances according to le Bouvier: the 100 lances of Pierre de Brézé, the 70 lances of Joachim Rouault, as well as those of Olivier de Coëtivy, Geoffroy de Couvran (probably 40 lances based on a muster roll from 1451), Olivier de Broon (probably 30 lances based on a montre from 15 October 1451), Oudet de Rie, and Jehan de Rossnyvinen, whose numbers are unknown.

Although accounts of the battle remain vague about its main phases and do not detail the actions of the various units, it was nevertheless the *compagnies d'ordonnance* and the companies from *Bretagne* that together secured victory at Formigny. Unfortunately, we do not know about how they fought.

The Battle of Castillon (17 July 1453)[30]

For the second campaign in Guyenne, which took place in 1453, Charles VII arrived in Guyenne with 'his army reinforced with a whole arsenal of war.'[31] This army included the companies of Amanieu d'Albret, Lord of Orval, Joachim Rouault, Jacques de Chabannes, Grand Master of the King's *Hotel*, Jean de Brosse, Lord of Saint-Sévère and Boussac, and the Count of Penthièvre, totalling 600 lances.[32] But Talbot managed to conquer 'most of the country,' including the town of Castillon.[33] The French companies were soon reinforced by those of *Maréchal* André de Lohéac, Philippe de Culant, Lord of Jaloignes, Jean de Bueil, and Louis de Beaumont, Seneschal of Poitou, for a total of 1,800 lances. The 'war machine' consisted of the artillery of Jean and Gaspard Bureau accompanied by *francs-archers*. On 14 July, the French army laid siege to Castillon, protecting its artillery with a fortified camp and a deep ditch. Upon hearing the news, Talbot left Bordeaux to come to the city's aid, leading 800 to 1,000 cavalry, followed by 4,000 to 5,000 infantry. Upon hearing this news, the French fortified their artillery. But Talbot surprised a troop of 400 *francs-archers* who were

29 Le Bouvier, *Les chroniques de Normandie*, pp.146–147.
30 For a detailed description of the battle see, Peter Hoskins, *The Battle of Castillon 1453* (Warwick: Helion & Co., 2023).
31 Basin, *Histoire de Charles VII*, Livre V, Chapter 6.
32 Le Bouvier, *Les chroniques de Normandie*, p.177.
33 Le Bouvier, *Les chroniques de Normandie*, p.177.

marching 'in disarray,'[34] 800 *francs-archers* commanded by Joachim Rouault according to de Coucy,[35] and killed 100 to 120 of them.[36] Fearing, at the sight of a cloud of dust, that the French were fleeing, and because those from Castillon were pressing him, Talbot resumed his march without waiting for his infantry. Meanwhile, the French reached the camp and got into 'good *ordonnance*' to defend themselves.[37] But when he arrived in front of the camp, he was 'greatly astonished' at the sight of the fortifications, moats and artillery deployed in front of him. 'Having arrived at the French camp with excessive haste and without waiting for his artillery and infantry, numbering, it was said, more than ten thousand men, he resolved to attack' despite the advice of his standard-bearer, Thomas Evringham, according to Thomas Basin.[38] 'Accustomed to being guided by his audacity and recklessness,' Talbot ordered Evringham 'to bring the standards he carried to the ditch of the French camp.'[39] According to le Bouvier, Talbot had his entire company stand at attention, with all eight banners unfurled: 'And then began a great and marvellous assault, and as long as they fought hand-to-hand, there were glorious feats of arms on both sides. But in the end, the English were defeated and their banners thrown to the ground.'[40] According to Basin, 'the French, very calm, greeted the English with stones, lead shot, and all kinds of projectiles, killing many with serpentines, culverins, and crossbows, and valiantly repelled the assault.'[41] The English seemed to have concentrated their efforts on the barrier that served as the camp gate, defended primarily by Joachim Rouault.[42] Talbot was hit in the leg by a culverin shot, and his horse was killed beneath him. The French took advantage of the hesitation in the English ranks to charge. According to Basin, as Talbot 'had fallen into the hands of foot archers who had lost their comrades-in-arms the day before because of his cruelty, they stabbed him repeatedly and slaughtered him without mercy.'[43] The English infantry following, learning of the disaster, then turned back. Thomas Basin believes that the Bretons who were in the service of the King of France, numbering 300 lances, distinguished themselves particularly.

Although the chroniclers' description of the battle is still superficial, it seems that artillery and *francs-archers* were the main contributors to the victory at Castillon. These accounts do not allow us to learn more about how the *compagnies d'ordonnance* actually fought.

34 Thomas Basin, *Histoire de Charles VII*, Livre V, Chapter 6.
35 De Coussy, *Chroniques,* p.121
36 Le Bouvier, *Les chroniques de Normandie*, p.178.
37 Le Bouvier, *Les chroniques de Normandie*, p.178.
38 Thomas Basin, *Histoire de Charles VII*, Livre V, Chapter 7.
39 Thomas Basin, *Histoire de Charles VII*, Livre V, Chapter 7.
40 Le Bouvier, *Les chroniques de Normandie*, p.179.
41 Thomas Basin, *Histoire de Charles VII*, Livre V, Chapter7.
42 De Bueil, *Le Jouvencel*, Tome premier, p.200 & Tome second, pp.295–296.
43 Thomas Basin, *Histoire de Charles VII*, Livre V, Chapter 7.

Battle of Montlhéry, 1465. Illustration from 'Mémoires de Philippe de Commines,' Musée Dobrée, Nantes, Ms 18, f. 7v. (Public Domain)

The Battle of Montlhéry (16 July 1465)

When Louis XI became King on 15 August 1461, he dismissed many of his late father's officers. These included Chancellor Guillaume Jouvenel des Ursins, the President of Parliament, several captains of military companies, bailiffs and seneschals. The growing discontent led to the creation of the *Ligue du Bien Public* in 1465. Among the main conspirators were Charles, Count of Charolais and heir to the Duchy of Burgundy, and François II, Duke of Brittany. But it was the King's brother-in-law, Jean II de Bourbon, who opened hostilities in March by giving the order to seize the King's people and money. The Duke of Bourbon had the support of Patrice Folcart, who managed to rally 60 to 100 Scottish lances.[44] Bourbon was soon joined by the Duke of Berry, Antoine de Chabannes, Count of Dammartin, and Jean, Count of Dunois. The royal troops, commanded by the Count of Maine and Pierre de Brézé, Count of Évreux and Seneschal of Normandy, took all the Bastard of Orléans' strongholds one by one. Louis XI then launched an army of 400 lances and a corps of *francs-archers* against the possessions of René d'Anjou and an advance guard of 200 lances, namely the companies of Philippe de Melun (replacing Louis de Crussol, who had fallen into disgrace) and Jean Salazar, against the Dukes of Berry and Bourbon. The Count of Maine, assisted by Pierre de Brézé, was put in charge of guarding the Breton border, while Joachim Rouault, *Maréchal de France*, was sent to Picardy with his 100 lances.

---

44 Delabos & Gaillard, *Montlhéry, 16 juillet 1465*, p.23.

The King was in Issoudun on 8 May, at the head of 800 lances, 10,000 *francs-archers* and artillery. His forces would reach 25,000 men on 22 June.[45] According to Maupoint, author of the *Journal Parisien*, the King's army in Bourbonnais numbered 2,000 lances totalling 18,000 combatants, or 20,000 according to another manuscript, including the *francs-archers*.[46] Ending his campaign in Berry and Bourbonnais, Louis XI headed for Paris, which was under threat from the Burgundians. Joachim Rouault, after leaving 500 *francs-archers* to guard Péronne in Picardy, came to reinforce Paris with 110 lances. On 5 July, the Count of Charolais was in Saint-Denis, where he was waiting for the Duke of Brittany. He took advantage of this wait to launch raids against Paris over five days. Under siege, Rouault and Brézé resisted the attacks. As Louis XI crossed the Loire on 11 July, Charles hoped that he would be joined by the Breton army. Numbering 12,000 to 15,000 men, the Breton army included seven of Charles VII's former *compagnies d'ordonnance*, then stationed on the lands of the Duke of Brittany, totalling 450 lances. Faced with such forces, the Count of Maine and his 300 lances, 700 to 800 men-at-arms according to Commynes, bided their time.[47]

On 16 July, Louis XI had with him an army estimated at 1,900 lances, divided into three *batailles*, positioned one behind the other.[48] The vanguard, destined to become the right wing, was commanded by Pierre de Brézé, while the rearguard, destined to become the left wing, was commanded by Charles, Count of Maine, and Admiral de Montauban. The King followed with the *bataille* destined to form the centre, which included the Dauphiné and Savoy contingents.[49] Opposite them, the army of Charles, Count of Charolais, numbered 1,400 men-at-arms, 8,000 to 9,000 archers and artillery. The Count of Saint-Pol formed the vanguard, which was to become the left wing. The Count of Charolais commanded the right wing, while Antoine of Burgundy and Jacques of Luxembourg commanded the centre.[50]

That day, the heat was intense. The King's vanguard arrived at Montlhéry, where the Count of Saint-Pol was staying. The latter alerted the Count of Charolais and asked him for help. Charles responded favourably and, at around seven o'clock in the morning, reinforcements consisting of 2,000 archers and four or five serpentines, according to Haynin, arrived on the scene and dismounted.[51] The Burgundian archers were deployed, each with a stake in front of them, the serpentines in front and the men-at-arms behind. Opposite them, five or six of the King's banners totalling 400

45 Delabos & Gaillard, *Montlhéry, 16 juillet 1465*, pp.27 & 32.
46 Jean Maupoint, *Journal Parisien* (Paris: Fagniez, 1878), p.53.
47 Godefroy, *Mémoires de Philippe de Comines*, Tome premier, p.17.
48 De la Marche, *Mémoires*, p.502.
49 Delabos & Gaillard, *Montlhéry, 16 juillet 1465*, p.48.
50 Delabos & Gaillard, *Montlhéry, 16 juillet 1465*, p.50.
51 Jean Haynin, *Les mémoires de messire Jean, seigneur de Haynin et de Louvegnies*, Tome premier (Mons: E.M. Hoyois, 1892), p.28.

men-at-arms, according to Commynes, deployed along a large hedge.[52] It was then that skirmishes began between the archers of both armies. The serpentine fire scattered the French somewhat, but they rallied. Poncet de Rivière's archers formed the vanguard. On the Burgundian side, the archers and men-at-arms were under the command of Philippe de Lalaing and Jacques du Maes. The Burgundians, who were more numerous, took a few doors from houses to use as shields and tried to set fire to the village, but with difficulty, as the French defended it. Faced with the threat, Poncet de Rivière's archers remounted their horses and retreated.

A long wait followed this episode, under a blazing sun. The Count of Charolais then ordered Saint-Pol to skirmish the enemy line with five to six lances and three to four thousand archers. It was then that, on the French side, the Count of Maine, blaming his nephew the King for wanting to fight, decided to leave the battlefield with 500 or 800 lances (500 according to Haynin and 800 according to Commynes) despite the murmurs of his men. Louis XI no longer had a left wing. Despite this betrayal, he nevertheless decided to fight before the arrival of the Duke of Brittany and the Duke of Berry. It was then that the Count of Charolais sent all his mounted *cranequiniers* at full gallop to deploy. They galloped past the hedge where the French were lined up in battle formation and took up position near the castle. The *cranequiniers* were followed by Saint-Pol's corps: foot archers followed by men-at-arms on horseback. This advance led his archers, in the heat, across fields of grain and up a slope. Facing them, the French retreated, climbing back up the hill.

Seeing the enemy retreat, the Burgundians were ordered to remount their horses and pursue the enemy: 'The Charolais climbed the mountain by force, pursuing the French as they thought, and there was a great encounter, and from then on there were many killed and captured on both sides.'[53] Indeed, as the Burgundians climbed the slope, breathless, the French turned around. The King's men-at-arms, led by Brézé, crossed the hedge at both ends and raised their lances: 300 men-at-arms charging 'lance on thigh' according to Olivier de la Marche .[54] In response, the Burgundian men-at-arms who were following their archers countercharged, running over them without even giving them time to shoot. 'I do not believe that among the twelve hundred men-at-arms, or thereabouts, who were there, there were fifty who knew how to hold a lance at the ready; there were not four hundred armed with cuirasses; and there was not a single armed servant,' recounts Commynes. [55] At the same time, Haynin relates:

> As the French in this encounter were mostly those of their vanguard, the others, seeing that our men were hastily retreating towards the

52 Godefroy, *Mémoires de Philippe de Comines*, Tome premier, pp.20–21.

53 Haynin, *Les mémoires*, p.36.

54 De la Marche, *Mémoires*, p.502.

55 Godefroy, *Mémoires de Philippe de Comines*, Tome premier, pp.22–23.

> top of the mountain and the castle, leaving their artillery behind, descended in full force and rushed upon the said artillery and carts, numbering two or three standards, and killed many of those who were around the said cartage, and many turned their backs, especially a large number of mounted cranequiniers, then many others both on horseback and on foot, even gentlemen of great name, shamefully leaving and abandoning their lord and prince. And this happened because those who had gone first with the Count of Saint-Pol to try to break through the French, seeing themselves so fiercely charged by the said French, and thinking to find the rest of the army near the said artillery and carts, slowly retreated towards them, defending themselves as best they could, and finding themselves frustrated, were forced to flee, thinking that the others had fled and were lost. Many fled as far as Saint-Cloud, others returned immediately, realising that they had been deceived, and came in time to finish the battle.[56]

On the French side, it seems that the King's battle, which followed the vanguard, took part in the pursuit: 'The main participants in this chase were the nobles of Dauphiné and Savoy, as well as many gendarmes,' wrote Commynes.[57] In his journal, Maupoint adds that, 'the King, on this day, performed great feats both in rallying his captains and men-at-arms three times and in fighting in person, for which he received great honour.'[58] After defeating the Burgundians '*à plate couture*' (i.e. soundly),[59] the royal troops reached the artillery and carts, pillaged the camp and brought the spoils back to their camp. They even came close to capturing the Count of Charolais. But he was saved by the fierce defence of the rest of his company. The count then led his company and the rest of his men, barely a hundred strong, into battle, taking cover behind his carts. They were soon joined by the men of Saint-Pol and other fugitives, totalling 800 men-at-arms.

After this *déculottée* (thrashing), as Haynin writes, the serpentines began to play on the enemy again.[60] Both opponents had lost their left wing, but the two centres still faced each other, lined up in battle formation, although the Burgundian line was now stronger in numbers. Things remained this way until nightfall. During the night, Louis XI withdrew to Corbeil, leaving the battlefield to the enemy.

As a skilled politician, Louis XI wrote to the people of Lyon on 17 July 1465, stating:

56 Haynin, *Les mémoires*, p.36.
57 Godefroy, *Mémoires de Philippe de Comines*, Tome premier, p.24.
58 Maupoint, *Journal Parisien*, p.57.
59 Godefroy, *Mémoires de Philippe de Comines*, Tome premier, p.24.
60 Haynin, *Les mémoires*, p.41.

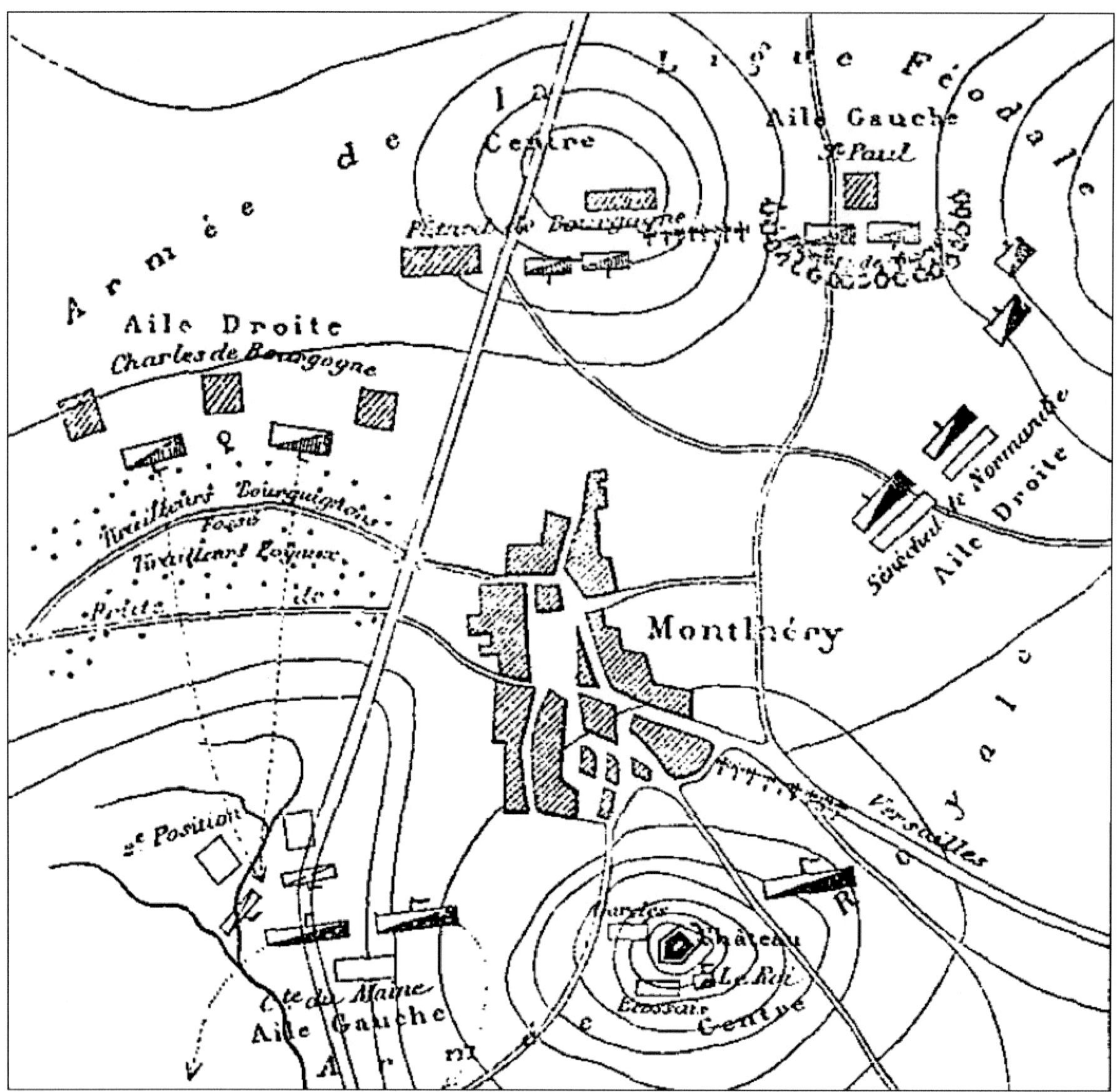

Battle of Montlhéry, 16 July 1465. (From Hardÿ de Périni, *Batailles Françaises*, Tome 1, (Paris: Plon-Nourrit & C., 1894), p.155. (Public Domain)

> About two hours after dinner, the Counts of Charolais and Saint-Pol, Atof de Clèves, the Bastard of Burgundy and all their men were in battle near Montlhéry, fortified with their carts, ditches, ribaudequins and other heavy artillery. We were advised to attack and fight them, and so we did. And thanks to God, we had the upper hand, and victory was ours, and twice or thrice the said Count of Charolais and most of his men fled, as did the said Count of Saint-Pol; and of these, both dead and captured, since the battle, a good two thousand fled.... Ten of their men died for every one of ours, as was found; and there were between fourteen and fifteen hundred dead on their side, and between two and three hundred prisoners, among whom there are many people of means. And as we have learned, the Bastard of Burgundy was killed [this is an error, he was not killed]; and furthermore, it has been reported to us that the said Counts of Charolais and Saint-Pol were seriously wounded. And we remained on the battlefield until sunset; and around sunset, when the field remained ours, we withdrew and came to the said town of Corbeil, and our whole army with us, except for some who thought things would turn out differently, and for that reason withdrew to various places.[61]

Jean Maupoint notes in his diary that around 1,800 prisoners and more than 2,000 horses entered Paris that day.[62]

In summary, the Battle of Montlhéry reveals that the *compagnies d'ordonnance* were disciplined units. These companies knew how to retreat in order, halt and counter-attack on command. The manoeuvres between men-at-arms and archers appear to be coordinated. Control by the chain of command also seems to be effective, as it appears that, after the pursuit, many units were maintained or redeployed in battle behind the hedge.

The Battle of Guinegatte (7 August 1479)

In 1477, Louis XI took advantage of the death of Charles the Bold, Duke of Burgundy, during the Battle of Nancy on 5 January 1477, to take possession of the Duchy of Burgundy. In response, Charles the Bold's daughter, Mary of Burgundy, married Archduke Maximilian of Austria. The King of France now had to face a coalition between the Habsburg Empire and Burgundy. The confrontation took place at Guinegatte on 7 August 1479.

Philippe de Crèvecœur d'Esquerde, the King's lieutenant in Picardy, who commanded the French army, was at the head of 1,100 *compagnies d'ordonnance*, or 6,600 men-at-arms, pages, archers and coustilliers, and

61 Vaesen et Charavay, *Lettres de Louis XI, Roi de France*, Tome II, pp.327–328.

62 Maupoint, *Journal Parisien*, p.57.

8,000 *francs-archers*, according to Commynes. Molinet, for his part, gives a much higher figure of 1,800 lances (although he later mentions two corps of 600 men-at-arms) and 14,000 *francs-archers*, making 22 standards, plus a large number of 'flying' artillery pieces, the main ones being *la Gringade* and *la Girade*.[63] This would give a total of 24,800 men excluding artillery, counting six men per company of foot soldiers. The Austro-Burgundian army, commanded by the Archduke, is estimated at 27,400 combatants, according to Molinet,[64] and was composed mostly of Flemish, 'up to 20,000 or more, as well as some Germans and some 300 Englishmen' according to Commynes.[65]

The day began with skirmishes. Jean Molinet describes the start of the battle thus:

> The duke, seeing his enemies lined up in terrible and cruel order, ... arranged his battle lines and instructed Salezar to engage in skirmishes, which proved to be a very brief task that day. His entire army was assembled into a single mass and arranged in a single battle line, drawn up in the manner of a portcullis; with 500 English foot archers at the forefront, led by Thomas d'Orican, accompanied by other archers, crossbowmen, culveriners and German arquebusiers, numbering 3,000 in total; then came the duke's engines, which did very well in firing on the French. Consequently, the prince's banner held its position.... Monseigneur de Nassau also had a very large force of Flemish pikemen.... The 825 lances that the duke had, all in groups of 25, were hastily deployed on the wings of the entire battle.[66]

The battle began around 2 p.m., in sweltering heat, with artillery fire. 'Because the artillery of His Grace the Duke of Austria was working hard on the French, His Grace d'Esquerdes was forced to divide his forces into large *esquadres* (squadrons) to surround the Burgundians, with five or six hundred lances and a large number of *francs-archers*, followed by the archers of *ordonnance*.'[67] Molinet's lines suggest that Crèvecœur divided his army into two battle formations of 600 lances followed by *francs-archers* (4,000 to 7,000 per *bataille*), with the archers of the *ordonnance* bringing up the rear, in order to 'surround' the enemy, i.e. to encircle or outflank them. The two *batailles* then marched 'in single file' towards Dunkirk and, upon reaching a wood, made a 'half-turn to the right' to flank the wings of the enemy army, where the Burgundian gendarmerie was stationed.[68] It is difficult to

63 Buchon, *Chroniques de Jean Molinet*, p.204.
64 Buchon, *Chroniques de Jean Molinet*, p.199.
65 Godefroy, *Mémoires de Philippe de Comines, Tome premier*, p.396.
66 Buchon, *Chroniques de Jean Molinet*, pp.204–206.
67 Buchon, *Chroniques de Jean Molinet*, pp.209–210.
68 Buchon, *Chroniques de Jean Molinet*, p.210.

understand the manoeuvre clearly here because, if it was an encirclement, one battle would have had to make a quarter turn to the right and the other a quarter turn to the left. But it is certain that at least one of the two Austro-Burgundian wings was attacked on its flank. The Burgundians faced them and 'powerfully' withstood the shock of the charge that follow:

> And the Burgundian companies joined them, which had previously marched in *esquadres* [i.e. squadrons] on the wing supporting the foot soldiers; but, due to enemy forces, the Burgundian company was separated and cut off from the Picards wing, so that they were forced to take the road to Therouanne.... They were pursued as far as the moats of the town of Aire by a company of Frenchmen, along with another band who began to attack the Burgundians' quartermasters. The French company had behind it the *francs-archers* with those of *ordonnance*, who found Monsieur de Nassau's company in their path, who dispatched them and took them so much by surprise that they had no time to draw their bows or draw their swords, and were rushed into a village near a hedge by the Germans, Picards, Burgundians, English and Flemings, who made a terrible slaughter of them. When the said archers were routed, the Burgundian foot soldiers wanted to come to their aid, and their captains had great difficulty in keeping them together, so as not to break up the large army for the adventures that might arise. It should be noted that, at the very moment when the French and Burgundian companies clashed, there were few deaths, but many broken lances. The French, archers from France and of the *ordonnance*, were dispatched by the Burgundians, as has been said.... At the first clash of this very fierce encounter, some Burgundians, about three hundred knights, broke away. Another three hundred French lances, seeing that the Burgundians were greatly occupied with the dispatch of the French archers to embrace them from another wing and give them new work, broke away from the main force [i.e. separated from the main body]; and passing in front of Viesville, they charged the duke's baggage train and killed the quartermasters, priests, seculars, mendicants, religious, pregnant women, pages, lepers and children who were still suckling. Those who were ordered to the rearguard to protect and defend them joined the main bataille; and they had such an ardent desire to fight their enemies that it seemed to them that they would never arrive in time; and they abandoned wealth to gain honour and prowess.[69]

Thus, the pikemen of the Counts of Nassau and Romont carried out several 'deadly' assaults on the French archers (*francs-archers* and archers of the

69 Buchon, *Chroniques de Jean Molinet*, pp.210–213.

ordonnance). At the same time, the French managed to reach Archduke Maximilian's artillery. However, it seems that the Count of Romont ordered the 'second company' of pikemen to come to the aid of the artillery, thus managing to recapture it after repelling the French. It was then the turn of the Burgundians to capture the French camp, taking 37 pieces of artillery, including serpentines and some *gros-bâtons* (hand cannons, literally 'big sticks').[70] The archers of *ordonnance* who had dismounted to finish off those who had been struck down by the men-at-arms did not have time to remount their horses and were themselves massacred by the pikemen, 'who gained hocquetons laden with rich gold and silver.'[71] The French fled, pursued by the Burgundians. Several French men-at-arms, returning from their pursuit in disorder, thinking the battle won, were then attacked by the Burgundian pikemen.

French chroniclers, of course, tell a slightly different story. Commynes simply reports that 'the King's horsemen, who were far more numerous than the others, broke through the duke's horsemen and chased them as far as Aire, and Monsieur Philippe de Ravestein, who was leading them, joined the duke among his foot soldiers.'[72] Commynes then regrets that Crèvecœur led the pursuit, 'since it is not the duty of the leaders of the vanguard and rearguard to chase.'[73] The *francs-archers* followed and began to plunder Duke Maximilian's waggons. However, the Burgundian infantry remained in place, for 'they had with them some 200 gentlemen of good standing on foot, who led them.'[74] This infantry then turned against the *francs-archers*, killing many of them and retaking the camp, as Jean de Troyes relates:

> And because some of the King's *francs-archers* who were following the said chase began to plunder the baggage and other goods left behind by the said adversaries, thus chased away as it is said, there came upon the said *francs-archers* and other men-of-war, the Count of Romont, who had some 14 to 15,000 foot soldiers, who killed some of the said *francs-archers* and other men-of-war. [75]

According to Commynes,

> the Duke suffered greater losses than we did, with many men captured and killed, but he retained his camp.... I was with the King when he received the news, and he was very saddened, for he was not

70 Buchon, *Chroniques de Jean Molinet*, pp.214–215.
71 Buchon, *Chroniques de Jean Molinet*, p.215.
72 Godefroy, *Mémoires de Philippe de Comines*, Tome premier, p.396.
73 Godefroy, *Mémoires de Philippe de Comines*, Tome premier, p.397.
74 Godefroy, *Mémoires de Philippe de Comines*, Tome premier, p.397.
75 Petitot, *Collection complète des mémoires relatifs à l'histoire de France*, Tome XIII, p.341.

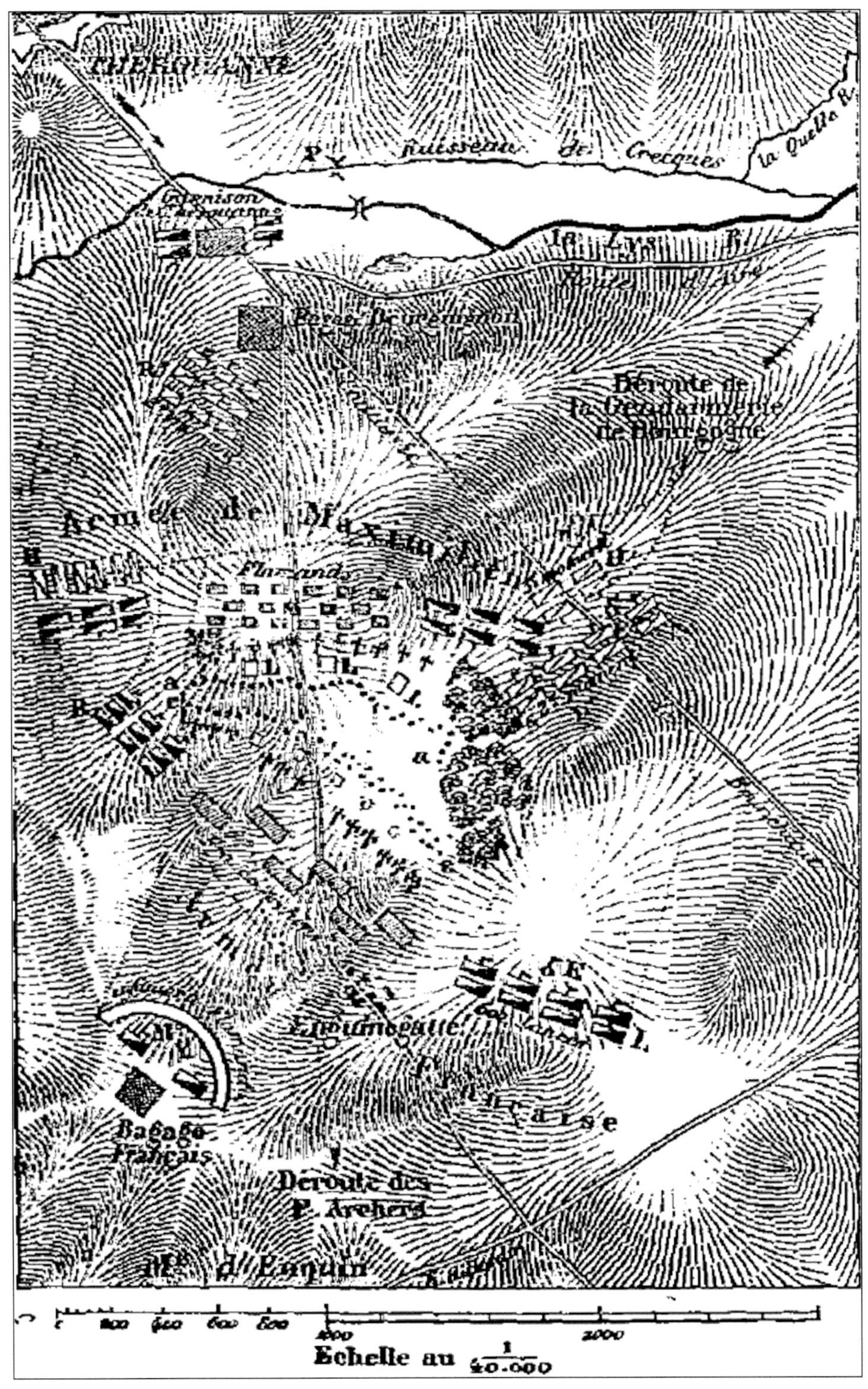

Battle of Guinegatte, 1479. (From Hardÿ de Périni, *Batailles Françaises*, Tome 1, (Paris: Plon-Nourrit & C., 1894), p.168. (Public Domain)

> accustomed to losing, but was so fortunate in all his endeavours that it seemed that everything went according to his wishes.[76]

Enemy losses are estimated at between 14,000 and 15,000, including 11,000 to 12,000 Burgundian, Picard and Flemish combatants and 900 to 1,000 prisoners, according to Jean de Troyes.[77] These figures are, of course, hardly credible. French losses amounted to 300 archers, not counting the *francs-archers*, according to the same chronicler. Jean Molinet clearly presents the Battle of Guinegatte, which he claims lasted only two hours, as a Burgundian victory. He estimates French losses at almost 10,000 men, including 6,000 to 7,000 *francs-archers*, and Burgundian losses at around 100 men-at-arms and 600 followers. Surprisingly, Commynes tells us that Louis XI was nevertheless pleased with Crèvecœur, his lieutenant. However, the outcome of this battle would determine Louis XI's decision to sign the peace treaty. In this sense, the Burgundian version of the battle is more credible. Guinegatte clearly proved to be a victory for the Flemish communal militias, mainly composed of pikemen, even if Maximilian was unable to take advantage of it.

This French defeat nevertheless remains an interesting testimony to the behaviour of the *compagnies d'ordonnance* and *francs-archers* on the battlefield. On that day, the French army demonstrated both professionalism and indiscipline. Crèvecœur's manoeuvre seemed well thought out, coordinated and executed: he divided his army into two equal corps, each composed of half of the *compagnies d'ordonnance* and *francs-archers*, in order to outflank the enemy battle line, which consisted mainly of an unshakeable corps of Flemish pikemen. Men-at-arms and archers *d'ordonnance* flanked the *francs-archers*, probably to bolster their courage, and the manoeuvre seemed to be going according to plan. However, Crèvecœur failed to keep his units in order: he allowed himself and his men-at-arms to be drawn into pursuing the enemy cavalry, leaving his archers vulnerable. For their part, the *francs-archers* broke ranks to plunder the enemy camp. It seems that at Guinegatte, in the absence of the King and experienced captains, or perhaps due to excessive confidence, the men-at-arms reverted to their bad habits.

---

76 Godefroy, *Mémoires de Philippe de Comines*, Tome premier, p.397.

77 Petitot, *Collection complète des mémoires relatifs à l'histoire de France*, Tome XIII, p.341.

Conclusion

At the end of this study, the creation of a standing army under Charles VII emerges as the culmination of a long process, marked by repeated crises, institutional adjustments and military lessons learned throughout the Hundred Years' War. Far from being a sudden 'invention', the reform of the army was part of a continuum that included the gradual monetisation of military service, the proliferation of *ordonnances* designed to regulate the men-of-war, and the gradual assertion of the monarchy's ability to recruit, control and pay troops on a regular basis. The disasters of Crécy, Poitiers, Agincourt and Verneuil, as well as the endemic violence of *routiers* and *écorcheurs*, highlighted the impasse of intermittent feudal mobilisation and the political necessity of containing private warfare.

The central issue addressed in this book – understanding why and how the idea of a stable, regulated armed force directly attached to the crown became established – can be answered here on several levels. First, on the military front, the experience of conflict imposed a new requirement: to retain troops that were immediately available, disciplined, and capable of prolonged campaigns and siege operations. Secondly, on the domestic front, the reform responded to an urgent public order issue: it was necessary to dry up the structural source of disorder represented by demobilised soldiers, who lived off looting, ransom and *patis*, and to restore security to the population, an essential condition for economic recovery and the legitimacy of power. Thirdly and finally, on an institutional level, the establishment of a standing army presupposed and accelerated the consolidation of a fiscal and administrative apparatus: a paid army required stable resources, collection mechanisms, control agents, *montres* (muster) procedures and a more transparent chain of command.

The *compagnies d'ordonnance*, the *francs-archers* and the rise of artillery crystallise this threefold logic. The former embodies the stabilisation of a professional core directly serving the King; the latter respond to the search for additional infantry that can be mobilised locally, while placing the defence of the kingdom in a more direct relationship between the monarchy and the communities; Finally, artillery illustrates the gradual shift in military superiority towards technical and logistical means requiring organisation, funding and expertise, and therefore centralisation. This combination helps to explain the new effectiveness of the royal military apparatus in the reconquest phase and in the ability of the authorities to hold territory, secure strongholds and impose stricter discipline on its military men.

However, the scope of these reforms goes far beyond the single issue of military effectiveness. The major challenge is political: war ceases to be primarily a feudal duty and becomes a function supervised by the state, supported by taxation and subject to standards. In this sense, the creation of a standing army was at the heart of a transformation of sovereignty: the monarchy tended to monopolise the legitimate use of force, reduce the military autonomy of princes and subordinate the warrior elites to an apparatus that was more administrative than feudal. This change also reconfigured the social status of war: it did not disappear as a noble pursuit, but it became increasingly bound by constraints of service, discipline, accountability and control, which heralded more modern forms of professionalisation.

Finally, it should be emphasised that this result, however decisive it may be, remains a step rather than a definitive outcome. The measures put in place under Charles VII set in motion a long-term process: they provided an institutional model and tools of government that would be consolidated, corrected or expanded under subsequent reigns. In other words, the standing army was not merely a temporary response to the Hundred Years' War; it was a structural turning point in the history of the monarchical state, because it permanently linked military power to taxation, administration and the centralisation of command.

Drawing from Honoré Bouvet, 'L'Arbre des Batailles,' *c.* 1493, showing men-at-arms of a *compagnie d'ordonnance*. BNF RES-R-272. (Public Domain)

The creation of this permanent army provides insight into the fundamental transformation of France in the fourteenth and fifteenth centuries: the gradual transition from an unstable feudal order to a more administrative monarchy capable of organising and financing warfare. By reforming the military, Charles VII did more than simply strengthen the army, he helped to reshape the very conditions of royal authority and lay one of the most concrete foundations of modern sovereignty.

Appendix I

Ordonnance of 8 January 1374[1]

1. Firstly, that our Constable of France, who is now or will be appointed, shall appoint and order certain persons to receive the *montres* of the people of his *hotel*, and each of our *maréchals*, four lieutenants to receive the *montres* of all kinds of people, and the master of the crossbowmen, one, to receive people from his *hotel* only; these clerks and lieutenants shall be wise and suitable and expert, and shall swear in the presence of the Holy Gospels, before they take up their offices, to uphold and keep the *ordonnances* relating to the said inspections, which are written below; and in the event of the death, transfer or other absence of those who are appointed, other suitable and competent persons shall be appointed in their place, who shall take the same oath as above.

2. Item.[2] Our constable, our *maréchals* the master of the crossbowmen and all the other captains of the armed forces shall, to the best of their ability and with the utmost loyalty, exercise and govern their offices and perform the duties pertaining thereto, to the honour and benefit of our kingdom and our war, as they would do for their own cause, and shall uphold and cause to be upheld and carried out our present *ordonnance* and all things contained therein, without causing any opposition to it by themselves or by others in any manner whatsoever.

3. Item. They, their lieutenants, clerks and deputies mentioned above, or others with authority to do so, shall not receive or allow to be received for montre or review any soldiers unless they are present in person, mounted and sufficiently armed with their own armour and on their own horse or that of their master; and also, when conducting the inspection or review, he shall swear on the Holy Gospels of God that he will serve in such a state or in such good state for the time that he receives our wages, unless he is out of

1 Secousse, *Ordonnances des Roys de France de la troisième race,* Cinquième Volume, p.658.

2 'Item' means 'likewise,' 'furthermore,' or 'in addition' in Old French.

his captain's command or in our service, or loyally exempted from his corps without any fraud, and they shall not receive, support or suffer any other person to be received, written or passed in montre.

4. Item. They shall take in their company and employ good men-at-arms, as they would take them for their own service, whom they know, and who are of such standing that they should be accepted *à nos gages* [i.e. at our expense or wages]; and they shall not dismiss or release them without reasonable cause.

5. Item. If none of them left before the time they were supposed to serve without leave and without loyal exemption, they shall reveal themselves and tell the treasurer of wars or his lieutenant who will make the payment, to have him reduced for the time he was away.

6. Item. They shall make the men-of-war under them swear that they will serve them continually and will not leave without their leave; and also that they will not cause any harm to their power over our people and subjects in any of the countries of our kingdom who are under our obedience, either by coming into our service or by remaining, as long as they are in our said service, or by returning to their countries and homes.

7. Item. They shall make their said men swear, when they are appointed, that they will govern themselves well, loyally and reasonably, without taking anything from closed towns, fortresses and other places, without paying a reasonable price and satisfying the hotels, so that they are satisfied; and also that they will not take or receive money, food or other things from our subjects and obedient subjects for capture or ransom, or for any other reason, other than as stated; and as soon as their wages are paid, they will return to their homes; and if they do not do so, they will lose their horses and their harnesses; and in all other respects they will do as we wish.

8. Item. If the captains send for men-of-war from other countries to serve them in the numbers ordered, and they commit a misdeed on their way to them, those captains shall be held responsible for the misdeed.

9. Item. If the men-of-war who are under no captain commit any pillaging, robbery, or damage during their service, the captains shall pay them themselves, when it comes to their knowledge, without seeking any cunning or malice on the contrary; and if they delay or refuse to do so, we want them to be compelled vigorously and without delay by our lieutenants, war chiefs, and other officers to whom the knowledge belongs; and in the event that it is not possible to identify the persons who have caused the said damage, the captains under whom the said offenders serve shall assemble all their men and make them swear and reveal those who have done so, in order to punish them; and the said captains shall swear to this effect.

10. Item. If any foot men or horsemen are found fleeing the army who are not craftsmen, merchants, or other persons necessary for the service of the

army, the lieutenants or warlords who are there shall compel them to leave and depart; if they refuse, they shall be punished according to the nature of the offence; and all other offenders in the host shall also be punished, without favour or deportation.

11. Item. That all payments to men-of-war shall henceforth be made in separate chambers; and no captain shall receive any payment, nor render account, except for the men of his own household alone; and it is our agreement that those who come at our behest to serve us, which behest shall be apparent from the fact that they shall conduct themselves in the manner described, shall be paid after their departure, arrival and return, as is reasonable.

12. Item. The *maréchals'* clerks shall receive nothing except the montres of captains who have one hundred men-at-arms or more under them.

13. Item. The men-of-war whom we shall henceforth employ in our service shall be divided into routes, each consisting of one hundred men-at-arms, and each company shall have a captain; and below the said number of one hundred men-at-arms, there shall be no captains; thus they shall form companies, according to how they wish to receive their payment.

14. Item. The said captains of one hundred men-at-arms, together with their men, shall be ordered by us to be under the command of lieutenants, war chiefs or other officers, at our pleasure and *ordonnance.*

15. Item. Henceforth, no one shall be captain of men-of-war without our letter and authority or that of our lieutenants and warlords or other princes and lords of our kingdom for our service, defence and security of their country, on pain of losing their horses and armour and all movable property and inheritance.

16. Item. No one shall have rank, except for the captains commanded over the aforementioned hundred men-at-arms, who shall each receive one hundred francs per month; and lieutenants or warlords who have a greater number of men-at-arms under their command shall be given state at our *ordonnance*, at our pleasure.

17. Item. As soon as the montres are made and the men-of-war have received their payment, the captains shall lead them straight away and as quickly as they can to the designated frontiers, without allowing them to linger in the country, and shall keep them in the most suitable places for the benefit of the war, and under the command and orders of the lieutenant or chief of our war, who shall be in that part at that time.

18. Item. Our lieutenants, constables, *maréchals*, masters of crossbowmen, and other captains of men-of-war shall swear; namely those who are presently and those who will come before the letters of office or captaincy are given to them, on the Holy Gospels of God, on their honour and by their faith and loyalty, that they will keep, hold and fulfil the above-mentioned

ordonnances and all things contained therein, point by point; and shall cause them to be kept and fulfilled loyally and truly, without causing them to be violated by themselves or by others (in any manner contained above). And we desire that the aforementioned *ordonnances* be published in Paris, at the borders and in other notable places in the kingdom where it seems expedient to our council and our officers in the matter of our war. In witness whereof, we have caused our seal to be affixed to these letters.

Given at the Bois de Vincennes, on the eighth day of January, in the year of grace one thousand three hundred and seventy-four, and in the tenth year of our reign.

Thus signed
By the King, in his council

Appendix II

Ordonnance of 22 April 1411 on the Matter of Artillery[1]

Paris, Arch. nat., JJ 166, fol. 262v°-263, n° 422; éd. *Ordonnances des rois de France de la troisième race*, t. 9, Paris, Impr. royale, 1755, pp.589–590.

Charles, etc. Let it be known to all present and future that as there was a certain dispute between our beloved and loyal *maréchals de France* on the one hand and the master of the crossbowmen of France on the other, saying that it belongs to our *maréchals* to have knowledge of the archers and gunners who, by our command, arm themselves and come into our service, and that the said archers and gunners must be received by them or by their clerks, for montres and reviewed, and that they must take and have letters from them, and also have knowledge of them as they have of the men of war who are commanded by us, the said master of the crossbowmen saying the contrary, and that it belongs to him and to no other to receive and cause to be received the said inspections and reviews of the said archers and gunners; and that through him their letters must be given to them so that they may be paid their wages.

Finally, to avoid any matters of disagreement and inconvenience that may arise from the above or in the future, our beloved and loyal Jehan le Maingre, known as Bouciquaut [*sic*], *Maréchal*, and Jehan, Lord of Hengest, master of the crossbowmen of France, appearing before us in person, have agreed that this matter should be discussed by and in our Grand Council and that whatever is decided by our said council should be declared and decreed by us to be binding and valid forever or in the future, and they have humbly begged us to do so; and we, at their request, have discussed the above-mentioned matter in our Grand Council, assembled in our presence, with a very large number of notable persons, both of our blood and of our said council, and the matter mentioned above having been discussed and

1 Bessey, *Construire l'armée française*, Tome I, pp.86–87.

debated, it was found and concluded by our said council that the knowledge of the said archers and gunners belongs and must belong to our said *maréchals* who are now and who will be in the future; and they must receive and cause to be received the muster and review when necessary.

For this reason, having heard the petition of the aforementioned Bouciquaut, *Maréchal*, and Lord of Hengest, Master of Crossbowmen, the said conclusion of our said council, have declared and ordered, and by these presents declare and order that the knowledge of these archers and gunners shall belong and remain perpetually to our said *maréchals* who are now and to their successors in said office, and that these archers and gunners shall henceforth receive montres and be reviewed by our said *maréchals* whenever the occasion arises, and shall be given a letter to be paid their wages by those to whom it may pertain; and we wish and decree that these declarations and ordinances shall be valid and upheld and maintained in our kingdom forever, so that no further dispute may arise between our officers mentioned above.

We hereby command our beloved and loyal subjects, the members of our present Parliament in Paris and those who will serve in future Parliaments, our accountants and treasurers in Paris, the general counsellors on the matter of the aid ordered for the war, the treasurers of our wars and all our other justiciars and officers present and future, or their lieutenants, and each of them, as befits them, that our declarations and ordinances mentioned above be recorded in the registers of our said Court of Parliament, of our said Chamber of Accounts and elsewhere where it may be appropriate, and that they be held, kept and observed perpetually without infringement in any way. And let this be a firm and established thing forever. We have affixed our seal to these presents, except in other matters our right and that of others in all.

Given in Paris, on the twenty-second day of April, in the year of our Lord one thousand four hundred and eleven, and of our reign the thirty-first.

By the King, in his council, where Monseigneur de Guyenne, Louis Duke of Bavaria, you, the bishops of Noyon and Tournay, the admiral, the lords of Omont, Rambures, Louroy and Savoisy, Sir Anthoyne de Craon and Regnault d'Angennes, were present.

[Signed:] Derian

Appendix III

Excerpts from the 13th account of Hémon Raguier, Treasurer of Wars, Relating to the Siege Of Gallerande in July 1426[1]

(copy of seventeenth century, ms. fr. 20.684, f. 548, another copy of the same account appearing in the manuscript fr. 32510, f. 59 v°)

To the captains and soldiers named below, who, from July 1426, were paid while serving in the company of His Lordship the Constable, laying siege to the fortress of Gallerande occupied by the English and that of Les Roches (?), which were surrendered to the English, namely:

> to Dizaroty the Jew for the payment of himself and 38 men-at-arms and 57 men-of-trait from the garrison of La Flesche,
>
> to Bouzon de Comerque, him and 75 men-at-arms, etc., 21 men-of-trait from the Craon garrison,
>
> to Sir Guillaume de Mauny, knight, him, two other knights, 15 men-at-arms and 22 men-of-trait from the garrison of Chasteau du Loir,
>
> to Louis Dolo, him, 16 men-at-arms and 9 men-of-trait,
>
> to Lois Mignon, him, 17 men-at-arms and 9 men-of-trait,
>
> to Sir André d'Averton, knight bachelor, him, 6 men-at-arms and 3 men-of-trait,

1 Planchenault, 'La Conquête du Maine par les Anglais', pp.149–151.

to Tugdual Bourgoys, him, 91 men-at-arms and 68 men-of-trait from the garrison of Durestal,

to Jehan Tibergeau, him, 12 men-at-arms and 9 men-of-trait,

to Jehan Rougebec, him, 5 men-at-arms and 9 men-of-trait from the garrison of Meaune (?),

to Geufroy le Breton, him, 17 men-at-arms and 18 men-of-trait,

to Jamet de Pernes, him, 16 men-at-arms and 23 men-of-trait from the garrison of Beaugé,

to Jehan Roy, 11 men-at-arms (7 men-at-arms, fr. 32510) and 9 men-of-trait from the Briolay garrison,

to Alain de la Chapelle, him, 29 men-at-arms and 21 men-of-trait from the garrison of Beaufort,

to Benegon de l'Estoille, him, 17 men-at-arms, including one knight and 12 men-of-trait,

to Jehan de Nevers, him, 16 men-at-arms, 20 men-of-trait from the garrison of Langés,

to Jocclin de Quitte, 16 men-at-arms, 9 men-of-trait,

to Jehan de la Chappelle, 45 men-at-arms, 18 men-of-trait,

to Sir Geufroye de la Haye, knight, another knight bachelor, 36 men-at-arms and 18 men-of-trait,

to the Bastard of La Bellière, 58 men-at-arms and 31 men-of-trait,

to Regnault de Lannoy, captain of Le Lude, 20 men-at-arms and 11 men-of-trait,

to Guion de Fromentières, 11 men-at-arms and 4 men-of-trait.

Appendix IV

Copy of the 1445 Order

Catalan version of the 'copy of the *ordonnance*' concerning the soldiers of King Charles VII of France, obtained by Étienne Petit. Undated. (Original drafted between 1 and 15 March 1445, copy made before 8 April 1445)

(f. 43r°)
Per metre a les gents d'armes e que lo Reyalme sia sens pullaria, lo Roy ordonen per governar los dits gens d'armes XV. o XVI. capitanes qui n'hauran lo carrech.

Primerament, lo Roy vol e ordone que totes les companyes de gents d'armes sien netejades de bagatge, e que tots los dits gents d'armes seran reduhits al nombre de XV cents lances e III^{m}. arches. e haura cascun hom d'armes III chevalx e I consetller e I patge, e II archiers hauran III chevalx. Qui es de combatents, los dits XV^{C} lances e archiers, VI^{m} combatents, los quals, a III chevalx per lance e III chevalx per II archiers, se monten en nombre tot VIIII^{m} chevalx.

Sequen-se los noms d'aquells que lo Roy vol que hajen lo carrech dels dits gents d'armes

Primerament lo Conestable (Arthur III de Richemont)	C lances II^{c} archiers
mossr lo mareschal de Loeac (André de Laval, seigneur de Lohéac)	C lances II^{c} archiers
moss. lo seneschal (Pierre de Brézé, sénéchal d'Anjou)	C lances II^{c} archiers
moss. Reynalt de Dresnay (Regnault de Dresnay)	C lances II^{c} archiers
moss. de Beauvau (Louis de Beauveau)	C lances II^{c} archiers

Ffloquet (Robert de Floques, Bailli d'Évreux)	C lances II^{c} archiers
Piere Louvain (Pierre Louvain, vicomte de Berzy)	C lances II^{c} archiers
moss. lo mareschal de Jaloynges (Philippe de Culant, sr de Jalognes)	C lances II^{c} archiers
moss. de Culant (Charles de Culant)	C lances II^{c} archiers
Lo cadet d'Alebret (Charles II d'Albret)	C lances II^{c} archiers
moss. de Bueil (Jean V de Bueil)	C lances II^{c} archiers
Poton (Poton de Xaintrailles)	C lances II^{c} archiers
Joaxin (Joachim Rouault, *Maréchal de France*)	LXX lances VII^{xx} archiers
mess. Johan de Totavilla (Jean d'Estouteville, sr de Torcy et Blainville)	LXX lances VII^{xx} archiers
Robiner Petitlo (Robin Pettylow, Ecossais) & Robert Coningan	
(Robert Conningham, capitaine de la garde écossaise)	LXX lances II^{c} archiers
moss. Marti Garayt (Martin Garcia?)	XXV lances L archiers
moss. Tealde (Theaude de Valpergue, Italien)	XXV lances L archiers
moss. Gui d'Alsigny (Guy d'Alsigny?)	XX lances XL archiers
Item, a dos qui's tindran ab lo rey	XX lances XL archiers

Ayxi monte lo dit nombre de gents d'armes XV cents lances e III^{m}. Archiers e ~~XV~~ cents consetllers, lo qual nombre de gents d'armes e de tret seran logatz e provehits en la manera seguent

(f. 43v)
Es a seber que lo rey fera loyats los dits gents d'armes per tots los pays de la sua obadiença, exceptat Languedoch, e seran fornits de viures de IIII. franchs per lance e II. franchs per archier pro mes.

Primerament, al bas pays d'Alvernia (Auvergne)	C lances II^{c} archiers
Item, al alt pais d'Alvernia	C lances II^{c} archiers
Item, en Roergua (Rouergue) o Querci (Quercy)	C lances II^{c} archiers
Item, en Arminyach (Armagnac) e Cominge (Comminges)	C lances II^{c} archiers

Item, en Borbonois (Bourbonnais) Forests (Forez)	C lances IIc archiers
Beaujolois (Beaujolais) e Lionnois (Lyonnais)	
Item, Gevalda (Gévaudan) Viverois (Vivarais)	
e Velay	CL lances II[c] archiers
Item, en Berry -----	C lances II[c] archiers
Item, en Poitou Xantonge (Saintonge)	
e Engemois (Angoumois)	CC (CL?) lances IIIc archiers
Item, en Torene (Touraine) desa o dela la	
Ribera de Lera (Loire) e la conte de Blois	C lances II[c] archiers
Item, entorn de la Ribera de Lera	C lances II[c] archiers
Item, en Nivernois (Nivernais), la contat de Gien e de Juyngny (Joigny), d'Estampes,	
de Montargis, de Niors, lo ducat de Nemors (Nemours) e tota la Bealte (Beauce)	
de Chartres fins a Vendosme (Vendôme), e lo ducat d'Orliens (Orléans)	
de la part dela la Bealte	C lances II[c] archiers
Item, al pais de Francha (Ile-de-France) de sa Seine	
en Brya (Brie) e Xampanya (Champagne)	C lances II[c] archiers
Item, en Limosi alt e bas (Limousin haut et bas)	C lances II[c] archiers
	Summa XIIII[c] lances logatz als pays dessus dits

A tota montbeliart, Bar e Lorraine que no son compres en aquell nombre, semble que lo Rey deu present despertir los pais, e dir a cascun dels caps dels dits gents d'armes e de tret on ilz seran lojats, assi que cascun trasmeta diligement al pais la ont ells deuran esser lojats per gardar los de pillaria e ansi per divisar lur logis. e que lo rey de present commete gents en cascun

[n° 44r°] pais qui stiguen ab les gents dels dits capitanes per fer lur dits logis, e axi mateix per avisar al fet dels viures, affi que, com los dits gents d'armes vindran al pais la ont seran logats, qu·ells troben viures per un mes on, per tal que ells no hagen causes de anar sobre los camps.

Item, los dits gents d'armes e de tret se logeran per lo pais aqui ont lo rey ordoneran, e cascun capitane de cent lances e IIc archiers aviseran en lur companya X. homens de be, als quals ells donaran lo carrech de VIIII°.

lances a cascun els archiers, e seran com cap de cambre, e seran lojats per Xnes de lances els archiers als millors villas e lochs del pais ont ells seran ordonats e ont haura justicia.

Item, per lo fet dels viures, lo Rey scriura als stats de cascun pais, es a seber fins al nombre de XII tan de glesia com nobles e altres, qui s'assemblaran ab los elegits e quils avisaran la manera dels lurs viures e del lur logis e en aquella manera los dits viures se pagaran, o que sia avisat de liurar los dits viures per castellania, e que de present sia avisat quals viures son rasonables per mes per cent lances e IIc archiers, qui son de nombre de gents e de chevalx, ço es a seber VIc homens e VIc chevalx. e que hom faça diligencia dels saber e, incontinent com hon haura vista e avisada la quantitat dels viures que son necessaris, que de continent en transmete per lo pais per fer que los dits gents d'armes sien provesits sitost quells arribaran a lur logis.

Item, sera ordonat que com los dits gents d'armes seran logiats aqui on lur sera ordenat, que degun d'ells no sia gosat ni ardit de cavalcar ne anar fora de la vila on sera logat sens licencia d'aquell qui sera cap de cambre, lo qual sia tengut60 de la venir dir an aquell de la justicia de la vila ont ells seran logats. Los quals de la justicia metran en scrit les noms d'aquells qui yran deffora e lo jorn que ells partiran aximateix lo jorn que ells tornara. e ayxi se sabra leugerament qual sera robador ni destrossador per lo pais.

Item, que lo Rey ordonen als capitanes que cascun tingue ses gents en tal orde e justicia que la mercadansa e la labor se pugen fer, en tal manera que cascun pugue anar segurament per los camps. e qui fara lo contrari, que lo Rey lo faça punir talment en bens e en cors que tots altres y prenguen exempli.

Item, que lo Rey fara fer mostres de mes en mes e par ayxi en sabra tots (n°44v°) jorns si les gents hi son, o que cascun mes sia feta revisitacio e de tres en tres mesos plena mostra, o de dos en dos mes com los pagaments d'argent se faran als dits gents d'armes.

Item, semble que valria mils fer lo pagament als dits gents d'armes de dos en dos mes, e per so se'n seguiria pus sovint mostra per que seria mils conegut si lo nombre dels dits gents d'armes y sera e en quin habillement ells se tindran."

(Arxiu Històric de la Ciutat de Barcelona, Consell de Cent, 1B X-15, f. 43r° - f. 44v°).[1]

1 Péquignot, 'De la France à Barcelone. Une version catalane de 'l'ordonnance perdue.' pp.825–828.

Appendix V

Poitou, to House Men-of-War, *Ordonnance* of 26 May 1445[1]

In order to put an end to the pillaging that has long been prevalent in our kingdom, to protect and preserve our lands and subjects from the evils and oppressions they have suffered in times past because of the bad and disorderly lives led by the men-of-war who occupied the fields and lived off them, we have, after much careful deliberation, made certain just and reasonable *ordonnances* concerning the manner and order of life of the said men-of-war and their lodgings, for the good and relief of our people, and so that everyone may come and go safely and without danger throughout all the lands under our obedience, to do their labour or trade and live according to their station.

By which [*ordonnances*], among other things, in order to complete the great destruction that was taking place, due to the large and excessive number of horses and worthless people who were in these companies and who were of no use, except to plunder and eat the people, it was ordered that all the said baggage be put and thrown out of the said companies and sent each to their hotels and homes to do their trades and live as they had been accustomed to do before they came to war, and that only a certain number of men-of-war and men-of-trait should remain, namely, for each man-at-arms: a squire, a page and three horses, and two archers: a page or a war servant and three horses; for the conduct of whom we have appointed and commissioned certain notables among our subjects, who are well-resident and have something to lose in our kingdom, who are experts and knowledgeable in such matters; who shall be bound to answer and give account for the men in their charge and that no harm be done by them to our said lands and subjects; and because, in order to keep the fields as they were accustomed to do, it was highly doubtful that they would not stray or

1 Bessey, *Construire l'armée française*, Tome I, pp.102–105.

refuse to obey their leaders, had it not been so easy to bring them to order as was necessary.

We have, moreover, ordered, for the sake of fairness and ease for our said people, that the said men-of-war shall be lodged in the good towns of all the countries of our kingdom, each according to what he can reasonably bear, as is more fully contained in our said *ordonnances*; and among others, we have ordered that in the country of Poitou, 190 lances and archers shall be lodged, that is to say, under our beloved and loyal seneschal of the said country [note: Pierre de Brézé], 60 lances under the *Maréchal de* Lohéac in Lower Poitou, and 30 lances from Floquet's contingent, and the archers, who are together, at three persons and three horses per lance, and, for two archers, three persons and three horses, 1,140 persons and as many horses.

They shall be provided with provisions by the people of the said country in the following manner: for each person, for a whole year, one and a half loads of wheat and two pipes of wine; item for a man-at-arms, the archers, who shall be six persons, per month two and a half sheep, an ox or a cow, or other equivalent meat, and per year four sides of bacon; item for salt and oil, candles, eggs and cheese for the days when no meat is eaten, with their other minor necessities, twenty sous tournois per month for the men-at-arms and the archers. And for each horse per year, twelve horses loaded with oats and four cartloads of hay and straw, that is to say, two parts hay and one part straw, or other such provisions as you deem necessary for the said men-at-arms and archers and their said horses.

In order to provide for, employ, impose, gather, raise and bring into lodgings the said men-at-arms, and, moreover, to carry out our said orders in these countries, we need to appoint people who are notable, powerful, expert and well-versed in such matters and who love the good of the public, knowing that we can fully trust your judgement, loyalty, prudence, diligence and experience in such matters, we have appointed and commissioned you, and by the terms of this document, we appoint and commission you, and two or three of you, in the absence of the others, to advise on the places and locations that you deem most suitable and appropriate for the lodging of the said men-of-war, and to lodge them in these places according to the contents of our said ordinances, and, with this to establish, impose and levy on all the said countries, as justly and equally as may be done, the strong bearing the weak, the provisions and money mentioned above which will be necessary for them, together with reasonable and moderate expenses, up to the sum of .... livres tournois, and to have these collected, raised and brought together and distributed to the said men-of-war, in the manner and form mentioned above, and to compel the lords and inhabitants of the towns where they are to be lodged, whether they be clergy or laymen or any other persons to whom it may pertain, to give you access and full obedience to this, to lodge the said men-at-arms and likewise those who have been assessed and taxed for the said provisions, money and expenses, exempt and non-exempt, privileged and non-privileged, and without prejudice to their privileges for this occasion, to pay their share and portions per quarter of a year, beginning their payment for the said quarter on the first day that the said men-at-arms enter the said towns, and by all the usual means used for our own debts, notwithstanding any opposition or appeals whatsoever.

And furthermore, in the event that there are none who refuse, deny or contradict the above-mentioned matters, we nevertheless wish, despite the aforementioned constraints and coercions that we have imposed in this matter, that you postpone or cause to be postponed their appearance in person, on a certain appropriate day, in the event that they cannot personally take and apprehend them, to execute the said constraints, before us and the people of our Grand Council, wherever we may be, under penalty of banishment and confiscation of body and property, to answer to our prosecutor for such purposes and conclusions as he may choose to bring against them and each of them, concerning the said disobedience, refusal or delay, proceed and go forward according to reason, as appropriate, taking and placing all their movable and immovable property, if they are lay people, and, if they are people of the church, their temporal property in our hands, in reality and in fact, and give them to sufficient and suitable persons to manage and govern, who can and know how to respond and give account when and to whom it may be necessary, notwithstanding the above, at least until we order otherwise, for thus we will and have ordered it to be done. To this end, we grant you power, commission, authority and special mandate, and we order and command all our justices, officers and subjects to obey you diligently in this matter and to lend you and give you advice, comfort, help and imprisonment if you need it and request it.

Given at Luppé-le-Chastel, on the twenty-sixth day of May, in the year of our Lord one thousand four hundred and forty-five, and in the twenty-third year of our reign.

Under our seal, ordered in the absence of the grand master
By the King, in his council
Delaloere

Appendix VI

Ordonnance of 28 April 1448, 9 November 1451 and 1459 Establishing the *Francs-Archers*[1]

Letter to raise the *francs-archers.*

Charles, etc., to the Seneschal of Poitou or his lieutenant and to the elected representatives regarding the aid (taxes) ordered for the war in the country and county of Poitou, to our beloved and loyal notary and secretary Master Jehan Besuchet, greetings.

After we had put an end to the widespread and disorderly pillaging that had long afflicted our subjects and had brought order to the affairs and maintenance of our men-of-war, we decided, after careful and mature deliberation by our council, advised that in order to provide for the safety and defence of our kingdom and lordship, in the event that by means of the truce which is now between us and our nephew of England we cannot achieve peace, be it offence, we may help and serve in the said act of war, without the need to seek help from others than our said subjects.

For this reason, after much careful deliberation with several of our lords of our blood and lineage, the members of our Grand Council, and other notable individuals, we have decided and ordered, and hereby decide and order, for the least burden and expense to our subjects, that in every parish of our said kingdom there shall be an archer who shall be and remain continually in sufficient and suitable attire, with a sallet, dagger, sword with *trousse*, jack or brigandine coat, and shall be called *francs-archers.*

Those who will be elected and chosen by you in the said election, the most skilled and proficient in the art and practice of archery who can be found in each parish, without regard or favour to wealth or to any requests that may be made to us in this regard.

1 Bessey, *Construire l'armée française, Tome I*, pp.114–121.

And they shall be required to maintain themselves in the aforementioned attire and to practise archery and to attend in their aforementioned attire all feast days and non-working days so that they may become more skilled and accustomed to the aforementioned exercise in order to serve us whenever we summon them.

And we shall pay them four francs per man for each month they serve us. And so that the said archers may have more resources and be more eager to wear and maintain the said state and clothing, we have ordered and do order by these presents that they and each of them shall be free, clear and exempt. And we hereby free, release and exempt them from all taxes and other charges whatsoever that may be imposed upon them by our kingdom and state for the maintenance of our said men-of-war, watchmen, gatekeepers and all other subjects whatsoever. Except for the aid ordered for the war and the salt tax. We hereby forbid the commissioners who will be appointed to impose and establish taxes and other levies on them on our behalf from subjecting them to such taxes. And to the lords and captains or castellans of the castellanies, that they shall not henceforth compel them to perform the said watch and guard duty, and for greater certainty of this, we desire and command you to grant them letters of exemption as you see fit. Which we desire to be valid as if they had obtained them from us.

And that they be more obliged to serve us and maintain themselves skilfully in the aforementioned manner. We desire and order that the said archers and each one of them shall take an oath in your hands to serve us well and loyally with their aforementioned clothing against all and to practise in the manner described, even in our wars and affairs, whenever we summon them. And none shall serve in war or in said manner without our order, on pain of losing their franchise and being punished.

And furthermore, we desire and order that the said *francs-archers* shall be registered by us by their names and surnames and the parishes where they reside, and that a register shall be kept in the court of your elected representatives, so that we may assist them and recover them promptly whenever we so require.

We hereby order and command you to carry out this *ordonnance* in the said election and in accordance with the instructions given to you in this regard. And to uphold and maintain this order, compel and cause to be compelled all those concerned by all customary means to do so for our own debts, tasks and affairs. Notwithstanding any opposition or appeals whatsoever, for which we do not wish to be delayed in any way in doing and executing the above-mentioned things, and each of them we have given and ordered full power, authority, commission and special mandate, we order and command all our justices, officers and subjects that they obey and diligently hear, promptly and give advice, comfort, assistance and imprisonment if such is required by you, and to the *vidimus* [i.e., 'we have seen', a certification of the conformity of the text] of these presents made under the royal seal, full faith shall be added as to this present original given at Montils-les-Tours on the twenty-eighth day of April in the year of grace one thousand four hundred and forty-eight and of our reign the twenty-sixth. Thus signed by the King in his council.

Instruction on the manner in which the King has ordered to be carried out, to raise and establish *francs-archers* and crossbowmen for the protection and defence of his kingdom.

1. Firstly, that the commissioners and elected officials, who will be appointed for this purpose in each country, will see from the election papers the number of parishes in the said country, and will know from their papers which are the most and least powerful; and according to this, they will draw up and write on a sheet of paper the assessment of the said archers by parish.

2. Item, in order to have no disparity in the assessment of the said archers, shall place one archer in each parish as reasonably as it can bear, having regard to the assessment of the poll tax, to those who will be more powerful and those who will be less, at their discretion.

3. Item, and since the plates of these archers cannot be divided equally as money can be, the said commissioners and elected officials shall not take into account three, four, five, six fires, more or less, either in number or in power.

4. Item, poor parishes, which are only taxed on two, three, four, five or six households, should not be included in this; however, if three or four parishes could provide one archer, this remains at the discretion of the commissioners and elected officials.

5. Item, this done, the said commissioners shall travel to all the parishes where the said archers are established, or at least to the castellanies, and shall speak to the inhabitants thereof, and shall ascertain and inquire which of them is the most skilled and fit to use a bow or crossbow, and shall not take them from among the wealthiest or at the request of the applicants; and when they have found him, they shall tell the parishioners that it is the King's pleasure, for the defence of the kingdom and several other good causes which they shall state, that the said archer shall be exempt from the King's taxes, from those of the men-at-arms, from watch, gate guard and all other subsidies, except for the aids and the salt tax, and they shall be forbidden, when dividing up the said taxes and subsidies, to impose them henceforth; and likewise the lord, captain, castellan or others to whom it may pertain shall not compel them to pay watch or gate guard duties; and this done, the said archer shall be accepted, if he is suitable for this; and in doing so, this archer shall be bound to maintain himself in point of hucque [i.e. a kind of cape with a hood] of brigandine or jack, sallet, sword, dagger, bow and trousse [i.e. a set of 18 arrows] or a loaded crossbow, as ordered, and to come into the service of the King, whenever the King summons him, paying him four pounds tournois per month for as long as he remains in the King's service; and he shall be commanded to be ready with all the aforementioned equipment within two months.

6. Item, the said commissioners and elected officials shall grant each archer a charter of franchise on the said land.

7. Item, The King shall appoint in each country a man of good character who shall be responsible for visiting all the archers after they have been thus set, and for ascertaining whether they are in good order, and for assembling them whenever the King summons them or whenever he pleases, to whom the said commissioners shall give the names and surnames of the said archers and the parishes where they have been residing.

8. Item, and in the event that the said commissioners and elected officials find in any good parish a good fellow accustomed to war who does not have the means to acquire the aforementioned clothing and is suitable to be an archer, the said commissioners and elected officials shall ask the inhabitants if they wish to help him obtain the said clothing, which may be to their advantage, as the exemption of the said companion is not very costly, and the said parish will not be greatly burdened by it; and if it should happen that the said companion should pass away or that he should be charged with providing another, in that case the said clothing shall remain with the said inhabitants, to be disposed of at their pleasure and given to whoever is appointed to wear it.

9. Item, the chosen archer shall be required to shoot with the bow at feast days or practice in the attire prescribed for him, together with others who wish to shoot for practice; and the said archer shall be required to attend all non-working feast days in full attire.

10. Item, the parishioners of each parish shall be required to ensure that the archer lodged in their parish does not dare to leave, sell or pledge his clothing; and if this should happen, they shall be required to inform the elected representatives; and likewise, if he dies, another shall be provided for him without delay.

11. Item, no one may seize or pledge the said archer's military clothing for any debt whatsoever; and if it should happen that any execution or seizure is made on his clothing, or that any sale is made by the said archer or by another, the person who has purchased it shall be required to return it and restore it free and clear, and shall pay the arbitrary fine to the King; and if any royal sergeant or other person executes any forfeiture on the said clothing, he shall be deprived of his office and shall pay the fine; and if the archer so desires, he shall be deprived of his franchise.

12. Item, the lord of the castle, or his captain acting on his behalf, shall be required to inspect the archers of his manor every month; and if he finds any fault, he shall be required to report it to the King's commissioners or elected representatives so that it may be remedied.

13. Item, the said commissioners and elected officials shall administer the oath and make the said *francs-archers*, and each of them, swear to serve the King well and loyally in their said capacity, against all others, in his wars and other affairs, whenever and wherever the King may command and inform them, and not otherwise, on pain of losing the said franchise, without the King's *ordonnance*.

14. Item, the said commissioners and elected officials shall be required to keep a register of the said *francs-archers*, their names and surnames, so that when the King wishes to enlist the help of the said *francs-archers*, he

may freely obtain and recover them by means of the paper and register of the said elected officials, by writing to them and sending a duplicate to the King.

Issued by the King, our Lord, while in council at Montilz-lez-Tours, on the 28th day of April, in the year one thousand four hundred and forty-eight.
Signed: J. Delaloere.[2]

Articles Added in 1451:

Instructions from the King regarding what the captains of the *francs-archers* shall henceforth do in every place, in the governance of the people under their command.

15. The said captains shall take an oath to the King, or to those whom he may appoint, and likewise shall take oaths before the Royal seneschals or bailiffs of the places where each of them shall be appointed captain.

16. Item and they, the captains, shall be required to know and inquire into the number of *francs-archers* who are assigned to their command and captaincy for these purposes, to know how they are dressed and armed. And if they are not well armed and dressed, they shall compel them to maintain themselves in good condition and attire, as has been customary hitherto.

17. Item and if, in searching for the said francs-archers, the said captains find none who are fit for military service, they shall record them all in a register. And this matter shall be dealt with by the elected representatives of the said places or their lieutenants. And by the counsel of each of them, others shall be appointed as they see fit among themselves.

18. Item and if the said captains find that in the countries under their charge the number of *francs-archers* ordered to be stationed there has not been or is not being stationed. That is to say, fifty fires or approximately one franc-archer, the said captains or elected representatives or both shall make up the shortfall. And they shall be dressed like the others named above, in accordance with the *ordonnance* of the country.

19. Item if any of the said *francs-archers*, after having been clothed and equipped, sell or redistribute their military clothing, the said captains shall compel them to clothe themselves and equip themselves again at their own expense. And if they do not have the means to equip themselves, they shall be punished accordingly. And in their place, others shall be appointed by the council and advice of the aforementioned and otherwise not.

20. Item and the said captains shall be required to conduct inspections and reviews of the people under their charge and to summon with them one of the elected representatives or lieutenants every four months, or every half-year. And they shall not assemble all their men together in one place to conduct montres, so as to minimise their work and prevent pillaging.

2 Bessey, *Construire l'armée française, Tome I*, pp.114–121.

But they shall assemble them by castellany or by fours or fifties and shall only bring them from four leagues or five at most, to avoid hardship and expense.

21. Item and immediately upon receiving the first watch made by each of the said captains of the people under their command, these captains shall send to the King the number of all their *francs-archers* under their command, along with everything they have found in these countries concerning the aforementioned matters, and their opinions and those of the elected representatives of each election. In order to provide the necessary provisions for this purpose.

22. Item and each of said captains shall receive, for their trouble and for the purpose of attending to and hearing the matters mentioned above properly and diligently, the sum of one hundred and twenty livres tournois for their wages and twenty livres tournois for their horsemanship, which shall be paid to them each year by the collectors appointed for the payment of men-of-war and by order of the King, along with the expenses incurred in each of the said elections, and by the receipt of the said captains.

Done at Villedieu le Comble near Saint-Maixent on the ninth day of November in the year one thousand four hundred and fifty-one.
Signed A. de Laloere

Ordonnance made in the year one thousand four hundred and fifty-nine.

23. Item and since several complaints have been made because it is said that the distribution of *francs-archers* has been uneven and poorly allocated across the electoral districts of this kingdom, we desire that everywhere the said elected persons within each electoral district shall be equal in the matter of the said *francs-archers* according to the number of households and the means and power of each parish, so that no parish shall be more burdened than the others, and shall, if necessary, issue another commission or order forthwith to comply with our present *ordonnance*.

24. Item and because several captains of the said *francs-archers* have sought and seek to compel the parishes from which they draw these *francs-archers* to provide them with various items that place a heavy burden on the poor people, we desire that the said parishes be required to provide nothing to the said *francs-archers* other than their military clothing and nothing else.

25. Item and when the said *francs-archers* have returned to their homes, they may only wear the clothing they have received from the parish on feast days, when they wish to practise archery or crossbow shooting or other skills in order to become more adept at serving in war. And on days when they are at work or otherwise as stated, they may not wear the said clothing.

26. Item because we have had several brigandines delivered to several captains of the said *francs-archers* to distribute to the said *francs-archers*, and may do so again in the future, we wish and order that the said elected

representatives or their clerks inquire how the said captains have distributed the said brigandines. So that the said distribution may be to the benefit of the said parishes. And with this, we want the said elected representatives or clerks to inquire whether these captains have taken any money as a gift for lending the said brigandines and that those of the said captains who have taken the said gift be required to return it. And with this, punish them according to the requirements of the case.

Appendix VII

The King's Entry into Rouen on 10 November 1449, According to Gilles (Jacques) le Bouvier[1]

The King of France, accompanied by the King of Sicily and other lords of the blood, celebrated All Saints' Day with great joy at the aforementioned place of Sainte-Catherine. And on the Monday following 10 November, the eve of Saint Martin's Day, he departed from there to enter his city of Rouen, accompanied by the aforementioned lords in many grand and rich garments, some covered and their horses draped in gold and velvet, the others in embroidery of gold, Damask cloth and satin in many styles and fashions, some with large white crosses and others with different decorations. Among them, after the King, were the Counts of Nevers and Saint-Pol, dressed in the finest garments. The Count of Saint-Pol was armed in white, on a horse harnessed in black satin studded with gold; and after him three pages dressed and their horses harnessed in the same manner as their lord, one of whom carried a lance covered in vermilion velvet, another covered in gold cloth, and another with an armet on his head made entirely of richly crafted fine gold. And after them was the groom, mounted, dressed and harnessed like the said pages, leading a great steed covered in gold cloth down to its feet. The Count of Nevers had eight gentlemen covered in vermilion satin with large white crosses.

The King of France rode, fully armed in white, on a steed covered from head to toe in azure velvet, embroidered with golden fleurs-de-lis, wearing a vermilion velvet hat topped with a gold tassel. Behind him rode his pages, carrying his head armour covered with fine gold in various styles of goldsmithing and ostrich feathers of many colours. At his head was the King of Sicily and on his left the Count of Maine, armed in white and their

1 Le Bouvier, *Les chroniques de Normandie*, pp.132–137.

horses richly adorned and covered with blankets resembling white crosses strewn with gold tassels, and their pages similarly.

Next came the Count of Clermont and other lords of France, each according to his rank, dressed in rich attire.

After him came the Lord of Culant, Grand Master of the *Hotel*, riding a noble covered steed, armed (in full armour), with a fine gold scarf hanging from his neck down to the croup of his horse, and his pages before him; he was the governor of the bataille, where there were six hundred lances, each bearing a small banner of vermilion satin with a golden sun.

The said pages of the King of France were dressed in vermilion, their sleeves entirely covered with white goldwork. Behind the said master of the hostel was a squire carrying the standard of the King of France, which was made of crimson satin strewn with golden suns; and closest to him were the said six hundred lances.

A little ahead was the King's cutler, mounted on a large warhorse, carrying the pennant, which was made of azure velvet with three gold fleurs-de-lis embroidered with large pearls.

Before the King of France stood Poton de Xaintrailles, Bailiff of Berry and squire of the royal household, mounted on a great steed harnessed in azure velvet studded with large silver-gilt *affiques* [*affiquet*: jewellery, fastener, ornament attached to clothing], armed entirely in white; who wore a large ceremonial sword with a gold pommel and cross, and a belt and scabbard covered in azure velvet studded with gold fleurs-de-lis, and the buckle and bit of the sword's hilt were likewise decorated in the same manner.

Near him in front was Pierre de Fonteuil [or de Fontenil], squire of the escutcheon, armed, mounted and harnessed like the other, wearing a pointed hat on his head, made of vermilion velvet lined with ermine [another version of the text specifies: who wore a scarlet purple cloak lined with ermine as a scarf].

Before him stood Sir Guillaume Jouvenel des Ursins, Lord of Trainel and Chancellor of France, dressed in royal robes and a fur-lined hood, with a scarlet cloak, and before him a white mare covered with golden fleurs-de-lis and embroidery on azure velvet similar to the King's, and on the blanket a small casket covered with azure velvet strewn with fine golden fleurs-de-lis, where were the great seals of the King of France, which mare was led by hand by a foot valet.

Before were nine trumpeters, with all the banners of their lords, who sounded one after the other. And between them and the said chancellor were several heralds and attendants of the King and other lords, who were richly dressed and clad in their coats of arms.

And at the very front were the King's Archers, all dressed in jackets studded with gold and silver and coloured red, white and green, those of the King of Sicily, the Count of Maine and several other lords who were there, numbering six hundred archers, well mounted, all wearing brigandines and jacks of various styles, leg armour, and all their swords, daggers and head armour covered and trimmed with silver. They were led by the Lord of Pruilly [or Prully], the Lord of Clère, Sir Théaude de Valpergue and others, whose horses were covered with satin of various colours, in several materials…

(Before the King) Came the Lord of Dunois, mounted on a horse covered in vermilion velvet with a white cross, dressed in a similar jacket lined with sable marten fur, wearing a black velvet hat, and with a sword at his side adorned with gold and stones, which was valued at twenty thousand *écus*; and the Seneschal of Poitou and Jacques Cœur, treasurer, mounted and dressed like the said Lord of Dunois.

Appendix VIII

Order from Charles VII to The Generals and Financial Advisers to Pay, For Three Months and Without Watches, Through Macé De Launay, 600 Lances and 450 Small Wages, Intended for The Expedition to Guyenne. La Guerche, 21 April 1451[1]

(Charles, by the Grace of God, King of France, to our beloved and loyal generals and counsellors...) have ordered and hereby order that six hundred lances and four hundred and fifty small lances [payments being made immediately] be supplied by our command and order to the said country of Normandy, to be paid for by the said Macé de Launay, without inspection or review, and by receipts from the said captains on behalf of themselves and their men for the said three months at the rate of thirty-one francs per month for each full lance, including the captain's status, and ten francs per month for each small lance, from the funds [ordered] by us to be placed in the said country for the above-mentioned payment, namely: under our cousin, the Count of Dunois, one hundred lances provided and only ninety-six small payments [*petites payes*], because Saquet de Jaucourt, knight, and Hector du Sel have only thirty-six, and the four remaining of forty [small] payments, which we thought that the said Saquet and Hector had, have

1 Bibliothèque nationale de France, ms. Fr. 25712, no.247; Gruel, *Chronique de Richemont*, pp.279–280.

always been paid under Charlot des Marés, in addition to the sixty that the said Charlot was accustomed to keep at the said place of Dieppe; under the sire de la Varenne, one hundred lances supplied and eighty small pay; under Floquet, one hundred lances supplied and forty small pay; under the sire de Torcy, one hundred lances supplied; under Odet d'Adie, twenty lances supplied; under the sire de Lohéac, sixty lances supplied; under Geoffroy de Couvran, knight, forty lances supplied; under the sire d'Estouteville, for Mont Saint-Michel, fifty small payments; under Jehan de Lorraine, for Granville, one hundred small payments; under Charlot des Marés, for Dieppe, sixty-four small payments; under ( ), for Fécamp, eight small payments; under Jamet de Tillay, two small wages; under ( ), for Arques, ten small wages. We want the said Macé de Launay to receive this payment from the private collectors of the said country and by his simple receipts, which we want to be valid as payment to the said private collectors in the rendering of their accounts…

Appendix IX

Regulations for the Maintenance and Discipline of Men-at-Arms, dated 6 June 1464[1]

And first, we want and order that, in order to carry out the montres and pay the wages of seventeen hundred lances of our order, there shall be six commissioners, five of whom shall each muster two hundred lances, which muster shall be carried out every three months at the places where the said soldiers are quartered, without removing them from the said places, unless we expressly order it. And the said men-of-war shall be lodged in enclosed places, if possible, or in large towns, without lodging in villages, so that they may be better kept in order; & we desire & order that the said commissioners shall reside continuously with the said men-at-arms & that with each of the said commissioners there shall be a clerk of the treasurer of war, well vouched for, for whom the said treasurer of war shall be responsible; who shall make payments to the said men-of-war individually to each person and to no other, and shall on his life give nothing to the captains or their pupils except the captain's pay and his status, whatever gifts the said men-of-war may give them. And there shall also be a notary appointed and ordained by us and at our expense, who shall receive the receipts from the said soldiers and, because of these, nor otherwise, shall take or demand anything from them.

Item & we want the commissioners, in making these montres, to ensure that the said men-of-war do not keep more men or horses than their *ordonnance* stipulate.

Item and we want each of these commissioners to have a lieutenant of the provost marshal, who, together with the bailiffs, Seneschals and other ordinary royal judges where there are royal judges, and where there are

1 De Reilhac, *Documents pour servir à l'histoire de ces règnes de 1455 à 1499*, Tome premier, pp.164–168.

no royal judges, the lieutenants of the provost marshal shall administer justice to the said soldiers; and when they commit any excesses, violence or offences, punish them according to the requirements of the case.

Item & if the said soldiers take anything without paying or exact anything from the people, the said clerk of the war treasurer, by *ordonnance* of the said commissioner, shall pay & restore from the wages of those who have done so or caused to be done all that has been taken & exacted & we want the payment made by the said clerk to be credited to the said treasurer of wars, bringing certification from the said commissioner and lieutenant and a receipt from the person to whom the payment was made by their order, just as if the said payment had been made to the man-of-war on whom the said reparation is ordered to be made; and notwithstanding the said reparation, justice shall be done to the person who has taken and demanded it, as the case may require, for we do not want the said men-of-war to do anything that is not lawful and proper for the nobles and other people of our kingdom; and when the said men-of-war do the contrary, we want them to be punished like the others.

Item & the said commissioner shall receive at the said montre only those who are present in person & in sufficient attire to pass; however, if any should be... ill or absent with the leave of their captain & for reasonable cause, they shall be excused & received at the said montre, provided that their horses & attire are in their lodgings & that the said commissioner sees them; & for those who are absent, he shall sign them as absent at the said muster & the said captains may not grant leave except to fifteen lances provided at one time out of the number of one hundred lances & more, more, & less, less & until the said fifteen lances are returned, he shall not grant leave to any other. However, when we see fit to summon the said soldiers, then the said captains shall not be able to grant leave to any of them, & if, when we summon them, any of these soldiers ask the said captains for leave & then wish to leave the said *ordonnance*, whoever does so shall be punished with capital punishment.

Item & if by chance no captain wishes to take on a new man to replace another, we want the new man taken on by the said captain not to be passed over & the clerk of the treasurer of war to retain his wages until he has notified us so that we may order as we see fit & no dismissal shall be valid unless the commissioner dismisses him.

Item & the said commissioner shall take great care that no crossbowmen pass in place of archers & also that no persons pass under borrowed names, nor that persons or clothing that have passed inspection under one company come to represent themselves at the inspection of another to fill the empty places; & we desire that all men-of-war & others who attempt to commit fraud in this matter be punished severely & according to the requirements of the case.

Item & with regard to the crimes, excesses & offences that will be committed by the said men-of-war, we want the said commissioner and lieutenant of the provost and each of them to collect complaints from the people and likewise to inquire on their behalf into the wrongs committed by the said men-of-war, and once this has been done, the said excesses and wrongs shall be punished and redressed by the said lieutenant, called our officers of our justice if there are none on the spot. And if any dispute should arise among the said men-of-war, the said lieutenant of the provost shall have knowledge thereof.

Item & if it should happen that any men-of-war disobeys his captain in any matter concerning our service, he shall be punished as before.

Item & every three months, the said commissioner shall certify to us truthfully & loyally, in letters signed by his own hand, the number of men he has found in each company & the clothing they are wearing, as well as any shortages & the names of those who are missing, along with this, he shall certify to us any excesses, crimes, and offences that the said soldiers may commit against the people, and the justice and reparation that has been done, as well as those whom he sees to be of ill will or who speak ill words sounding of sedition or disobedience, or who wish to be with others than us, or who would support those who would pillage or rob the people.

Similarly, the aforementioned clerk of the treasurer of wars shall certify the payments he has made to each of the aforementioned montres; and if it transpires that the said commissioner, lieutenant of the provost marshal, clerk of the treasurer of wars and notary above-mentioned have made false certification, or otherwise committed any fault or abuse relating to the above matters, they shall be punished by capital punishment as defrauders of the defence of public affairs & criminals of the crime of lèse-majesté.

Item & so that the said men-of-war may live better & clothe themselves & pay for what they take, we issue a general prohibition to all captains of the said men-of-war that they shall not be so bold as to take, retain, or demand anything from the said men-of-war, whether in the form of a gift, a loan, or in any other manner whatsoever, & if there is anyone who does the contrary, he who does so shall be deprived & dismissed from his office & from this moment forth we declare his said office & all offices, benefits & pensions that he might have from us to be forfeited & confiscated & he shall incur our indignation.

Item & we wish & intend that henceforth the said men-of-war shall be provided with lodgings & household utensils and shall pay for them from what they receive from us; that is to say, those who receive their pay & payment in hard currency shall pay thirty sous tournois per month for the said lodgings & utensils, as has been customary according to the old *ordonnances*; & those who are paid in low currency current in Normandy, as long as their said payment is made in said currency, shall pay forty sous tournois per month of said currency, as they did previously. And upon paying the said amount, the said commissioners & the justice of the places where they shall provide them with said lodgings and utensils, reasonable and without excess.

And we decree that the said men-of-war, on pain of being deprived of their orders and punished corporally, as the case may require, shall not be so bold as to take or compel the people to give them any lodging or utensils other than those ordered by the said commissioners and the justice of the said places.

We hereby command our beloved and loyal *maréchals de France*, all captains and military leaders, the commissioners appointed by us to enforce these *ordonnances*, and all our justices, officers and subjects, that they keep and maintain and cause to be kept and maintained this ordonnance in every respect according to its form and content, without in any way doing or allowing anything contrary to it to be done. In witness whereof, we have caused our seal to be affixed to these presents; given at Lihons in Santerre on the sixth day of June in the year of grace one thousand four hundred and sixty-four and of our reign the third.

By the King in Council
J. de Reilhac

Appendix X

Schedule of the State of the Troops in the King's Pay for the Year Beginning 1 January last and Ending on 31 December 1464[1]

Men-at-arms on high pay receive fifteen pounds per month each, and each archer seven pounds ten *sous*; those on low pay receive only ten pounds, and each archer or crossbowman five pounds per month.

Monseigneur le Comte du Maine *a dix lances fournie* (1)	
Poncet de Rivière (2)	100
Monseigneur de la Tour (3)	100
Monseigneur le Comte de Comminges (4)	100
Jean de Carguesolle, *grand écuyer* (5)	100
Joachim Rouault, *maréchal* (6)	100
Monseigneur de Crussol (7)	100
Tristan l'Hermite (8)	100
Geoffroy de Saint-Belin (9)	96
Gaston de Lyon (10)	50
Étienne de Thoulerette (11)	30
Le Bailiffs de Bourbonet (12)	
Regnauld du Chattelet (13)	20
Thomas, écuyer (14)	50

1 De Reilhac, *Documents pour servir à l'histoire de ces règnes de 1455 à 1499*, Tome premier, pp.158–164.

Robert Conegham (15)	50
Jean de Sallesart (16)	100
Guille Chenuet (17)	
Monseigneur de Candale	70

(1) His Lordship the Count of Maine is not required to conduct any muster or review and is required, upon receipt of payment, to pay him nine hundred and fifty pounds per quarter for thirty archers, at the rate of ten pounds per archer, according to letters issued in Paris by the King on 8 March 1463.

(2) Poncet de Rivière, one hundred lances, according to letters signed in Bordeaux on 10 February 1462, the last review of which took place in Bordeaux on 14 January 1463.

(3) Monseigneur Bertran de la Tour, Count of Boulogne and Auvergne, has one hundred lances, including himself, the second review taking place in Villefranche de Rouergue on 15 April 1464 and 23 July, the third in Saint-Gaultier in Berry on 17 and 18 November, the fourth in Saint-Laresne au Moine on 28 January 1464, in Domphront and Vire on 3 and 4 February.

(4) Monseigneur le Bastard d'Armagnac, Count of Comminges, adviser and vice-chamberlain to the King, *Maréchal de France*, lieutenant general for the King in his lands of Dauphiné and the Duchy of Guyenne and having charge of one hundred lances provided to him, as stated in letters given at Saint-Thierry-les-Reims on 12 August 1461. First review in Bordeaux on 15 March 1463; second in Blaye and Bordeaux on 11, 14 and 16 July; third in Montréal, Armagnac and Barbezieux on 25 and 26 October 1464 and 10 November 1464; fourth in Bordeaux on 3 and 4 February 1464 [1465]; each quarter nine thousand livres for one hundred men-at-arms and two hundred archers, at 15 livres per man-at-arms and 7 livres 10 sols per archer.

(5) Jean Gargueselles, first squire in charge of one hundred lances by letters given at Amboise on 3 November 1461: the first review at Laberelle on 15 April 144; the second in Forez, Lyonnais & Beaujolais from 12 August to September; the third in Château-Gontier, Laval and Maine at the end of October; the fourth in the same places on 17 February 1464.

(6) Joachim Rouault, Lord of Boimenard, Viscount of Fronsac and *Maréchal de France*, in charge of one hundred lances, by letters granted at Avesnes in Hainaut on 2 August 1461. First review in Saint-Lô and Villedieu on 16 and 19 April 1464, the second in Saint-Lô Villedieu Pont-au-Bas in August 1464, the third in Saint-Lô Villedieu and Avranches at the end of October 1464, the fourth in Brissac, Thouars Chemille & Beaupreau on the last day of February 1464.

(7) Louis Seigneur de Crussol, *Grand Panetier de France*, in charge of one hundred lances, by letters given at Montlhéry on 25 September 1461. First

review in Poitou at Saint-Maixent & the village of Souldant in the county of Poitou on 14 March 1464, the second in Poitiers, Niort & Lussac at the end of August, the third in Montaigu-Roche-Serrière Tiffauges at the end of October; note that in this review he takes on the role of Seneschal of Poitou, which he did not take on in the two previous ones, the fourth in Garnoche & other similar places on 3 & 4 February 1464.

(8) Sir Tristan L'hermite, Knight Provost Marshal of France, in charge of 10 [100 in the list above] lances provided by letters given at Saint-Denis on 28 August 1461. He has no commissioners and is paid on his receipts by letters given at Nogent le Roy on 25 April 1464.

(9) Sir Geoffroy de Saint-Belin, Knight of Saint-Belin & Bailiff of Chaumont, responsible for 86 lances [96 in the list above] by letters given at Lussac on 6 July 1463, paid by the first review by the receipts of the Lord Bailiff of Chaumont, given the great distance at which they are lodged, some being in Anjou, the others in Roussillon, & this by letters given at Isle en Flandres on 23 February 1464, [at the] 2nd review they are scattered in Champagne & Burgundy, 3rd review in Caourgi & Gien-sur-Loire, 4th they are paid on the captain's receipt by letters from the King given at Chinon on 13 January 1465.

(10) Gaston du Lion, Seneschal of Saintonge, Lord of Besaudun and 1st King's Cupbearer, in charge of 50 lances, according to letters issued at Saint-Thierry in Reims on 12 August 1461, the 1st review in Bayonne on 20 April 1464, the 2nd in Dax in August, the third at Pierre Forade at the end of October, the fourth at Bayonne on 15 January 1464 [1465].

(11) Estevenot de Tauleresse, squire of the King's *decury* and Bailiff of Montferrand, in charge of thirty lances by letters given in Paris on 9 September 1461. First review in Bayonne on 20 April, second review in Dax on 12 August 1464, third review in Pierre Forade at the end of October, fourth review in Bayonne on 15 January 1464 [1465].

(12) Louis Bastard de Bourbon, Lord of Roussillon, in charge of 20 lances by letters of retainer given in Paris on 4 September 1461. First review in Lyon on 18 September 1464, second in Dauphiné on 10 and 12 August by letters given in Neuville-près-Arques on 28 July 1464.

(13) Regnault du Chastelet, squire and royal cupbearer, 3rd review of archers, exempt from the 4th by letters from the King given at Chinon on 15 January 1464 [1465].

(14) Thomas, squire of Caen, in charge of 50 lances, according to letters issued in Bordeaux on the 24th day of March 1461. First review in Issoire on 15 April 1464, second in Saint-Poursain, Cuisset, Escurolles, Aigueperse, Clermont, Maringues, Lerone, Thiart, Corpierres, etc. from 9 to 22 August, third review in the same places in November, fourth.

(15) Robert Coningham was responsible for 50 lances according to letters given at Saint-Thierry-les-Reims on 13 August 1461. First review in Saint-Flour on 1 May 1464, the second in Brioude, Laniac, Alègre, etc., and at the end of August the third in the same places, and at the end of November the fourth.

(16) Jehan de Sallezart [Sallazar], Lord of Saint-Just, one hundred lances, by letters given to (   ) on (   ) one hundred lances. First review in Vienne in Dauphiné on 7 April 1464, second review *ibid.* on 8 July.

(17) Guillaume Chenu, Lord of Portneau, 70 lances by letters given at Amboise on 1 November 1462. First review carried out at (   ) by Jean Foucault, knight, governor of Orléans and commissioner for this review by His Lordship the Count of Dunois and Longueville, Lord of Partenay, lieutenant of the King on this side of the mountains, on 8 February 1463, & these 70 lances were granted by letters given at Rouen on 13 August 1462 to Jean de Foix, Count of Candale, Benauge de Lavau, Captal de Buch. First muster in Roussillon and Cerdagne conducted by Gabriel de Saint-George, squire Bailiff of Perpignan, appointed for this purpose by special commission of the King issued in Lions en Santerre on 6 June 1464. Second in the same manner, and likewise the third conducted in February 1465.

Other lances from the countries of Normandy:

Monsieur le comte de Dunois (18)	100 lances
Monseigneur du Lau (19)	100
Monseigneur de Laborde (20)	100
L'amiral de Montauban (21)	100
Monseigneur du Pont Labbé (22)	70
Floques *dit* Floquet (23)	100
Jean du Fou (24)	30

(18) His Lordship the Count of Dunois and Longueville having charge of 100 lances by letters given to the Porcherons on 29 August 1461. First review in Romans in Dauphiné, on 23 April 1464; the second *ibid.*, in August 1464; the third *ibid.* On 1 December, the King detached nine men-at-arms and 18 archers, whom he gave to Artus de Longueval, by letters given in Paris on 22 May 1462. The King, by letters given at Beaugency on 2 December 1464, exempted six men-at-arms and as many archers from attending the reviews. Hector d'Uselles, same exemption by letters given at Sauve on 12 August 1464, two men-at-arms and four archers, on 6 January 1465 by letters given at Tours.

(19) Sir Antoine de Chasteauneuf, Lord of Lau, Seneschal of Guyenne & Captain of Falaise, having charge of one hundred lances by letters granted to ( ) 1461. These men-at-arms in Normandy & the reviews at the times marked approximately as above.

(20) Jean Deteuil, knight, Lord of La Borde and Seneschal of Limousin, in charge of one hundred lances by letters of retainer given at Aveines on 3 August 1461. First review in Tulles on 15 April 1464; the second in Cadenat, Limoges, Tulle, etc., on 21 and 22 July; the third in Saint-Denis en Anjou on 23 October; the fourth in Craon, Prouencé, Segré on 20 February 1465.

(21) Jean, Lord of Montauban, Admiral of France, in charge of one hundred lances by letters given to ( ) 1462: 1st review in Valognes, 25 February 1464; the 2nd in Valogne, Montebourg, Carentan in July 1464; the 3rd in Avranche, Montebourg, on the 3rd of November; 4th review of only 86 men ibidem. Note: by letters signed in Tours on 24 April 1465, the King gave the Admiral of Montauban everything that might be due until 1st April to the men-at-arms and archers of his company who had left and gone to Brittany.

(22) Jean, Lord of Pont & Rostrenen, Bailiff of Cotentin, in charge of 70 lances, according to letters issued in Paris on 11 September 1462. First review in Caudebec, Montivilliers, Fécamp, Neufchâtel. The second *ibid.*, for 68 men only. But the King, by letters given at Abbeville on 10 October 1464, wants Olivier Plusquellec, man-at-arms, and eight archers to be paid, even though they are absent, and by others given at Novion near Abbeville on 15 September 1464, he wants Brun de Bouteville to be paid. The third *ibidem et eodem modo*. The fourth, made in Rouen, found only 51 men-at-arms: six men-at-arms and 15 archers were excused; the others had gone to Brittany & the King gave Guillaume de Ricarville, his maître d'hôtel & clerk for the review of this company, what was owed to these deserters, on condition that he would pay what they might have borrowed during their last quarter & owed to certain merchants. By letters given at Montargis on 23 July 1466 and confirmed by others given at Orléans on 5 October 1471.

(23) Robert de Floquet, known as Floquet, bailiff of Évreux, in charge of 100 lances by letters given at Saint-Thierry-les-Reims on 12 August 1461: 1st review at Honfleur, Pont-l'Evêque, Pont-Audemer, in March 1464. The 2nd *ibid.*, in July; the third *ibid.*, in October; the fourth at Saint-James de Beuvron, Saint-Guillaume de Mortain & Honfleur in February 1465. Only 96 men were found there, but the King, by letters given on 19 May 1465 at Montluçon, ordered that the other four be excused & paid.

(24) Jean du Fou, the King's chief cupbearer, had thirty lances according to letters issued at Saint-Thierry on 12 August 1461. The first review took place at Cherbourg, the second and third likewise, and the fourth was also held at Cherbourg on 19 January 1465, but only 21 men-at-arms were present; nine and thirteen archers had gone to Brittany, and the King, by letters signed at Razilly on 29 January 1465, gave the captain what might be due to them from their pay.

Appendix XI

Ordonnance of 1466 Establishing Four Captain Generals of The Francs-Archers[1]

Reproduced in R. P. Gabriel Daniel, *Histoire de la Milice Françoise* (Paris: Jean-Baptiste Coignard, 1721)

And first, to lead the said *francs-archers*, four captain generals were appointed and appointed, whose names are as follows. Sir Aymar du Puyfieu, known as Cadorat Chevalier, Councillor and Master of the Household of our Lord the King, and Bailiff of Mante. Pierre Aubert, Lord of La Grange and Bailiff of Melun. Messire Ruffec de Balzac [*sic*] Chevalier, Seneschal of Beaucaire. Messire Pierre Comberel, Lord of L'Isle. And that there shall be a chief above all the said four captains, whom the King shall appoint.

Item. It has been ordered that sixteen thousand shall be raised throughout this Kingdom *francs-archers*.

Item. Each of the four captains shall be responsible for four thousand *francs-archers*, to be taken as stated below, where there shall be seven captains, each of whom shall lead five hundred, and the other five hundred to make up the four thousand, each of the said captains shall have five hundred.

Item. And to raise the aforementioned sixteen thousand *francs-archers*, the Kingdom was divided into four parts, so that each of the four captains could be given a quarter, as follows.

And firstly, that the said Sir Cadorat Bailly de Mante, because his bailiwick is near Normandy, shall have, for one of the four parts of this Kingdom, the country of Normandy, including the lands of Monseigneur d'Alençon,

1 Bessey, *Construire l'armée française*, Tome I, pp.125–130.

Maine and Mortain, because they are joined together, the bailiwicks of Mantes, Chartres, Estampes and Dourdan, the counties of Dreux, Dunois and Blois on this side of the Loire, and the other lands on this side of the Somme and Oise rivers, including the Election of Beauvois and Amiens on this side of the Somme, the County of Eu, and the Pays de Vimeu, without touching the Bailiwick of Vermandois.

Item. The aforementioned Aubert Bailly de Melun shall receive the four bailiwicks of Champagne for the second of the four parts. Namely Chaumont, Vitry, Troyes and Meaux, the Bailiwicks of Vermandois and Senlis up to the River Oise, the Counties of Rethel and Porcien, Marle, Vertus, Brenne, Roussy, Grantpré and Joigny, the Duchies of Valois, the counties of Beaumont and Soissons, the Provostship and Viscounty of Paris, the Bailiwick of Montargis, including the duchies of Orléans and all of Gastinois: the bailiwicks of Melun and Sens, with the lands of Nivervois, Donziois and Tournonoys, Morvant, Puysoys, and the Election of Langres.

Item. The aforementioned Sir Ruffec shall receive, for the third part of the aforementioned four parts, the province of Berry, and that which comprises the Bailiwick of Chartres and the County of Blois from there to the River Loire in Sologne; the Bailiwick of Saint Pierre le Monstier, Bourbonnais, Rouennais, Foree, Beaujolais, Lyonnais, Upper and Lower Auvergne: La Marche, Combraille and Rouergue, with the lands of Monseigneur d'Armagnac on both sides of the Garonne; the Seneschalsy of Bazas; the Counties of Comminges, Lestrac and Perdriac.

Item. The aforementioned Sir Pierre Comberel shall receive Poitou, Anjou, Touraine, Limosin haut et bas, Saintonge, Aunis, Angoumois, Périgord, Quercy, Agenois, Condomois, with the Seneschalsy of Guyenne, the Seneschalsy of Lannes, the County of Bigorre, the lands of Monseigneur de Foix that he holds in Lannes, in Guyenne, and from there the Garonne, Bayonne and the Bourg.

Item. It has been ordered that the *francs-archers* shall be raised and stationed along the entire coastline of Normandy, as in other places.

Item. To ascertain the number of *francs-archers* the King has, he has ordered that each of the four captains shall go in person to all the bailiwicks and elections in his district, and shall issue orders compelling the elected representatives to truthfully report the numbers of their elections, so that all the *francs-archers* of those elections may be registered, without any compromise or deception. And in the event that the said captains are unable to go to any of the said places, they shall send their men there, in order to better and more reliably raise the said *francs-archers*. And once this has been done, the said captains shall each ascertain in their own district the number of their said *francs-archers* in order to inform the King whether they have their full number.

Item. The said four captain generals shall swear that they will rightly establish and place the said *francs-archers* in places and parishes where they have not yet been established, without committing fraud. And in this they shall follow the will and intention of the King, as has been ordered. And with this they shall not suffer the elect or any others to make any agreements or appointments that derogate from or prejudice the King. And all this on pain of confiscation of their lands, offices and any property whatsoever. And each of the four captains shall deliver a document signed by his own hand, which the Lord Chancellor shall keep. And the Lords Marshals shall be present to draw up the said document or obligation.

Item. It has been ordered that in each district there shall be a lieutenant of the said captains: who shall have the power that if any *francs-archer* returns without leave from the captain general, he shall have him hanged by the neck: and shall be brought before no other court of justice than that of the said lieutenant.

Item. It has been ordered that henceforth each of the twenty-eight captains who will be in command shall have 500 *francs-archers* under their charge and shall receive for each year the usual wages of 120 pounds and 20 pounds for their mounts, as they had in former times and in the time of the late King, and since then. And likewise, when they ride and are at war, they shall receive fifteen francs per month, and their lieutenants ten francs, as they have been accustomed to receive.

Item. It has been ordered that all *francs-archers* who are newly recruited shall be equipped with jacks, sallets, gauntlets, swords, daggers and vouges, or other sticks that they may find useful. Those who are already equipped with brigandines shall remain so, on condition that when they are broken or damaged, they shall be equipped with jacks.

Item. It has been ordered that henceforth each of the four captain generals of the Francs-Archers who will have 4,000 *francs-archers* under his command will each receive the ordinary wages of 800 livres and, in addition, when they are employed in the army, each of the said captains will be paid for a lance fournie in addition to the said wages. And each of these captains shall be required to have under his said lance two archers in good and sufficient clothing. These two archers shall not be included in the number of the said *francs-archers*.

Item. It has been ordered that each of the four captain generals shall have a lieutenant, who shall receive a salary of 10 pounds per month, as do the lieutenants of the said captain.

Item. It has likewise been ordered that henceforth none of the said *francs-archers* shall lead horses or pack animals. But they may assemble in groups of 8, 10, 12, 20, or whatever number they see fit, and have a cart or carts to carry their clothing or provisions: provided that they maintain and feed the said cart at their own expense.

Item. It has been ordered that each of the four captain generals shall have a rider from the stable with him to carry letters and orders in order to ensure greater obedience.

Item. It was likewise ordered that the said four captain generals shall assemble in their respective quarters the elected representatives, bailiffs, Viscounts and other officers, together with the individual captains of the said *francs-archers* in four locations within their said quarters, in order to assemble a thousand men in each of the said locations and to make a montre.

It is known that, with regard to the office of Lord Chamberlain Cadorat, it has been announced that one of the four locations in his district will be in Rouen, where the Bailiwicks of Rouen, Caux, Évreux and Gisors will be brought together; the other will be held in Beauvois, where those from the County of Eu, the Pays de Vineu, the Election of Beauvois and that of Amiens, on this side of the River Somme, may come; together with those from the Bailiwick of Senlis between the Oise and Normandy, and as far as the said River Somme, without touching the Bailiwick of Vermandois. The third part shall be held in the town of Saint-Lô because it is more central to the region. Those from Caen, Falaise, Bayeux, Coutances, Avranches and Valognes shall attend, as well as those from the County of Mortain, the Election of Alençon, and the Viscounty of Domfront. And the fourth part will be held in Chartres, where those from the counties of Maine, Perche, Dreux, Dunois, and the county of Blois on this side of the Loire will go, as well as those from Mantes, Estampes, and Dourdan.

Item. With regard to the office of the aforementioned Pierre Aubert, it appeared that he should hold his four seats as follows. One in the town of Sens, where those from the Duchy of Orléans, the Bailiwick of Montargis, the County of Gien on this side of the Loire, the regions of Nivernais and Donziois, the Counties of Joigny and Vézelay, the region of Morvant, and the Bailiwick of Sens will gather. The other seat shall be held in Melun, where those from the Viscounty and Provostship of Paris, the Bailiwick of Senlis on this side of the River Oise, the entire Bailiwick of Meaux, and the whole region of Gatinois, Nemours, and everything that does not belong to the Bailiwick of Sens may go. The third seat may be held in Reims, where those from the Bailiwick of Vermandois, the Duchy of Valois, the Counties of Rethel, Porcien and Guise, and all the lands that depend on them, and the Bailiwick of Vitry will go. And the fourth seat will be held in Troyes, where the Bailiwick of Chaumont, the Duchy of Langres, the Counties of Tonnerre and Brie, and all that belongs to the Duchy of Nemours together with the Bailiwick of Troyes will gather.

Item. Each of the said captains shall remain in one of the said four places until the said *francs-archers* have been raised and assembled, and until they know the number that the King will be able to use.

Do not in any way warn the said four captain generals ordered to assemble the *francs-archers*; it seems that when they are in the places ordered by the King to bring the elected, bailiffs, Viscounts or their lieutenants before them; and where there are no Viscounts, to bring the ordinary judges or their lieutenants, and the sergeants who are deemed necessary; after they have in the roll of the particular captains of the said *francs-archers*, and of the parishes of which they are: and also the rolls of the elected officials to know how many parishes there will be in their elections, each in his own regard, and the taxable fires and taxpayers to the said *francs-archers* enrolled by the bailiffs, Viscounts, ordinary judges in their elections, and the sergeants who may be of assistance; and that all shall be done without fraud or abuse of the penalties decreed by the King and declared in the Mandements on this matter; the said four principal captains, each in his office, shall see that they have in their charge the number ordered by the King, that is to say, 4,000 *francs-archers*.

Item. And if they do not have their full complement, they shall have nothing else to do but keep their registers of the specific number of said *francs-archers* in each election, and see the muster of said *francs-archers* in each election, and whether they are suitable persons for that purpose, and in sufficient condition to serve the King. And if they find that they are not suitable persons to serve in war, they shall replace those who are to be replaced and shall put others in their places who are good and suitable, without taking any money, as they are obliged to do. And with regard to their clothing, both those who remain and those who are replaced, the commissioners shall provide for them according to the terms of their commission.

Item. And if the said captains see that they do not have their full complement in the countries for which they are responsible, they shall consider how many they will need, and which countries are the least burdened in terms of the number of households, the means of the people, and the poverty or wealth of the countries and parishes that will be least burdened, as they will need *francs-archers*, and they shall have them placed in good and suitable positions; the strong supporting the weak as best they can.

Appendix XII

Instruction by Aymar Cadorat (*c.* 1466)

Reproduced in R. P. Gabriel Daniel, *Histoire de la Milice Françoise* (Paris: Jean-Baptiste Coignard, 1721)

Memo of the King's wish that the *francs-archers* of his Kingdom be dressed in jacks from now on. And for this purpose, he has instructed the Bailiff of Mantes to draw up a plan. And it seems to the said Bailiff of Mantes that the wearing of jackets would be good, profitable and advantageous for them in warfare, given that they are foot soldiers; and that, having brigandines, they have to carry many things that a single man on foot cannot carry.

Firstly, they need jacks made of 30 or 25 pieces of cloth, and at least one piece of deer leather. If they are made of 30 pieces of cloth and one piece of deer leather, they are good. Moderately worn and unbound cloth is best, and the jacks should have four quarters. The sleeves must be as strong as the body, except for the leather. The sleeves must be large, and the sleeve cap must be close to the collar, not on the shoulder bone, wide under the armpit, and full under the arm; fairly loose and wide on the lower sides. The collar must be like the rest of the jacket, and the collar must not be too high behind the armour of the sallet. And the said jacks must be fastened at the front and have underneath a piece of cloth of the same strength as the said jacks. Thus shall their said jacks be comfortable: provided that it has a doublet without sleeves or collar; of two pieces of cloth only, which shall be only four fingers wide at the shoulder. To this doublet he shall attach his breeches. Thus his jacks will flow inside, and he will be at ease. For no one has ever seen six men killed by hand or arrow inside said jacks: and if people were to fight well there.

(2) Item. It seems to bailly that the *francs-archers* should be divided into four equipments. Some with halberds, others with spears, others with bows, and others with crossbows.

(3) Item. It seems to him that those equipped with vouges should have them moderately wide, and that they should have a little belly. And also that they should be sharp and good daggers. And that the said guisarmiers should have visors, gauntlets and large daggers, without swords.

(4) Item. Those who carry spears must have sallets with visor, gauntlets and moderately long, stiff and sharp swords. Their spears should be the same length as the lances of arms. They should not be too thick, and should be almost straight, except for a small *deraillis* at the bottom, a small half-finger-high stop behind the tailoring, to give them shape. The iron must be sharp and slightly long, and all must be strong.

(5) Item. Archers shall have sallets without visors, bows and quivers, and fairly long, stiff and sharp swords called bastard swords. And if they wish to carry shields, there shall be no harm in that, and they shall have medium-sized daggers, and the shields should not be too high.

(6) Item. Crossbowmen should have sallets with visors, which they can raise high enough when they wish. And the underside of the visor should not be so deep that it covers their vision. And also that the right side should not come down as low on the cheek as the left, so that they can rest their crossbow on their cheek at ease. And they shall have swords that are not too long, stiff or sharp. And the belt shall hold the sword from behind, so that it does not touch the ground much. And their crossbows shall have ten bolts or thereabouts. And they shall draw with four pulleys or two, if they are good drawers. And they shall have quivers with at least eighteen arrows and shall have no daggers.

Appendix XIII

Letters Concerning the Clothing of the *Francs-Archers* and the Sums Levied by Their Captains, Paris, 12 January 1474

LOYS, by the Grace of God, King of France, to all those who shall see these prescriptions, greetings. As several complaints and grievances have been made to us by the nobles and countless evils, damages, pillaging, extortion, and exactions, which have been and still are committed and perpetrated every day in various ways, for the benefit and maintenance of our *francs-archers*, and under the pretext and on the occasion of the same, to the great harm, burden, and oppression of our subjects and inhabitants of our kingdom; and for this reason, we, desiring with all our heart to suppress and completely abolish and remove the said evils, pillaging and other forbidden misdeeds, and to relieve our said subjects of undue burdens and oppression, have, on the advice and deliberation of several lords of our blood, our warlords, the people of our kingdom, our Grand Council and our treasury, made the following *ordonnances*:

And first. We forbid all captain generals and captains of the said *francs-archers* from taking or causing to be taken anything for the new admission and transfer of *francs-archers*, and from granting any commission to impose any sum of money on our subjects for the sake of the said *francs-archers*, in any manner whatsoever; in this manner, if any have been given by them or by others, we have revoked and annulled them, and we revoke and annul them, together with all the power that the said captains or any others may have from us to do so, by these presents, and we wish that no one should obey them, except only our patens, signed by one of our secretaries signing in finance.

(2) Item. That the said captain generals and captains particular shall no longer compel our subjects to pay the wages of the said *francs-archers*, nor to take or purchase from them or others on their behalf, at their pleasure and will, pikes, spears or other military equipment for the clothing of the said *francs-archers*, as they have done hitherto; we therefore wish that, when any new *francs-archer* is appointed, our said subjects shall have the said clothes made, and shall purchase the said pikes and vouges, brigandines and other military clothing wherever they see fit, and the said *francs-archers* shall have the said only every two years, when theirs are worn out, to wear on their armour only, and at a price of twenty *sols tournois* per piece and below.

(3) Item. And once the said *francs-archers* are sufficiently equipped, we want that, from then on, nothing else be given to them for harness or other clothing of any kind, except in cases where they have lost their military clothing or part thereof in the course of war, in which case they shall be required to provide certification from their captains of the loss of said harness; otherwise, if the said *francs-archers* lose, sell, pledge or damage the said armour or part thereof, they shall be compelled by the said captains and elected representatives, by seizure of their persons and property, to restore the said harness.

(4) Item. We desire and order that the inhabitants of the parishes shall provide carts at their own expense to transport the clothing of the said *francs-archers* when they go to war, that is to say, one cart for every fifteen francs-archers, and the said fifteen *francs-archers* shall be required to purchase and provide at their own expense horses and harness to drive the said carts, together with a cart driver to drive them; and with regard to the *francs-archers* of the Counties and Duchies of Normandy and Guyenne, they shall not take the said carts with them if they go to war outside the said duchies and countries.

(5) Item. We maintain that no swords, vouges, crossbows, traits, brigandines, hocquetons, or any other items used for their military attire should be left in the hands or possession of the said *francs-archers* when they are in their homes and in times of peace, but we want the inhabitants of the parishes where they live to keep them safe, and for everything to be stored in a secure place so that it is ready whenever the said *francs-archers* are called upon to go to musters and to war.

(6) Item. We further forbid the said captain generals and captains, elected officials and their clerks, and other judges of whatever kind, from compelling or causing to be compelled our said subjects to give to the said *francs-archers*, when they are sent to war or otherwise, at any time whatsoever, one *ecu* per man, or any other sum, or likewise doublets, breeches, shirts, hats, caps or any other clothing whatsoever, except only to each *francs-archer* the sum of six *livres tournois*, which shall be given and paid to them, each year, both in times of war and peace, by our said subjects, in four instalments per year,

that is to say, thirty *sols tournois* at each instalment, for their maintenance, including the exemption and franchise they have from us from paying our taxes and other aids and subsidies.

We hereby command our beloved and loyal *maréchals de France*, all our bailiffs, seneschals and other officers and justiciars or their lieutenants, present and future, each of them as it may concern him, that they maintain and uphold our said ordinances and all the contents herein, and cause them to be maintained and upheld, each in his own right, inviolably and without infringement, and cause them to be published in their bailiwicks and seneschalships, and elsewhere where necessary, so that no one may claim ignorance, and that transgressors or infringers of the same shall be punished or make restitution according to the contents of the said ordinances, and to compel or cause to be compelled all those whom it concerns, truly and in fact, vigorously and without delay, as is customary in such cases, notwithstanding any opposition or appeals; for which we do not wish to be delayed in any way. And because these presents may be needed in various places, we wish that the vidimus thereof, made under the royal seal, be given the same faith as this original present. In witness whereof, we have caused our seal to be affixed to these prescriptions.

Given in Paris, on the twelfth day of January, in the year of our Lord one thousand four hundred and seventy-four, and of our reign the fourteenth. Signed above the fold: By the King, AVRILLOT

Appendix XIV

Letters Concerning the Raising, Pay, Armament and Obligations of the *Francs-Archers*, 30 March 1475

LOYS, by the Grace of God, King of France, to all those who shall see these letters, greetings. We hereby declare that, as our late beloved lord and father, may God rest his soul, had issued several ordinances concerning the maintenance and upkeep of the *francs-archers* of our kingdom, and likewise, since our accession to the throne, we have done the same, and even more recently, in response to complaints and grievances we have received concerning the exactions and pillaging they carried out on our subjects for the maintenance of the said *francs-archers*, we have made certain declarations and *ordonnances*, but since then we have received several complaints and remonstrances, both from the captain generals and several individuals and on behalf of the said *francs-archers*, regarding the content of these *ordonnances*, saying that, due to the manner and form in which they were made, it would be impossible for the said *francs-archers* to maintain themselves, and also that there were some things that were not sufficiently clarified, requesting us to have these, and similarly the others made previously, be reviewed and examined by our council, and if there were anything in them that required further clarification or improvement, that we would do so and make such provision as would enable the said *francs-archers* to be reasonably maintained when necessary: know that we, wishing to give orders and police the matter of the maintenance of the said *francs-archers* and remove all the pillaging that might be involved, and to protect our subjects from undue charges, after having shown by the people of our council, in our presence, several *ordonnances* concerning the said francs-archers, and especially those made in our city of Paris last January, and, having sought the advice and deliberation of our Grand Council and our finance officers, we have corrected the ordinances previously made concerning the said *francs-archers*, which could derogate from the present ones, and have made the following *ordonnances* concerning their maintenance:

Firstly. That the muster of the said *francs-archers* shall be carried out immediately, as it has not been done recently, by the captain generals or their clerks, by the elections and viscounties, and in the most convenient place possible, and at these *montres* the said *francs-archers* shall be found in their clothings, and with them, for the sole purpose of presenting themselves at the said montre, one man from each fifty, and if it is necessary to make any amendments to the brigandine, sallet, hocquetonn and other war clothing of the said *francs-archers*, it shall be repaired and put in sufficient condition at the expense of the said fifty, and the said captain general or his clerk, or the one who comes for the said fifty, shall give orders to have it done with all diligence; and the said inhabitants shall not be required to repair or provide the said *francs-archers* with any doublets, hose, bonnets, or anything else, except for proper military clothing and hocquetons.

(2) Item. And once they are thus dressed and equipped, the *francs-archers* shall henceforth be required to maintain themselves adequately in all respects

(3) Item. To help carry their weapons and clothing, as has been ordered on other occasions, the said *francs-archers*, when they go out to war, shall have for the fifteen of them a cart with iron wheels and drawn by three horses, which for this first time shall be provided and paid for out of the money that has been collected for this purpose, and thereafter, said cart shall be maintained at the expense of the inhabitants who shall make up said fifteen *francs-archers*, and shall be brought back by said *francs-archers* at the end of each journey and given into the custody of such person as the inhabitants who shall have provided it shall advise; but the horses, collars, harnesses and other items necessary to drive the said cart shall be found and provided by the said fifteen *francs-archers* at their own expense, without these inhabitants having any work or trouble in keeping them, nor making any effort for these horses, collars, or other equipment for the said horses.

(4) Item. And so that these *francs-archers* may better maintain themselves in clothing and also the said horses, the said inhabitants of each fifty shall pay for each year from now on to their *francs-archers*, whether in times of peace or war, the sum of nine livres tournois at the two montres that shall take place twice a year, and no more, at the time and in the manner ordered by the captain general; and, in return for this sum, the said inhabitants shall not be required to provide any war clothing, doublets, hose, money for montre journeys or any other items whatsoever: but, in return for the said nine livres tournois, after the said *francs-archers* have been provided, as stated, with military clothing, the said inhabitants shall be released from all payments and deposits for the said francs-archers, except for the maintenance of the said cart. However, if, by the fortunes of war, any francs-archer should lose his military clothing or part thereof, in that case, upon

certification of the said loss by the said captain general, by his command, these inhabitants shall be obliged to provide the *franc-archer,* at their own expense, with whatever has been lost of the said military clothing; but if they were lost through negligence or otherwise, the said *francs-archers* shall provide them at their own expense, and they shall be compelled to do so by the said captain generals, in reality and in fact, by seizure of their bodies and property.

(5) Item. To provide for the said *francs-archers* and help them to live and maintain themselves when they are called to go to war, the captain general shall order, if he sees fit, that of the said sum of nine livres tournois, each franc-archer shall be paid his share of up to thirty sols tournois for his attendance and maintenance on the spot, pending our provision and order for their payment.

(6) Item. And, wherever said *francs-archers* may reside, assuming that it is not in the parishes for which they are francs-archers, they shall be exempt from taxes and shall enjoy all the privileges of *francs-archers*, provided that it is not outside the district for which they are *francs-archers*, without the inhabitants of the said parishes having any recourse or reversion, because of their residence, against the inhabitants for whom they are francs-archers; and also, when determining the specific rates of taxation, the elected representatives shall take care to grant a reasonable rate and portion to the inhabitants of the parishes where these *francs-archers* reside.

(7) Item. We forbid the said captain generals to allow the captains-particular to transfer or replace any *francs-archers* with others, nor to appoint any new ones themselves, unless and when a vacancy arises for any reason whatsoever, the captain generals and captains shall fill them themselves, at their own expense, without taking anything from the said *francs-archers* or from the inhabitants.

(8) Item. When the time comes for the vacancy of any position of *franc-archer*, the captain general shall choose the said free archer and take him into the fifty or elsewhere in the election, as he sees fit, provided that there is no one skilled to serve as a *franc-archer,* for which, for the letter of retention, the said captain general or private individual or any other shall have no claim whatsoever.

(9) Item. And after the said franc-archer has thus been chosen, he shall be given and delivered all the harness in good condition that belonged to the previous one, and the previous one or his heirs shall be compelled to do so by the captain, unless it was lost in war, in which case, and in no other, the inhabitants shall provide him with war clothing only for the first time, and thereafter shall maintain him as stated.

(10) Item. We forbid the said captains, both general and particular, from taking or allowing to be taken from the said *francs-archers* or inhabitants anything by way of arrow tax or otherwise.

(11) Item. And likewise, we forbid the said captains from accepting any *francs-archers* to send men to war for them, but we want those who are appointed as *francs-archers* to go in person, unless they are ill; and, if otherwise done, we desire and command by these presents that they be subject to taxation for the parishioners and punished by the captain generals and deprived of being *francs-archers*, and that the said elected persons immediately certify this to the said captain generals so that they may be punished so severely as to serve as an example to all others.

(12) Item. And when it happens that the said inhabitants have to provide anything for the said *francs-archers* in the manner described, whether it be military clothing or hose, they may purchase or make them wherever they see fit and wherever they can get them at the best price, without the said captains having any involvement in the matter, nor shall they be delivered by their hands; however, if the said clothing is not good and sufficient, the said captains may compel the said inhabitants and parishioners, and also the said *francs-archers*, when the occasion arises, to provide other clothing that is sufficiently good.

(13) Item. When the said *francs-archers* go to war, they may not leave without leave from the captain general, on pain of imprisonment; and if any are found to be doing or having done otherwise, the bailiffs and judges of the places shall have them taken and made prisoners and shall keep them prisoners until they have notified the captain general, under whose charge and conduct they shall be, to punish them as above stated

(14) Item. When there are certain *francs-archers* who, due to impotence, mutilation, or accident sustained during a military expedition, or due to old age, can no longer serve and are removed from the said order of *francs-archers*, having certification from their captain general of the good service they have rendered us, they shall have their letters of franchise as we have ordered for the said *francs-archers*, and the secretary of our finances shall give them to them, as we have commanded.

We hereby command all bailiffs, seneschals, captain generals and individuals of the said *francs-archers*, elected on the basis of our aid, and all other justiciars and officers or their lieutenants, or each of them as appropriate, that our present edicts, ordinances and wishes, and the contents of the said present, be maintained and upheld, and cause them to be maintained and upheld inviolably, without compulsion and without regard to other ordinances that may be contrary to and derogate from the said present, and that they be published immediately in their bailiwicks, seneschals and elections, wherever they may be, so that no one may claim just cause of ignorance, and that they punish and make restitution for transgressors and violators of the same, as required by the circumstances, following the contents of our said *ordonnances* without any concealment, so that it may serve as an example to all others. And furthermore, provided that the end of the truce between us and Charles of Burgundy, our rebellious and disobedient subject, his allies and accomplices, will be brief, and that we must act promptly to resist the harmful undertakings that he and his allies, accomplices and adherents are endeavouring to carry out to burden and damage us, our kingdom and service, and our good and loyal vassals and subjects, and to help us with the said francs-archers, we command and order, by committing by these presents to all the said elected representatives of our said kingdom, that, immediately after the said publication, they shall compel, each in his own place, the inhabitants of the towns and parishes to deliver and prepare all the war clothing of the said *francs-archers* for whom they are responsible, in accordance with the above, and to have them all ready and clothed, as stated, by the twentieth day of April next, and to compel or cause to be compelled to do so, as is customary for our own works and affairs, notwithstanding any opposition or appeals, for which we do not wish to be delayed in any way. And, since it may be necessary to carry out the work referred to herein in several and various places, we wish that the vidimus thereof (in witness thereof), made under the royal seal, be given the same faith as this original, to which, in witness whereof, we have affixed our seal.

Given in Paris, on the xxxth day of March, in the year of our Lord one thousand four hundred and seventy-five, after Easter, and in the xiiii year of our reign. Thus: By the King, the Lord of Beaujeu, the Lord of Curion.

Colour Plate Commentaries

Plate A

Mounted man-at-arms, *c.* 1445–1455, reconstructed after Viollet-le-Duc. He wears a sallet with visor; a *colletin* with *bavière* protecting the neck and chin; *spalières* or *espalières* (shoulder guards); *garde-bras* (arm defences); and *gantelets* (gauntlets) protecting the hands. His body defence consists of a brigandine reinforced by a steel corset known as a *pansière*, together with a *braconnière* at the waist. The lower limbs are protected by *cuissots* (thigh defences) with *genouillères* (knee guards), *grèves* for the legs, and *solerets* (foot defences). This equipment is characteristic of the men-at-arms serving in the *compagnies d'ordonnance.*

Plate B

Two men-at-arms of a *compagnie d'ordonnance*, in white harness, are shown mounted on horses equipped with plate *harnois* (horse armour), still comparatively uncommon in the French army at the time. This horse armour comprises *chanfreins* (chamfrons), *tétières* (headpieces), and mail or plate protection for the neck and chest, together with *croupières* protecting the croup. The riders are wearing German armour.

Plate C

Two men-at-arms of a *compagnie d'ordonnance* in white harness, wearing German armour and different patterns of sallet. For the horse armour, see Plate B.

Plate D

Two complete armours for men-at-arms, shown in front view. The example on the left, dated to *c.* 1440, and from the Château de Pierrefonds, was described by Viollet-le-Duc as 'a marvel in terms of both design and craftsmanship'. He further observed that the harness did not impede movement, owing to the precision with which it fitted to the body. The leg harness, in particular, is notably slender. The example on the right, by contrast, dated to the early fifteenth century, has more rudimentary *spalières*, each composed of two plates. This armour is also illustrated after Viollet-le-Duc.

Plate E

Two further complete armours, dated *c.* 1470–1480, display more elaborate arm defences in a range of patterns. The right arm, unlike the left, was devised to permit greater freedom of movement, allowing the wearer to couch the lance while remaining capable of fighting with sword or mace. The left arm is furnished with more substantial shoulder defences, intended to compensate for the absence of a shield. This type of armour, which became widespread among German and English men-at-arms from *c.* 1440 onwards, appears to have been less common in France before 1450.

Plate F

Busts of men-at-arms wearing breastplates and brigandines studded with rivets over *hocquetons*, together with various forms of sallet. The shoulder guards represented here follow a model dateable to *c.* 1420, reproduced in Viollet-le-Duc's *Encyclopédie médiévale*. They conform closely to the shoulder and incorporate an upper defence intended to deflect spear thrusts. This arrangement was, however, rapidly superseded by forms affording more effective protection, such as those shown in the preceding plates.

Plate G

Chapels and *capacetes* in the fifteenth century. Iron chapels remained in use throughout the fifteenth century, particularly in Southern France. The anonymous author of the *Costume militaire des Français* refers to this type as the 'chapel de Montauban', after the town in Southern France. The examples at lower left, shown with two different *bavières*, have strongly sloping brims and, according to Viollet-le-Duc, were generally associated with men-at-arms engaged in assaults on fortified places. The other examples, shown above and in the right-hand columns, are Spanish types worn in the second half of the fifteenth century. In Spain they were designated *capacetes*, and their form would subsequently develop into that of the morion. It is possible that they were also used by some soldiers from Southern France. These reconstructions are based on specimens preserved in the Real Armería, Madrid.

Plate H

According to Viollet-le-Duc, the armet appeared around 1440. Although apparently less common than the sallet, numerous examples survive in museum collections; it is also attested in fifteenth-century paintings and in written sources. Le Bouvier, for example, records that a page in the retinue of the Count of Saint-Pol wore an armet at the royal entry into Rouen in 1449. The upper example, dated *c.* 1440, is reproduced after Viollet-le-Duc and derives from the armoury of the Château de Pierrefonds. The middle example, from the same collection and likewise reproduced after Viollet-le-Duc, dates from *c.* 1470. The example at lower left, formerly in the Musée de l'Artillerie in Paris at the end of the nineteenth century and cited by Viollet-le-Duc, dates from *c.* 1490. The final example, at lower right, is Italian and is reproduced from a painting by Pedro Berruguete depicting Federico da Montefeltro, dated 1476.

Plate I

Archers during the reigns of Charles VII and Louis XI. In contemporary miniatures, archers are most commonly represented wearing vermilion *hocquetons* charged with a white cross. In his account of the royal entry into Rouen in November 1449, Gilles Le Bouvier notes that the Count of Nevers had 'eight gentlemen clothed in vermilion satin with large white crosses.' The *francs-archers*, for example those of Compiègne, likewise wore red tunics. Illuminated manuscripts also depict red banners charged with white crosses, two examples of which are reproduced here. At the same time, the illuminations in the Froissart manuscripts and in Martial d'Auvergne's 'Vigiles du roi Charles VII' also show archers wearing *hocquetons* in a wider range of colours, including red, blue, ochre, grey, and green, all marked with a white cross. It remains difficult to determine whether this variety of colours reflects historical practice or merely pictorial convention.

Plate J

Archers *d'ordonnance* during the reigns of Charles VII and Louis XI. In his description of the royal entry into Rouen in November 1449, Le Bouvier states that the king's archers were 'dressed in jackets studded with gold and silver and coloured red, white and green'. The Scottish Guards of Louis XI would later adopt a tricolour livery of green, white, and red. French Ms 2609 in the BNF and Martial d'Auvergne's 'Vigiles du roi Charles VII' depict such archers dressed in red and green *hocquetons*. Several illuminations in the 'Vigiles du roi Charles VII' similarly show a red and green banner of this type. In one instance, however, a small white cross appears on the red field.

Plate K

Archers during the reign of Charles VII. Other colours were probably employed to distinguish the archers of different *compagnies d'ordonnance*. An illumination in the manuscript 'Les Vigiles du roi Charles VII' (f. 208), intended to represent those who 'had the honour of conquering Normandy', shows some archers of *ordonnance* wearing grey and green *hocquetons*, while others are clad in brown and grey examples, as represented here. The same illumination also includes a green and grey banner, together with the banner of the Constable of Richemont. The white banner semé of ermine of Brittany occurs in several illuminations in the manuscript.

Plate L

According to Le Bouvier, at the royal entry into Rouen on 10 November 1449, the king's tailor carried a pennant 'made of azure velvet, embroidered with three gold fleurs-de-lis and large pearls'. Such standards occur frequently in manuscript illuminations of the period. Chartier similarly states that Roger Blosset carried the King's Standard, described as being of 'crimson satin, with Saint Michael in the field, and also strewn with golden suns'. Le Bouvier further records that, following the Lord of Culant, there were 'six hundred lances, each bearing a small banner of vermilion satin charged with a golden sun'. He also notes that the Standard of the King of France was made of crimson satin strewn with golden suns. The Banner of Saint-Denis is reproduced here after a miniature in a manuscript of Froissart and after Viollet-le-Duc's *Encyclopédie médiévale*.

Bibliography

Published Books

Basin, Thomas, *Histoire des règnes de Charles VII et de Louis XI* (Paris: Renouard, 1855)

Belleval, René de, *Du costume militaire des Français en 1446* (Paris: Auguste Aubry, 1866)

Bernage, George, *Encyclopédie médiévale d'après Viollet-le-Duc* (Bibliothèque de l'image, 1996)

Bessey, Valérie, *Construire l'armée française*, Tome I (Turnhout: Brepols Publishers n.v., 2006)

Bonnault d'Houët, Baron de, *Les francs archers de Compiègne 1448–1524* (Compiègne: Publication de la Société Historique de Compiègne, 1897)

Bréquigny, *Ordonnances des rois de France de la troisième race, recueillies par ordre chronologique, quatorzième volume* (Paris: Imprimerie royale, 1790)

Buchon, J. A., *Branche des royaux lignages, chronique métrique de Guillaume Guiart*, Tome VIII (Paris: Verdière, 1828)

Buchon, J. A., *Chroniques de Jean Molinet* (Paris: Verdière, 1828)

Buchon, J. A., *Choix de chroniques et mémoires relatifs à l'histoire de France* (Paris: Delagrave, 1835)

Bueil, Jean de, *Le Jouvencel* (Paris: Renouard, 1889)

Champollion Figeac, M., *Documents inédits historiques tirés des collections manuscrites de la bibliothèque royale*, Tome second (Paris: Didot Frères, 1843)

Chartier, Alain, *Quadrilogue* (BNF)

Chartier, Jean, *Chronique de Charles VII, Roi de France, Tome I* (Paris: Vallet de Viriville, 1858)

Contamine, Philippe, *La guerre au Moyen Âge* (Paris: Presses Universitaires de France, 2eme édition, 1992)

Contamine, Philippe, *Charles VII* (Paris: Perrin collection Tempus, 2021)

Contamine, Philippe, *Guerre, État et Société à la fin du Moyen Âge. Tome 2. Études sur les armées des rois de France 1337–1494* (Paris: EHESS, 2024)

Daniel, R. P. Gabriel, *Histoire de la milice françoise et des changements qui s'y sont faits depuis le début de la monarchie dans les Gaules jusqu'à la fin du règne de Louis le Grand* (Paris: Jean-Baptiste Coignard, 1721)

Delabos, Christian & Gaillard, Philippe, *Montlhéry, 16 juillet 1465* (Annecy: Historic 'One Editions, 2003)

Favier, Jean, *La guerre de Cent Ans* (Paris: Marabout, 1980)

Froissart, Jean, *Les chroniques de Jean Froissart*, Collection des Chroniques Nationales Françaises, livre second, Tome IX (Paris: Delagrave, 1824)

Godefroy, Denis, *Histoire de Charles VII par Jean Chartier, Jacques le Bouvier dit Berry, Roy d'armes, Mathieu de Coucy et autres auteurs du temps* (Paris: Imprimerie Royale, 1661)

Godefroy, Denis, *Mémoires de Philippe de Comines*, Tome premier (Bruxelles: François Foppens, 1723)

Gruel, Guillaume, *Chronique d'Arthur de Richemont* (Paris: Société de l'histoire de France, 1890)

Haynin, Jean de, *Les mémoires de messire Jean, seigneur de Haynin et de Louvegnies, Tome premier* (Mons: E.M. Hoyois, 1892)

Hélary, Xavier, *L'armée du Roi de France – La guerre de Saint Louis à Philippe le Bel* (Paris: Perrin, 2012)

Hoskins, Peter, *The Battle of Castillon, 1453*, Retinue to Regiment series no.21 (Warwick: Helion & Co., 2023)

Lecestre, Léon, 'en introduction de Jean de Bueil,' *Le Jouvencel*, Tome premier (Paris: Renouard, 1887)

Lobineau, Dom Gui Alexis, *Histoire de Bretagne,* Tome II (Paris: Veuve François Muguet, 1706)

Maupoint, Jean, *Journal Parisien* (Paris: Fagniez, 1878)

Monstrelet, Enguerrand de, '*Chronique d'Enguerrand de Monstrelet*' in J. A. Buchon, *Collection des chroniques nationales Françaises*, 11 volumes (Paris: Delagrave, 1824–1826)

Nicolle, David, *French Armies of the Hundred Years War*, Men-at-Arms series no.337 (Oxford: Osprey, 2000)

Paris, Paulin (ed.), *Les grandes Chroniques de France*, Ttome sixième (Paris: Techener, 1838)

Petitot, M., *Collection complète des mémoires relatifs à l'histoire de France, Tome XIII, les chroniques de Jean de Troyes* (Paris: Foucault, 1820)

Thorey, E. Pilot de, *Catalogue des actes du dauphin Louis II devenu le Roi de France Louis XI*, Tome deuxième (Grenoble: Imprimerie de Maisonville, V. Truc, successeur, 1899)

Reilhac, Jean de, Secrétaire, Maître des comptes, Général des finances et ambassadeur des rois Charles VII, Louis XI & Charles VIII, *Documents pour servir à l'histoire de ces règnes de 1455 à 1499*, Tome premier (Paris: H. Champion, 1886)

Roque, Gilles André de la, *Traité du Ban et Arrière-ban* (Paris: Michel le Petit, 1676)

Savy, Nicolas, *Bertrucat d'Albret ou le destin d'un capitaine gascon du Roi d'Angleterre pendant la guerre de cent ans* (Pradines: Archeodrom, 2015)

Savy, Nicolas, *La guérilla Anglaise en Languedoc, Auvergne et Limousin – Les cavaliers de l'Apocalypse* (1369–1393) (Pradines: Chez L'auteur, 2022)
Secousse, M. de, *Ordonnances des Roys de France de la troisième race,* quatrième volume (Paris: 1734)
Troyes, Chrétien de (Jean-Pierre Foucher, trans.), *Romans de la Table Ronde* (Paris: Gallimard, Folio, 1970)
Vaesen, Joseph & Charavay, Étienne, *Lettres de Louis XI, Roi de France,* Tome II (Paris: Renouard, 1885)
Vilevault, *Ordonnances des rois de France de la troisième race, treizième volume* (Paris: 1782)
Viriville, Auguste Vallet de, 'Notices et extraits de chartes et de manuscrits appartenant au British Museum de Londres', Bibliothèque de l'École des Chartes (1847)

L'ordonnance cabochienne (1413) – Documents sur le règne de Charles VI (Clermont-Ferrand: Paleo, 2008)
Recueil des historiens des Gaules et de la France, Tome 20 (Paris: 1840)
Recueil des historiens des Gaules et de la France, Tome 21 (Paris: 1855)
Recueil des historiens des Gaules et de la France, Tome 23 (Paris: 1876)

Articles and Chapters

Anonymous, 'Le charroi de Nîmes', in A. Pauphilet (ed.), *Poètes et Romanciers du Moyen Âge* (Paris: Gallimard, La Pléiade, 1952)
Beauvillé, Victor de, *Recueil de documents inédits concernant la Picardie, deuxième partie* (Paris, 1867), Ch. 1, p.95
Bouvier, Jacques (Gilles) le, 'Recouvrement de Normandie' in *Les chroniques de Normandie* (Rouen: Hellot, 1881)
Contamine, Philippe, 'Les compagnies d'aventure en France pendant la Guerre de Cent Ans' in *Mélanges de l'école française de Rome*, 87:2 (1975)
Contamine, Philippe, 'La Guerre de Cent Ans: le XIVe siècle. La France au rythme de la guerre', in A. Corvisier (ed.), *Histoire militaire de la France, 1: Des origines à 1715* (Paris: Presses Universitaires de France, 1992) pp. 125-152
Contamine, Philippe, 'La Guerre de Cent Ans: le XVe siècle. Du "Roi de Bourges" au "Très Victorieux Roi de France"', in A. Corvisier (ed.), *Histoire militaire de la France, 1: Des origines à 1715* (Paris: Presses Universitaires de France, 1992) pp. 171-208
Contamine, Philippe, 'La première modernité. Louis XI, tensions et innovations,' in A. Corvisier (ed.), *Histoire militaire de la France, 1: Des origines à 1715* (Paris: Presses Universitaires de France, 1992) pp. 209-232
Coussy, Mathieu de, Chroniques, in *Choix de Chroniques et Mémoires relatifs à l'Histoire de France* (Paris: Delagrave, 1835)
Froissart, Jean, 'Chroniques' in Jean Yanoski (ed.), *Collection de chroniques, mémoires et autres documents* (Paris: Firmin Didot Frères, 1865)

Hélary, Xavier, 'Pourquoi combattre?' in G. Traina (ed.), *Mondes en Guerre – Tome I: De la préhistoire au Moyen Âge* (Paris: Perrin, 2025)

Hélary, Xavier, 'Combats et opérations militaires', in G. Traina (ed.), *Mondes en Guerre – Tome I: De la préhistoire au Moyen Âgee* (Paris: Perrin, 2025)

Lassalmonie, Jean-François, 'L'abbé Legrand et le compte du trésorier des guerres pour 1464: les compagnies d'ordonnance à la veille du bien public' in *Journal des Savants* (2001) 1

Marche, Olivier de la, 'Mémoires' in *Nouvelle collection des mémoires pour servir à l'histoire de France*, Tome troisième (Paris: publisher not stated, 1837)

Milot, Jean, 'Évolution du Corps des Intendants Militaires (des origines à 1882)', *Revue du Nord*, 198 (1968)

Mirot, Léon, 'Dom Bévy et les comptes des trésoriers des guerres; Essai de restitution d'un fonds disparu de la Chambre des Comptes', *Bibliothèque de l'École des Chartes* (1925) 82

Péquignot, Stéphane, 'De la France à Barcelone. Une version catalane de "l'ordonnance perdue" de Charles VII sur les gens d'armes (1445)', *Revue Historique*, 4:276 (2015)

Perroy, Édouard, 'L'artillerie de Louis XI dans la campagne de l'Artois (1477)', *Revue du Nord* (1943), 103

Planchenault, René, 'La Conquête du Maine par les Anglais: les campagnes de Richemont 1425–1427' in *Revue historique et archéologique du Maine*, 2:13 (1933)

Troyes, Chrétien de, 'Yvain ou le chevalier au lion', in A. Pauphilet (ed.), *Poètes et Romanciers du Moyen Âge* (Paris: Gallimard, Bibliothèque de la Pléiade, 1952)

Uncredited, 'Montres inédites de gens d'armes Bretons', *Extrait de la Revue Historique de l'Ouest*, années 1885 à 1887

About the author

Stéphane Thion holds a PhD in Human Sciences from Toulouse Capitole University. Passionate about history and strategy, and well-versed in research methods (he is currently Director of a Doctorate of Business Administration programme), he has been conducting research in the historical field for over 15 years. He is the author of several historical works including *French Armies of the Thirty Years' War, The Battle of Fribourg 1644* and *The Armies of Ptolemaic Egypt* published by Helion & Company.

A Time of Knights 400 CE to 1453 CE

The Battle of Adrianople (378 CE) marked the dominance of heavy cavalry over infantry, signalling the decline of the Western Roman Empire and the rise of feudalism. Nobles, in exchange for land, provided knights who became Europe's primary military force, clad in increasingly advanced armour. Beyond Europe, the Mongols relied on disciplined light cavalry, while the Islamic Caliphates combined light and heavy cavalry with trained infantry. China pioneered gunpowder weapons.

Castles and fortified cities shaped siege warfare, leading to increased use of artillery. By the late Medieval period, longbows, pikes, and firearms challenged knights' battlefield dominance, ushering in military innovations that paved the way for the Early Modern era of warfare.

Submissions

The publishers would be pleased to receive submissions for this series. Please email info@helion.co.uk, or write to Helion & Company Limited, Unit 8 Amherst Business Centre, Budbrooke Road, Warwick, CV34 5WE

You may also be interested in: